Other fields,

other grasshoppers:

readings
in
cultural
anthropology

edited by
L. L. LANGNESS
University of California, Los Angeles

EDGAR V. WINANS
consulting editor

J. B. Lippincott Company
Philadelphia
New York · San Jose · Toronto

Copyright © 1977 by J. B. Lippincott Company

All rights reserved.

This book is fully protected by copyright, and, with the
exception of brief extracts for review, no part of it may
be reproduced in any form, by print, photoprint, microfilm,
or any other means, without permission of the publishers.

ISBN 0-397-47363-X

Library of Congress Catalog Number 76–55310

Library of Congress Cataloging in Publication Data
Main entry under title:

Other fields, other grasshoppers.

    Bibliography: p.
    1. Ethnology—Addresses, essays, lectures.
2. Ethnology—Field work—Addresses, essays,
lectures.   I. Langness, Lewis L.
GN378.085   301.2   76-55310
ISBN 0-397-47363-X

Photography credit:
Cover illustration courtesy of
Paul G. Hiebert

dedicated to the
memory of my father

CLEVELAND W. LANGNESS

Contents

Preface

I have been more and more frequently asked in recent years, by people teaching anthropology at virtually all educational levels, for books that will actively stimulate beginning students to a further interest in anthropology. It has been made clear that ordinary introductory textbooks are not what they have in mind. While there are a few truly stimulating works available, some of them well known, there is no single book that provides the broad coverage of different peoples, *cultures*, and topics that most teachers and students would find desirable. There are, in addition to the now very large number of introductory texts, readers such as George Peter Murdock's *Our Primitive Contemporaries* (1934), Wendell Oswalt's *Other Peoples, Other Customs* (1972), and Carleton S. Coon's *A Reader in General Anthropology* (1956); but these are very attenuated *ethnographies* that attempt to give a description of an entire culture in far too few pages. And, as they are meant to be straightforward ethnographic descriptions, they tend to suffer from being not very captivating or readable.

The more humanistic and more interesting accounts, such as Elenore Smith Bowen's *Return to Laughter* (1954), Colin Turnbull's *The Forest People* (1961), and K. E. Read's *The High Valley* (1965), are impossible to put together in sufficient numbers to require as reading for a single course. Furthermore, there is no readily available combination of such books that would adequately cover the many different kinds of questions that beginning students might well wish to ask about anthropology.

Although this collection cannot fulfill these requirements perfectly, it does attempt a somewhat broader perspective than has been heretofore available. The selections have been chosen first of all for readability; but they also attempt a broad geographical and topical coverage. At the same time they present different styles of ethnographic reportage and try to give insight into the "anthropological experience" itself. Naturally, these selections cannot possibly give a complete account of the cultures they describe; they are no more than cross-sections or glimpses of other ways of life in what anthropologists call the *ethnographic present*. They do, however, suggest further questions and readings and, taken together, will tell you a great deal about anthropology, anthropologists, and the myriad peoples they study. Above all, if you approach them with an open mind, you will gain an appreciation of human diversity and of the dignity of human life wherever it is found.

Acknowledgments

I am indebted to Ms. Cecile R. Edgerton for her help with certain of the selections, as well as for her many insightful comments as this book began to take shape. I would also like to acknowledge the very helpful suggestions I received from Ms. Jill E. Korbin and Ms. Gelya Frank. Professor Robert B. Edgerton has been more than encouraging from the beginning, and Ms. Jae Stewart has, as always, been patient and unfailing with secretarial assistance. The three unknown (to me) readers of the original manuscript should also be thanked for their thoughtful if anonymous advice.

Introduction

Well . . . the Oriental . . . doesn't put the same high price on life as does the Westerner. Life is plentiful, life is cheap in the Orient . . . and, uh . . . as the, uh, philosophy of the Orient, uh . . . expresses it, uh . . . uh . . . life is, uh, is not important.

GENERAL WILLIAM C. WESTMORELAND
Hearts and Minds

The lamentable ignorance revealed in this statement leaves the audience stunned. How could these words have been spoken by a mature, intelligent, and otherwise well-educated man at this late date in the twentieth century? Yet shock may not be an appropriate response, after all. For how much solid knowledge about other people do most of us possess? And how did we acquire the information—or the misinformation—that we claim to have?

Earlier societies had an excuse for their ignorance. Before the age of exploration, in the fifteenth and sixteenth centuries, the various peoples of the world had little knowledge of each other. Mostly they were familiar with only their immediate neighbors, who were basically just like themselves. Traveling great distances was hazardous if not impossible. Only rare and brave individuals journeyed more than a scant few miles from where they were born. This is not to suggest that earlier people had no curiosity about other groups; rather their natural curiosity was perforce focused on peo-

1

ple who were close by. It was not until some particular group of people had arrived at a reasonable idea of the true extent of human variation, that their curiosity could be either fully stimulated or satisfied.

Saint Augustine had asserted in his famous work **The City of God** that there could be no people at all in the remote corners of the world. Other writers had long ago reported on the existence of various kinds of semihuman monsters that might be found there—creatures with a single large eye, with only one huge foot, with enormous ears, with tails, with bird-like heads, people who had been raised by wolves or other animals, and creatures far more fanciful even than these. Thus, when the earliest explorers actually encountered people very different from themselves, people living in Africa, Asia, South America, the Pacific and Arctic regions, and so on, some of whom wore no clothing of any kind, some of whom drank fresh blood and ate raw meat, anointed themselves with animal fat, grotesquely distorted their lips, noses, and ears, mutilated their genitals, and practiced what appeared to be an almost endless variety of seemingly bizarre and irrational customs, they did not know quite what to make of it all. They were struck by the diversity, but not always quite certain whether they were dealing with people or with some kind of semihuman or nonhuman beings.

The Spaniards quickly and remorselessly tortured and murdered the inhabitants of the New World, rationalizing that they were not really human beings. North American Indians, Australian aborigines, Tasmanians, Bushmen, Hottentots, and others later suffered unbelievable atrocities largely for the same reasons. Slavery, of course, was justified on similar grounds.

There were arguments in these early days over whether certain of the newly discovered (by Europeans) people could mate with the great apes (also relatively newly discovered by Europeans), whether they had souls like Europeans—if they had any semblance of religious feeling at all—and whether, perhaps, they might have cyclical breeding seasons like the animals. However Europeans might have disputed points like these, there was unanimous agreement that such peoples were inferior to themselves and were "obviously less intelligent," "rude," and "uncivilized." But as more and more information was obtained it became clear that by most or all of the criteria employed all of these individuals were, indeed, human beings. The question then became, how could all of these obvious but strange differences be explained? Why, for example, were some people living in a so-called civilized way while others—so-called savages and barbarians—were traipsing about nude or seminude in the deserts and forests eating raw or barely cooked foods and sleeping wherever night found them? Why did some people insist that a man could have only one wife, while others believed that the more wives a man had the better? Why did some people submit their sons and daughters to excruciatingly painful initiation rites, whereas others found such customs repugnant almost beyond belief? Why did some call their father's brothers by the same term they used for their father, although they called their mother's brothers by quite a different and special term? How could it be that some people were cannibals, whereas their neighbors, not far away, were not? How in short, if all people were members of the same species, could the enormous variation be explained?

It was out of experiences and questions such as these that the science of man, **anthropology,** was conceived. Anthropology is a recent development in the history of science. Prior to the early 1900s there were no professional anthropologists, and even those serious but amateur scholars who considered themselves anthropologists relied for their information almost exclusively on the biased and generally inaccurate accounts of traders, missionaries, explorers, and other travelers. **Fieldwork,** now the anthropological stock-in-trade, did not develop as an integral part of the anthropological tradition until after 1900. Since that time, and particularly since about 1930, literally hundreds of anthropologists have done fieldwork and have returned to write scientific treatises on what they have learned. But even so, what anthropological science has discovered about the fundamental unity of mankind appears to have aided but little in overcoming people's animosity to one another. The world, at this moment as in the past, remains torn by hatred, suspicion, and fighting, all of this fueled by ubiquitous age-old beliefs that others are somehow not as human as we are, and that life is, for them, unimportant.

Much of the problem stems from **ethnocentrism,** which although related to ignorance, is not the same as ignorance. It is a curious fact of human life that all groups of people tend to judge others from the perspective of their own culture. Thus they do not hesitate to make value judgments based on their own sense of value even though the circumstances in which others must exist, adapt, and behave can by very different indeed. That ethnocentrism is found not only among Europeans can be readily seen in the following:

> In Java, for example, where I have done much of my work, the people quite flatly say, "To be human is to be Javanese." Small children, boors, simpletons, the insane, the fla-

grantly immoral, are said to be **ndurung djawa,** "not yet Javanese." A "normal" adult capable of acting in terms of the highly elaborate system of etiquette, possessed of the delicate aesthetic perceptions associated with music, dance, drama, and textile design, responsive to the subtle promptings of the divine residing in the stillness of each individual's inward-turning consciousness, is **sampun djawa,** "already Javanese" that is, already human. To be human is not just to breathe; it is to control one's breathing, by yoga-like techniques, so as to hear in inhalation and exhalation the literal voice of God pronouncing His own name—**hu allah.** It is not just to talk; it is to utter the appropriate words and phrases in the appropriate social situations in the appropriate tone of voice and with the appropriate evasive indirection. It is not just to eat; it is to prefer certain foods cooked in certain ways and to follow a rigid table etiquette in consuming them. It is not even just to feel, but to feel certain quite distinctively Javanese (and essentially untranslatable) emotions— "patience," "detachment," "resignation," "respect." [Geertz, 1965]

That anthropologists have been able to do so little to overcome ethnocentrism is due in part, no doubt, to the apparently natural reluctance of human beings to change their basic values and attitudes. But it has also to do with the failure of scientists to communicate with others. Although Jacob Bronowski did not have anthropologists in mind when he commented as follows, his statement is to the point and worthy of consideration:

There is a division in the mind of each of us, that has become plain, between the man and the brute; and the rift can be opened, the man submerged, with a cynical simplicity, with the meanest tools of envy and frustration. . . . It helps to create the conditions for disaster. And I think science has contributed to it. Science, the fact that science is there, mysterious, powerful; the fact that most people are impressed by it but ignorant and helpless—all this seems to me to have contributed to the division in our minds. And scientists cannot escape the responsibility for this. They have enjoyed acting the mysterious stranger, the powerful voice without emotion, the expert and the god. They have failed to make themselves comfortable in the talk of people in the street; no one taught them the knack, of course, but they were not keen to learn. And now they find the distance which they enjoyed has turned to distrust, and the awe has turned to fear; and people who are by no means fools really believe that we should be better off without science. [1962:282]

It is true that during their struggle to gain recognition as scientists, from approximately the 1930s on, anthropologists gradually came to deem it inappropriate to talk to "people in the streets." There emerged a negative attitude towards "popularization," an attitude so strong within the profession that those who attempted to write personal, subjective, or humanistic accounts felt compelled to preface them with apologies or, in some cases, to write under pseudonyms. Margaret Mead's **Growing Up in New Guinea** (1930) and Ruth Benedict's **Patterns of Culture** (1934), two of the most influential and widely read books ever written by anthropologists, were severely criticized by many, if not most, professional anthropologists, because they were "too novelistic," "too artistic," "too unscientific." The result of all of this was that most anthropological books came to be written in an anthropological jargon for other members of the profession, and that nonprofessionals who attempted to write ethnographic books were very commonly denigrated. Scientific objectivity, often spurious in any case, was pursued at the expense of readability. Anthropology, which deals with the most intrinsically interesting subject matter of all the sciences, became and tends to remain a dull subject. And most unfortunately of all, outside of its own limited circle, anthropology seems to have contributed little to our understanding and tolerance of each other. The public's great interest in the lives and cultures of others has not been well served. The responsibility that anthropologists should have assumed was shouldered, if at all, by those whose motives were often more pecuniary than scholarly.

In spite of the generally negative attitude of the profession in the past (the present attitude might be characterized as more ambivalent than completely negative) there has always been a perfectly respectable tradition of a more literary approach to anthropological writing. This tradition has a humanistic rather than a scientific emphasis. It is a small tradition and not as well known as it might be, but it does convey, nonetheless, an acceptable and much more human picture of both anthropologists and those they write about than does the more sterile scientific literature. It might be said that the tradition began with Adolph Bandelier's novel of the Keresan Pueblos of the American Southwest, **The Delight Makers** (1890). It includes not only other **ethnographic novels,** but also short stories, biographies, first-person accounts of fieldwork, chronicles, and even an occasional play. These efforts share with more standard ethnographic writings the primary task of presenting an accurate account of another way of life. They differ, however, in that there is an attempt to present characters and plots, both inevitably missing from the more traditional ethnographies. Thus they have an intimate and personal flavor, and they provide a psychological dimension that has usually been ignored. I have attempted to draw from this literature in such a way as to capture and stimulate the reader's interest in other people, in the books from which the selections are taken, and in the ethnographic record in general. Above all, I hope to make clear that however much anthropologists reduce their materials to abstractions, generalizations, and scientific jargon, still, in the process of doing fieldwork and learning about other ways of life, they deal fundamentally and always with other individuals, fully human beings just like themselves.

The great puzzle of anthropology has always been how to reconcile unity and diversity. How is it that people can be so fundamentally similar and yet at the same time so fantastically different? Naturally enough, when people first became aware that other people existed in far parts of the globe they were immediately struck by the differences. Later, when more information was forthcoming, anthropologists became interested in the similarities. They began to speak of **universals of culture,** a topic that has tended to predominate in recent years. As scientists have always believed that they must deal with universals rather than with particulars, this is perhaps understandable. But why, as Clifford Geertz has recently challenged (1973), is what it means to be human more clearly revealed in universals than in particulars? The most important thing we know about human nature is that it reveals itself only in particulars—in individuals and in their particular interactions with each other and with the universe. People are born with the potential to be members of any culture, but they in fact become members of only one particular culture.

Culture consists essentially of a set of controls for organizing and directing human behavior. These controls are transmitted to us extra-genetically from previous generations and peers. They come to us in the form of a system of symbolic meanings that we must acquire before we can become fully human. Symbols can be words or objects, even gestures, expressions, and acts—provided they impose meaning upon experience. In the process of becoming human you acquire only certain symbol systems and thus you must become only a certain kind of person—an American, a Chinese, a Tahitian, a Papua New Guinean, or whoever. To be human means to incorporate such symbolic systems into your very being. And as no individual acquires and understands precisely the same system of meanings, you cannot become a universal person, you must become a very special person; you become not only an American or an African, but a very special or unique American or African. Thus, however different people have become, and however cultures vary as systems of meaningful symbols, people do not differ with respect to their fundamental humanity—they are in this dimension entirely equal. As man is even in his most basic biological form a product of his own culture, every culture that has survived to the present day represents a success. And as no one can predict with certainty which cultures or peoples will survive into the future, statements like the following cannot be taken entirely seriously:

> The simple tribal groups that are living today are not primitive, they are stultified. Truly primitive tribes have not existed for thousands of years. The naked ape is essentially an exploratory species and any society that has failed to advance has in some sense failed, "gone wrong." [Morris, 1967]

The problem here is not the absence of "primitives," but the presence of the same ethnocentric standard that helps to keep us from truly "advancing." Technology is the only standard of "progress" that has ever been seriously employed. It would be ironic indeed if the most technologically advanced were the next to disappear. From the standpoint of human evolution, which we only dimly comprehend, this is not entirely farfetched.

Individual variation among members of the same species is a biological given for all species, including man. Without it there could be no evolution. Cultural variation is not so easily understood. Although all people could in principle share a common culture, in fact they do not and have not. It would surely be undesirable from an evolutionary point of view. To believe that others could be or even should be like "us," and to disrespect the lives of others because they are not, is not only to ignore what we know about human nature, but also to miss much of the meaning of human existence itself. So that—

> To be human is thus not to be Everyman; it is to be a particular kind of man, and of course men differ: "Other fields," the Javanese say, "other grasshoppers." [Geertz, 1965]

1

The song of the forest

COLIN TURNBULL*

Perhaps one of the best known works of humanistic anthropology is Colin Turnbull's **The Forest People** (1961), from which the following selection has been adapted.

The Ituri Forest, the home of the Pygmies about whom Turnbull writes, lies virtually in the center of the African Continent in what is now the Republic of the Congo. The Pygmies, a classic example of what anthropologists call a **hunting and gathering** society, take their sustenance directly from the forest where they can find it instead of cultivating plants or raising domestic animals. They move about the forest in small groups for much of the year, but they periodically spend some time with their more sedentary Bantu neighbors, with whom they trade. Turnbull, who lived intimately with the Pygmies for many months, was obviously much attracted to their gentle life—so much so that he seems to have identified with them and to have taken on their attitudes towards the non–forest-dwelling Bantu. In this book he gives a fascinating account of how he began to learn about their religious system.

Lewis Henry Morgan, said by some to have been the father of American anthropology, made the following comment on the religion of **"primitive"** peoples: "Religion deals so largely with the imaginative and emotional nature, and consequently with such uncertain elements of knowledge, that all primitive religions are grotesque and to some extent unintelligible" (1877:5). In spite of this unfortunate early dis-

* Reprinted by permission of Simon & Schuster, Inc., from *The Forest People*, by Colin Turnbull. Copyright © 1961 by Colin M. Turnbull.

9

claimer, anthropologists have always been interested in the subject of religion. You might note in this selection, however, just how difficult it is for anthropologists even now to be completely free of the enthnocentrism expressed by Morgan.

I noticed that only men sat at this fire and asked Kenge why this was. He told me it was the *kumamolimo*, "the place of the molimo," and now that everyone was here we were going to start the festival. The food that had been collected from hut to hut was to feed the molimo, because the molimo was a hungry animal that ate a great deal. He added pointedly that it smoked a great deal too, and when I gave him several packets of cigarettes he solemnly put them with the food in the molimo basket.

About an hour later, when I was in my hut, I noticed that Makubasi and Ausu were standing outside, obviously wanting to say something. Usually they were not backward about interrupting, and I was puzzled when Ausu beckoned with his head that I should come outside. He whispered in my ear that a few of them were going off to get the molimos, as we were to start the festival that night. Masimongo, Kenge's brother-in-law, had said that he, as well as Manyalibo, wanted to bring out his molimo, and make it a doubly great festival. Half a dozen youths were waiting to see if I would go with them, but they told me that the place where the molimo lived was a long way off and we would have to run all the way and return when it was dark.

Of course I said I would go, and we started off immediately. But halfway across the camp Masimongo leaped into my way and shouted that I was not to go. For a moment there was a loud and sharp argument, most of which I could not follow. Finally Njobo, to whom everyone always listened, said that he had seen me in the forest and knew I could travel as well and as fast as the others, so that I would be safe. Masisi then objected with a shrill torrent of words, saying that the molimo was none of my business. For a moment I felt like saying I would not go, as I certainly did not want to cause any bad feeling. The others were already moving off at a run, down the path through the glade, not waiting for me.

Njobo pushed me on the shoulder and said to follow quickly, if I was sure I could keep up and would not be afraid of traveling in the forest in the dark. He said the others would not be able to wait for me if I dropped behind; this was a serious matter. As I hesitated he added, in a loud voice directed at everyone in general, but particularly to Masimongo and Masisi, that the molimo had already sung to me and no harm had come of it. I was after all an adult, and of the forest, so there was no reason why I should not go with the others.

He was still talking as I caught up with Makubasi, who was hanging back to see if I was coming. We jumped into the Lelo, more swollen than ever, and struggled across. The water came up to my waist, nearly up to his shoulders. My shoes filled with sand and grit, but there was no time to take them off. As we made our way through the water the others ducked their heads and washed themselves, and I did the same.

When we climbed out on the far side, Ausu, leading, was halfway up the hill while I was still splashing around trying to find a foothold in the slippery bank. The forest was not dark yet, but it was very silent, and for once no one made a sound as we ran, following the antelope trails, toward the north.

The trails we followed were narrow, and in places even the Pygmies had to stoop and bend. We ran at a steady pace without slowing up once. There was never any hesitating as to direction, even though there were times when it was difficult to see any trail at all. When we climbed upward we went faster because that made it easier to keep a footing. I was the only one whose feet made any noise; the others ran so lightly that they barely touched the ground but rather seemed to skim along just above it, like sylvan sprites.

After about forty-five minutes we came to a stream that was larger than the others we had crossed, though it was only a few yards wide and very shallow. For the first time we slowed to a walk and stepped through the bubbling water, lifting our feet high so as not to splash. The forest was silent now, except for the evening chorus of crickets and frogs, and on the far side of the stream we halted while Ausu and Makubasi looked around and listened, to reassure themselves that we were alone.

I had no idea of how far we had come or in what direction, but I knew we had left the camp far behind. It was the first time I had known a group of Pygmies to be so silent. Normally, unless hunting, they are deliberately noisy, but now, just at the time that leopards would be prowling about in search of food, they seemed unwilling to disturb the forest or the animals it concealed. Just the opposite, in fact. It was as if they were a part of the silence and the darkness of the forest itself and were only fearful lest any sound might betray their presence to some person or thing *not* of the forest.

They stood there, quiet and still, and it struck me with a sudden shock that not one of them carried a spear or bow and arrow. As they peered into the dusk and cocked their heads first on this side then on that, satisfying themselves that we were really alone, it seemed that they felt themselves so much a part of the forest and of all the living things in it that they had no need to fear anything except that which was not of the forest. One of them said to me, later, "When we are the Children of the Forest, what need have we to be afraid of it? We are only afraid of that which is outside the forest."

We stood there, water from the stream still running down our legs, until they were satisfied that all was well. Then Makubasi nodded to Madyadya and to another boy. They ran on ahead, and after a whispered discussion two others followed. The rest of us walked slowly on until we came to a small clearing nearby, the far side of which was only just visible as the last glimmer of daylight dwindled away into blackness. We stood there waiting, saying nothing. Ausu and Makubasi wandered about aimlessly, poking here and there from habit to see if there was any tasty fruit to be had for the picking, but it was too dark to see.

Just as I was about to ask where the others had gone they reappeared, announcing their presence with low whistles that sounded like the call of a night bird. They were in two pairs, each pair carrying between them, over their shoulders, a long slender object. Even at that moment I wondered if they would veer off into the complete blackness of the forest before I could see more closely, but they came on toward us. Madyadya was carrying the rear end of what proved to be a huge tube of some kind, fifteen feet long. He gestured proudly and said, "See, this is our molimo!" Then he turned and putting his mouth to the end of the trumpet, which it was, he blew a long, raucous raspberry. Everyone doubled up with laughter, the first sound they had made since leaving camp.

I was slightly put out by this sacrilege and was about to blame it rather pompously on irreligious youth, when I saw something that upset me even more. I do not know exactly what I had expected, but I knew a little about molimo trumpets and that they were sometimes made out of bamboo. I suppose I had expected an object elaborately carved, decorated with patterns full of ritual significance and symbolism, something sacred, to be revered, the very sight or touch of which might be thought of as dangerous. I felt that I had a right, in the heart of the tropical rain forest, to expect something wonderful and exotic. But now I saw that the instrument which produced such a surprisingly rude sound, shattering the stillness as it shattered my illusions, was not made of bamboo or wood, and it certainly was not carved or decorated in any way. It was a length of metal drainpipe, neatly threaded at each end, though somewhat bent in the middle. The second trumpet was just the same, shining and sanitary, but only half the length.

Everyone was looking at me to see what my reactions would be. I asked, keeping my voice low, how it was that for the molimo, which was so sacred to them, they should use water piping stolen from roadside construction gangs, instead of using the traditional materials.

Evidently now that they had the trumpets in their possession there was no longer any need for silence, for they answered calmly and loudly with a counter-question. "What does it matter what the molimo is made of? This one makes a great sound, and, besides, it does not rot like wood. It is much trouble to make a wooden one, and then it rots away and you have to make another."

Ausu, to prove how well it sounded, took the end of the longer pipe, which evidently belonged to Manyalibo, and all of a sudden the forest was filled with the sound of trumpeting elephants. The others clapped their hands with pleasure and said, "You see? Doesn't it sound well?"

The molimo was often referred to as "the animal of the forest," and the women were supposed to believe that it really was an animal, and that to see it would bring death. That of course is why they were all bundled off to bed with the children before the trumpet was ever brought into camp. And even when it *was* brought in it was often shielded by a number of youths so that if any woman should happen to look, she would see nothing. The animal sounds it produced were certainly realistic, but I wondered what the women thought when it sang. What kind of animal was it that one moment could make such threatening sounds, and the next instant sing more beautifully than anything else in the whole forest?

I remembered again Ausu's saying that the only important thing about the trumpet was the fact that it had a good voice and could sing well. I was reminded of the Pygmy legend of the Bird with the Most Beautiful Song. This bird was found by a young boy who heard such a Beautiful Song that he had to go and see who was singing. When he found the Bird he brought it back to the camp to feed it. His father was annoyed at having to give food to the Bird, but the son pleaded and the Bird was fed. The next day the Bird sang again; it sang the Most Beautiful Song in the Forest, and again the boy went to it and brought it back to feed it. This time the father was even more angered, but once again he gave in and fed the Bird. The third day (most Pygmy stories repeat themselves at least three times) the same thing happened. But this time the father took the Bird from his son and told his son to go away. When his son had left, the father killed the Bird, the Bird with the Most Beautiful Song in the Forest, and with the Bird he killed the Song, and with the Song he killed himself and he dropped dead, completely dead, dead for ever.

There are other legends about song, all telling how important it is, and I wondered just why. I looked at the others sitting with me around the kumamolimo. The flames from the fire flickered, lighting up the serious faces, shining brightly in their large, honest eyes. Some gazed straight into the fire, others leaned back and looked up into the trees as they sang. A few lay down on their hunting nets, but they were awake and they sang with the rest. Then I saw that Makubasi had his infant son on his lap, holding the boy tightly against him, wrapped in his powerful arms, rocking backward and forward. He was singing quietly, with his mouth up against his son's ear. The words of the song, like the words of most molimo songs, were few. They simply said, "The Forest is Good."

The Pygmies seemed bound by few set rules. There was a general pattern of behavior to which everyone more or less conformed, but with great latitude given and taken. Even on this occasion, when all women and children were supposed to be abed, if Makubasi felt like getting his son and singing to him at the kumamolimo, nobody objected or thought anything of it. Possibly this was because the baby was too young to know what was going on, and so could not tell the others what he saw; possibly simply because it did not matter very much anyway, for the Song was not only Beautiful, it was Good and Powerful.

It took me some time to realize just how important song was. That first night I just thought of it as being a beautiful sound. After we had eaten the food that had been offered to the molimo we sang again, and at one point the younger men got up and danced around the fire, excitedly, but without any of the frivolity that would come later. This was the first night of the molimo and everyone was on his best behavior. Then when the dancing was over we heard the trumpet again, and as we sang it sang back to us, getting farther and farther away. As it went it carried our song with it, deeper and deeper into the forest. Finally we could hear it no more, and only the echoes of our own voices came back to us from the night.

Not long after that old Moke stretched and yawned and said that he was tired and that everyone should go to sleep and let him sleep. But the younger men paid no attention and went on singing, so Moke resignedly joined in. But after another half-hour, when it was not very long before dawn, even the younger men decided to quit. Moke picked up the log he had been sitting on, the end of which was glowing in the hot ashes, and shuffled back to his hut, swinging the log so that it glowed brightly and lit his way across the camp. Manyalibo simply stretched out where he was, right beside the molimo fire, and went to sleep there. A number of youths did likewise, their hunting nets making comfortable beds, but I went back to my hut. I found Kenge there, fast asleep. He was on my bed, wrapped in my blanket, snoring contentedly, and the hut was filled with smoke from the fire he had lit beside him.

For a month I sat every evening at the kumamolimo; listening, watching, and feeling—above all, feeling. If I still had little idea of what was going on, at least I felt that air of importance and expectancy. Every evening, when the women shut themselves up, pretending that they were afraid to see "the animal of the forest"; every evening, when the men gathered around the fire, pretending they thought that the women thought the drainpipes were animals; every evening, when the trumpet drainpipes imitated leopards and elephants and buffalos—every evening, when all this make-believe was going on, I felt that something very real and very great was going on beneath it, something that everyone else took for granted, and about which only I was ignorant.

It was as though the songs which lured the "animal" to the fireside also invoked some other kind of presence. As the evenings wore on toward morning, the songs got more and more serious, and the atmosphere not exactly tense but charged with an emotion powerful enough to send the dancers swirling through the molimo fire as though its flames and red-hot coals held no heat, as though the glowing embers were cold ashes. Yet there was nothing fanatic or frenzied about their action in dancing through the fire. Then there was always that point when the "animal" left the camp and returned to the forest, taking the presence with it. I could feel it departing as the mellow, wistful voice of the molimo got farther and farther away.

The morning rampages carried no such presence with them; they seemed more tangible both in actuality and in purpose. I learned that after these rampages the trumpets were brought back to the Lelo River, just above where the men bathed, and immersed there during the daytime so that the women would not see them. One day there was a terrible storm and the Lelo rose four or five feet, transformed into a torrent. When the rain abated in the late afternoon Madyadya went to look for the trumpets and found that one of them had been washed away. This caused tremendous hilarity, though of course everyone tried to disguise what they were talking about in front of the women. The women, playing the same game, pretended not to know what was going on. Eventually the trumpet was found some distance downstream, full of sand and gravel and mud.

But that night, in spite of its prosaic experience, it was a mysterious thing again, alive and awe-inspiring and wonderfully beautiful; something that made the eyes of young and old alike light up with pleasure as they heard it sing. And, as always, there was that look in Amabosu's eyes as he worked his magic with the drainpipe. He was no longer Amabosu; he had some other personality totally different, and distant.

One day, when I was beginning to wonder if I would ever find out what it was all about, I was out with Kenge and his half-brother, Maipe. We had left at dawn, as we wanted to go to a distant part of the forest, about five hours' walk if one carried no load, and return by nightfall. About halfway there, far to the north of the Lelo and near the great falls of the Kare River, we stopped for a rest. We were in an *idu*, a small natural clearing used by the forest animals as a salt lick. For some reason we started talking about water and I asked again why the molimo trumpets always drank when they crossed a stream. Maipe, who seldom said much, said, as Ausu had, that they always gave wooden trumpets water to drink because it made them sound better. So, he said, it had become a custom and they still followed it even if the trumpet was metal. I then asked why the trumpets were kept in water and was again given a practical answer—it was the easiest place to hide them. I finally arrived at the question I had been leading up to—what happened to the molimo trumpets at the end of a festival? Did they go back to live in the water?

This struck both Maipe and Kenge as terribly funny. They said certainly not; if the trumpets were kept in the water always they would rot right away and everyone would be spending all their time making new ones instead of hunting. Without any further prompting they went on to tell me how the trumpets are normally made, from the young straight molimo tree, a tree with a soft center that can be bored out laboriously, using different vines and woods as drills, twisting them between the palms of the hands. It took a very long time, they said, but this was the real molimo, and its voice was the best of all. Njobo used to have such a trumpet, but it had rotted away, and now all he had was a short bamboo one.

Kenge told me that the trumpet which Masimongo owned had originally belonged to Kenge's father, Adenota, and by rights belonged to him. But he said he couldn't be bothered with it. "It costs too much, and it makes too much work. Always going around collecting food to feed everyone. . . . " He shook his head in disgust. He had given it to Masimongo when Masimongo married his sister. He could have it back if he wanted, or he could make another, but it was all really too much trouble.

Maipe said nothing, but after a while, when we were moving off, he asked me if I would like to see the sleeping place of a trumpet. He led me along an antelope trail, so low that I had to go almost on hands and knees. It followed the banks of a stream and the mongongo plants grew thickly. After a while the stream descended a slope in small cascades, and the undergrowth cleared. We stood up and saw that water was all around us, rippling over rocks and coming together at the bottom in a sizable pool. Maipe looked around, then walked surely into a patch of undergrowth and called me. I found him at the foot of a tall tree, the base of which was hidden by thick bush. Through the bush ran a vine, looped around the tree about three feet off the ground. Maipe said that any Pygmy seeing that would know that it marked the sleeping place of a molimo trumpet and would keep away, for it did not concern him and the molimo should not be disturbed while sleeping. I asked where the trumpet was, and Maipe pointed up above his head. I could see nothing except the immense branches of the tree spreading out high above, more than a hundred feet up. "That is where it sleeps," he said. "It is safe there. It sleeps there until it is needed."

I asked when it was needed, but Maipe had said all he was going to say. He looked up at the tree for a last time, then motioned with his head that we should be on our way. Kenge whispered to me that when we got back he would ask Moke to tell me more. It was better for old men to talk about these things.

That same night, just before the singing started, Moke was sitting outside his hut, whittling away at a new bow he was making, and talking to himself because there was nobody else for him to talk to. Kenge had spoken to him when we got back to the camp at dusk, but I did not expect anything to come of it, and Kenge had said nothing to me. Moke looked up and stared in my direction, then he looked back at his bow and continued whittling away with a rough stone. But he spoke a little louder, so that I would hear.

"Ebamunyama," he said, using the name I had been given, "*pika'i to*." ("Come here.")

He spoke as if he was addressing the bow, and when I got to him he still did not look up but just told me to sit down. Talking to the bow in his soft old voice, he said that he had been told I was asking about the molimo, and that this was a good thing and he would tell me whatever he could.

He went on to tell that the Pygmies call out their molimo whenever things seem to be going wrong. "It may be that the hunting is bad," he said, "or that someone is ill, or, as now, that someone has died. These are not good things, and we like things to be good. So we call out the molimo and it makes them good, as they should be."

Kind, quiet old Moke, all alone and without a wife to look after him, still working away at his bow, occasionally looking along the shank to make sure he was keeping the line true—he told me many things that evening. But, most important, he told me, or rather showed me, how the Pygmies believe in the goodness of the forest.

"The forest is a father and mother to us," he said, "and like a father or mother it gives us everything we need—food, clothing, shelter, warmth . . . and affection. Normally everything goes well, because the forest is good to its children, but when things go wrong there must be a reason."

I wondered what he would say now, because I knew that the village people, in times of crisis, believe that they have been cursed either by some evil spirit or by a witch or sorcerer. But not the Pygmies; their logic is simpler and their faith stronger, because their world is kinder.

Moke showed me this when he said, "Normally everything goes well in our world. But at night when we are sleeping, sometimes things go wrong, because we are not awake to stop them from going wrong. Army ants invade the camp; leopards may come in and steal a hunting dog or even a child. If we were awake these things would not happen. So when something big goes wrong, like illness or bad hunting or death, it must be because the forest is sleeping and not looking after its children. So what do we do? We wake it up. We wake it up by singing to it, and we do this because we want it to awaken happy. Then everything will be well and good again. So when our world is going well then also we sing to the forest because we want it to share our happiness."

All this I had heard before, but I had not realized quite so clearly that this was what the molimo was all about. It was as though the nightly chorus were an intimate communion between a people and their god, the forest. Moke even talked about this, but when he did so he stopped working on his bow and turned his wrinkled old face to stare at me with his deep, brown, smiling eyes. He told me how all Pygmies have different names for their god, but how they all know that it is really the same one. Just what it is, of course, they don't know, and that is why the name really does not matter very much. "How can we know?" he asked. "We can't see him; perhaps only when we die will we know and then we can't tell anyone. So how can we say what he is like or what his name is? But he must be good to give us so many things. He must be of the forest. So when we sing, we sing to the forest."

The complete faith of the Pygmies in the goodness of their forest world is perhaps best of all expressed in one of their great molimo songs, one of the songs that is sung fully only when someone has died. At no time do their songs ask for this or that to be done, for the hunt to be made better or for someone's illness to be cured; it is not necessary. All that is needful is to awaken the forest, and everything will come right. But suppose it does not, suppose that someone dies, then what? Then the men sit around their evening fire, as I had been doing with them for the past month, and they sing songs of devotion, songs of praise, to wake up the forest and rejoice it, to make it happy again. Of the disaster that has befallen them they sing, in this one great song, "There is darkness all around us; but if darkness *is*, and the darkness is of the forest, then the darkness must be good."

As Moke looked at me and spoke I wondered if this was how he had once explained things to his own son. Now I began to understand what happened at night when fifteen feet of drainpipe was carried into the camp and someone blew or sang into it; and I began to understand what the "presence" was—it was surely the presence of the Forest itself, in all its beauty and goodness.

The Pygmies and a few other similar groups still live very close to nature. They represent a way of life different in the extreme from our modern, urban, complex, and in many ways artificial mode of life. Even so, the Pygmies' great love for the forest and the powerful religious sentiments that are associated with it do not appear unintelligible. And, although their worship of the forest may eventually be extinguished, since the forest itself is beginning to disappear, it is a religious sentiment that can scarcely be described as "grotesque." How much more grotesque, perhaps, is Turnbull's expectation (shared most probably by many of us) that the *molimo* should be a precious material object rather than an ordinary length of drainpipe. It is to his credit, however, that Turnbull came to realize his own ethnocentrism in this respect. He describes this deeper awareness in a memorable anecdote:

One night in particular will always live for me, because that night I think I learned just how far away we civilized human beings have drifted from reality. The moon was full, so the dancing had gone on for longer than usual. Just before going to sleep I was standing outside my hut when I heard a curious noise from the nearby children's bopi. This surprised me, because at nighttime the Pygmies generally never set foot outside the main camp. I wandered over to see what it was.

There, in the tiny clearing, splashed with silver, was the sophisticated Kenge, clad in bark cloth, adorned with leaves, with a flower stuck in his hair. He was all alone, dancing around and singing softly to himself as he gazed up at the treetops.

19

Now Kenge was the biggest flirt for miles, so, after watching a while, I came into the clearing and asked, jokingly, why he was dancing alone. He stopped, turned slowly around and looked at me as though I was the biggest fool he had ever seen; and he was plainly surprised by my stupidity.

"But I'm **not** dancing alone," he said. "I am dancing with the forest, dancing with the moon." Then, with the utmost uncon-cern, he ignored me and continued his dance of love and life. [1961:272]

This will perhaps not impress those who see the forests only in terms of "board footage," or those who have been raised exclusively on concrete and steel, but it surely repre-sents human values that should be treasured by all.

In terms of the anthropological experience and of the **personal equation** in fieldwork, a most instructive lesson can be drawn from comparing Turnbull's account of his life with the Pygmies with his later sojourn among the Ik. The latter experience, described in **The Mountain People** (1972), was as distasteful to him as the previous one had been pleasant. The Ik, as Turnbull describes them, represent an almost unbelievable contrast to the Pygmies, and this fact raises many questions about the essence of human nature.

In addition to **The Forest People** and several articles, Turnbull has written a more traditional ethnography of the Pygmies, **Wayward Servants** (1965). He is also the author of a series of life-sketches of modern Africans, **The Lonely African** (1962); of the previously mentioned book on the Ik, **The Mountain People** (1972); and, more recently, of a general book on Africa, **Man in Africa** (1976).

For other accounts of the Pygmies see G. Burrows, **The Land of the Pigmies** (1898); P. B. du Chaillu, **The World of the Great Forest** (1900); P. Schebesta, **Among Congo Pygmies** (1933) and **Revisiting my Pygmy Hosts** (1937). There is a brief account by Patrick Putnam, "The Pygmies of the Ituri Forest," in **A Reader in General Anthropology,** edited by Carleton S. Coon (1948).

An ethnographic film that deals with the life of the Ituri Pygmies, **Pygmies of Africa,** was made in 1939. A some-what more ambitious French attempt, **Au Pays des Pygmées** (In Pygmy Country), appeared several years later. Although neither of these is outstanding, they do give considerable in-formation on the day-to-day life of this exceptional group. The most comprehensive film to date on these remarkable people is **Pygmies,** produced by Jean Pierre Hallet.

2

An eskimo takes a bride

PETER FREUCHEN*

No people on earth, not even the Pygmies, have captured the imagination of others as the Eskimo have. To survive in their harsh arctic environment they have had to develop not only exceptional hunting skills and a remarkable technology, but also elaborate customs relating to sharing and cooperation. As men cannot survive in the arctic without women to aid them, nor women without men, the institution of marriage takes on an unusual significance. The following short story, taken from Peter Freuchen's **Book of the Eskimos,** gives us an entertaining account of an Eskimo marriage and at the same time allows us a glimpse of some Eskimo personality traits.

Peter Freuchen was eminently, even uniquely, qualified to tell us about the Eskimo. He first visited them in 1906 with the Danish Expedition to Greenland. He returned in 1910 with Knud Rasmussen to found a trading station at Thule. He married an Eskimo woman and spent the rest of his life living and working with the Eskimo. During the Fifth Thule Expedition (1921—1924) Freuchen lost one of his feet. It was during his convalescence that he became interested in writing about the Eskimo. Not all of what we know about other peoples has come to us from trained anthropologists, of course. Much of the best information we have on the Eskimo came from the labors of Rasmussen and Freuchen, who were much better known as explorers and traders than as anthropologists. As such, they were not con-

* Reprinted from Peter Freuchen, *Book of the Eskimos*. Copyright © 1961 by the Estate of Peter Freuchen. Reprinted by permission of Harold Matson Company, Inc.

strained always to write in an academic format or in anthropological jargon. This did not prevent them from presenting
accurate ethnographic information, and in fact it allowed
them to tell us many things about the Eskimo, especially
about Eskimo personality and thought, that we would not
find in the more typically dehumanized accounts of anthropologists.

Two little girls brought the exciting news from tent to tent: "Imenak
has arrived! He has left his sled down by the ice and he doesn't un-
load it!"

Nobody could fail to understand the meaning of this. Imenak
wanted to get away in a hurry. He had already given himself away by
paying too much attention to Arnaluk, the beautiful daughter of
Otonia. And there was no doubt of her feelings. It was common
knowledge that she had several times lately eaten the lice which she
removed from his hair when he put his head in her lap to be relieved of
the annoying little animals. What then could be more obvious than
that she loved him.

Imenak was a very good hunter, he was young and he was good
looking. His father was highly regarded and lived with his brothers at
a settlement farther north. He had given his son a number of good
dogs and the young man already had several bears and walrus to his
credit. No wonder that Imenak was now looking around for a wife to
take care of all his skins and to make clothes for him. As long as he remained single his mother did it for him which meant that Imenak
always had to wait until his father had been taken care of. His
younger sister and old grandmother made him his mittens and sometimes a pair of kamiks, but a young man who is a great hunter needs a
great deal of clothes. A wife is a necessity.

Arnaluk was free and unattached. She might not yet know all
there is to know about sewing and she was far from being an expert in
preparing the skins. She was still failing in many of the duties of a
woman. But she was strong, hard working and good looking. Her
teeth were pure white, her full cheeks were always smudged from the
skins she was chewing in order to make them soft enough for kamik
soles. The brown and black smears looked rather cute. And Arnaluk
had the flattest little nose—and thus the most beautiful—of all the
girls in the village.

Many young men had tried in vain to become a son-in-law in
Otonia's house, since Arnaluk's father would only accept a man
whose fame and family were equal to his own. A few quiet words had

22

been enough to turn down the suitors. No scenes were permitted and an outright quarrel was out of the question.

The suitor would pay a visit and stay as a guest in Otonia's house. Sometimes the men spent the night in the Young People's House where Arnaluk slept, but the girl took no interest beyond the friendly smiles she gave everybody. The boys would never pay any attention to her. They would not make themselves the laughingstock of all the listeners by talking to a girl or even looking at her except to let her dry their boots or mittens and once in a while to let her pick the lice out of their hair when the animals were getting too vicious. Arnaluk was very good at catching the little gray bugs, but she always threw them in the fire and laughed when they exploded with a tiny "crack."

The eager young men would always sit quietly on the side bench over their meal. It was not seemly for them to speak first when there were older people present. But if a man was very set on his errand, he might finally speak up.

"One should have mended a pair of kamiks," he might say. "Unfortunately one has nobody to do the sewing."

There would be a few minutes of silence. The meaning of the words was obvious.

"There might perhaps be a woman further north," Otonia would finally answer. "Somebody might be found there to take care of a pair of kamiks."

Thus it was said, the refusal was public and the suitor had been told off. He would never show a thing, only continue his meal and maybe say a few words about his useless dogs which would make them all exaggerate their praise of his animals. The man would prolong his meal as much as possible since his departure had now been made quite difficult. He knew that roars of laughter would follow him out. The best was to wait until somebody else had an errand outside and then try to sneak out unnoticed. The suitor would never say goodbye, just drive off with his dogs as quietly as possible. A young man did not carry much luggage and nobody could tell whether he was going hunting or was a rejected suitor going home empty-handed.

Gossip travels fast, however, and the moment a suitor had left Otonia's tent the news made the rounds: "Otonia has turned down another man again!" The names were mentioned, each new and unsuccessful proposal was whispered about up and down the coast. The Arctic Eskimos are not numerous, it is far between their villages and they thrive on gossip.

But everything was different the day Imenak arrived. It was well known that last spring Otonia had spent quite some time with Imenak's father. They had stayed together in an igloo while they were waiting for walrus. The evening had been very long with nothing to do but talk.

Imerasuk was proud of his son Imenak who had just caught a walrus that same day. It was the first one they had caught and it was a fat and glistening animal.

"This poor boy of mine," Imerasuk had said. "By the merest chance he has happened to catch this walrus today. It's a great pity for him since he'll now be expected to have the same luck all the time. And it is well known to us all that he is totally lacking in any kind of skill."

The other men praised Imenak and said that the young man would surely become a great hunter like his father.

"Nothing of the kind," Imerasuk went on. "What a misery! Now in my old days it seems that I shall have to move to another settlement since my fellow settlers are given to lies. My son is not the only member of my family who would surely starve if the neighbors did not help. The boy is utterly dependent on his luck. I fear for the fate of my son when he grows old. No father can possibly trust him with his daughter since she would be bound to starve."

There was a breathless pause since they all knew the importance of Otonia's answer. At last the old man spoke up:

"If the girls in my village were only not so miserably useless and at the same time so ugly that they have to hide their faces! Otherwise they would have had a chance of being fed in their old age."

The question was settled. The faces in the igloo were set in masks of frozen calm. No hint of expression revealed the faintest interest in a conversation which merely dealt with women and thus could be of no importance. But two of the men went outside, saying that they had to look after their dogs. Once outside, they took a careful look at the sky and decided it would be too windy for the ice to settle tomorrow. There would be no good hunting and they might just as well go home right away. As they drove off, the other men knew that this latest news was going out in the world with them. Soon it would be known all along the coast that Otonia had promised his daughter to Imenak, the great son of Imerasuk. All the other young men would know that there was no hope for them any more since Imenak was stronger than them all and came from a great and powerful family.

Imenak had been lying on the floor in the igloo while his father talked with Otonia. He soon began snoring to show that he had not heard a word they had said and that in any case the whole subject did not concern him in the least.

The next few days he could not help noticing, however, that the girls began eying him curiously and small hints popped up in everything that was said to him. Imenak felt quite shy and wanted to get away from it all. At last he got one of his friends to go bear hunting with him in the region of the Humboldt Glacier far to the north. Thus he would be left in peace and at the same time show that he did not depend on any woman.

They did not return until the ice was breaking up. Imenak brought back with him a number of good bearskins, but it was noticed right away that he had cut off the long mane hair which the Eskimo women use for the tops of their stockings. His sisters felt quite hurt and told their girl friends about it:

"A bear hunter returns but, of course, he must throw away the mane hair of the bear which we could use for stockings!"

It was easy enough to figure out. People giggled and talked and Imenak felt their eyes constantly on him—which is the worst kind of torture for an Eskimo. And so at last he went down to Cape York where Otonia and his daughter Arnaluk lived.

The girl had had her troubles too. She had felt the curiosity all around her and had taken to sleeping more often in the Young People's House instead of with her parents in order to show her independence. Her mother laughed at her but was proud of her modesty.

From the moment Imenak arrived, Arnaluk did not show herself outside. She stayed in her tent all the time. Outwardly she was calm but she felt as if she was going to burst. Soon she would be the wife of a great hunter, she would be able to invite all her new neighbors, urging them to eat while she complained bitterly that nothing in her house was worth eating since her husband did not know the first thing about hunting. Alone in her tent she was dreaming about all the things that make life wonderful for a young Eskimo girl.

Imenak had to call on all the people in Cape York. He did not go first to Otonia's house, nor did he make it his last visit. Either way he would have revealed his eagerness and showed that his visit had a special purpose.

When he finally called on his future father-in-law, Otonia received him in a friendly way without giving him any special attention. Otonia's wife served auks in rich oil and when they had all eaten a while, their tongues loosened. Most of the people at the settlement were present since they did not want to miss anything.

"Well, well," sighed Imenak at last. "One certainly would like to settle down close to a bird cliff this summer and fill up the bags with such good auks."

Nothing was said since they all knew that one cannot decide whether to settle down until one has a woman. Imenak had had his say.

That night Imenak slept in the Young People's House, but Arnaluk remained in her parents' tent. The next night the same, and the following one. Imenak did not seem to be in a hurry. He went seal hunting during the day, caught a great many and drove by Otonia's house with a sled loaded with seals. But Arnaluk did not appear, nor did she turn up at the communal meals. She ate by herself in her tent.

One day an old woman finally commented to Otonia's wife on the long absence of her daughter.

"She is such a shy girl!" said the mother proudly and everybody heard her. A few of them laughed, but hurried to explain that it was only because some of the puppies playing by the fire seemed so funny.

Finally it was discovered that Arnaluk had to leave her tent for a few minutes in the evening to follow the call of nature. She always looked around very carefully first. Imenak was waiting for her and pounced on her the moment she appeared. But he was not fast enough. Arnaluk jumped back in the tent and the young man could hear her say in a loud voice that she had just taken a look at the weather but it did not seem very inviting.

Imenak waited a moment before he went back to his sled where he now decided to spend the night. It was quite warm, the Arctic sun was in the sky all night long and Imenak could stay outside and keep an eye on the entrance to Otonia's tent. But Arnaluk did not come out any more. She only lifted up the bottom flap of her tent now and then and did not have to let him see her at all.

The excitement was growing in Cape York since they all knew it would be too bitter a defeat for Imenak if he had to return home without his girl. But they never discussed it with him, they only talked about hunting and the weather. Imenak made only very short hunting trips now and spent most of the time in the settlement playing with the other young men. Arnaluk paid no attention to their games, she remained stubbornly out of sight and was highly praised for her maidenly modesty. She could be heard singing to her young sisters, telling them that she would play in the snow with them next winter. This was an open challenge and at last Imenak was forced to take the offensive.

In the winter it is impossible to get a woman out of a stone house and, consequently, a marriage can take place only in summer. There is only a small hole in the floor of the winterhouses and if a woman just spreads out her arms and legs, nobody can force her out. In the summer it is different since a tent is no great obstacle.

Finally Imenak went into action. With a great jump he was in the middle of Arnaluk's tent. The children screamed and their mother told them to be quiet. Otonia sat on his bed and greeted his future son-in-law with a smile.

"We seem to have visitors today," he remarked but he quickly left the tent while his wife remained quietly in her corner.

Imenak jumped on the bed where Arnaluk had withdrawn as far as possible, clutching the tent pole with all her might. Two old women sitting next to her were screaming with laughter.

Imenak grabbed the girl who screamed and kicked in vain. He got hold of one knee and one arm and pulled her to him. She held on to the tent pole and the whole tent was trembling as he pulled her. The mother called out that Arnaluk was not playing fair and that the whole tent would fall down.

"I don't care! Nobody can get me out of here!" Arnaluk screamed in a wild fury, and bit him in the hand. Imenak pulled and she kicked until finally the pole gave way and tore a gaping hole in the wall of the tent.

"An opening should be used!" cried Imenak jubilantly and with one kick he split open the entire wall of the tent. He rolled her through and now they were both on the outside where they were met by shrieks of laughter. The whole settlement knew what was happening and they were waiting to see the couple come out the regular exit. This way it was even more exciting.

Outside there was more room for fighting. Arnaluk still held on to the tent pole, but he got one of her hands loose by beating her over the knuckles. He tried the same thing with the other hand which flew suddenly from the pole straight into his face. The sharp nails tore five long gashes from his eye down the whole cheek and the blood was streaming down his face. The Eskimos cheered for this honorable feat.

At last Imenak got the wild woman up on his shoulders while she still beat him over the head and tore out fistfuls of hair. She was kicking wildly but he had her in such a grip that she could not stop him from walking.

The audience knew that the end of the show was approaching. Down by the meat rack two young men were looking casually at the sky apparently without having seen or heard a thing. Judging from their faces they did not even notice the kicking, screaming girl on Imenak's shoulder. The proud bridegroom stopped for a moment to show that nothing unusual had happened although he carried a shrieking bride on his shoulders.

"It is not unlikely," he said casually, "that one might go away for a while."

"Oh? Somebody is leaving?" they answered with a disinterested air. Imenak's face remained calm although he had to use all his strength to keep her in place.

He got her down to the place he had prepared and threw her down on the sled. But still the crazy girl did not give up. She jumped up and tried to run away from him. Imenak had to run after her and grabbed her in such a way that they both fell down. She kicked him in the face and soon blood from his nose mixed with the blood running down from the gashes in his cheeks. He got her on the sled once more and this time he gave her a real beating, but as soon as he stopped she got up again, spit in his face and took up a defensive position once more.

At last Arnaluk's mother had had enough. She had enjoyed the fight immensely, she was very proud of her daughter's modesty and defiance which she knew would be praised up and down the coast to the honor of her family. But enough is enough.

She called down from her tent: "It's time to give in! A young woman has given sufficient proof of her fear of marriage which is the terrible fate of all women. Alas, resistance is of no avail. All men are pitiless brutes and the masters of our weaker sex! It has been seen once more that there is no escape!"

The words had been said. The mother had given the signal and Arnaluk subsided at once. She settled down on the sled, still gasping from the struggle. People returned to their tents and Imenak made the dogs ready for the trip. When one of them tried to get away and return to the tents, Arnaluk grabbed the whip and lashed out viciously like a man.

"Miserable dogs!" she called out. "Don't you know we are going home!" She was a wife already and as such had the right and duty to berate her husband's property to win the praise of others.

They made the return trip in a leisurely pace to have a few days to repair their clothes and let their faces heal. Imenak had some sewing things along, since the young wife had nothing. She had been robbed and carried off by force and her husband had to look after her.

When they arrived at the first settlement no questions were asked. They were received as if Imenak had always had Arnaluk with him wherever he went, but as soon as they left, the talk began. The obvious signs of damage to Imenak's face and clothes were all to the honor of the bride.

Imerasuk met them as soon as they arrived at the settlement. He had been out hunting and brought home a great many delicious seals.

"There is reasonable hope that my skins will be cleaned faster now that my son has someone to help with the work," was all he said.

But this was the welcome greeting and the recognition of the marriage.

Arnaluk entered the tent of her parents-in-law and sat down. Nobody greeted her and she said nothing. Imenak had caught a few seals on his way home. Now he cut open one of them and brought the liver into the tent. He put it on a flat stone and cut it in beautiful, pink slices.

"Perhaps one would condescend to taste the liver of this measly little seal I had the undeserved luck to catch," he said.

"What a misery! It's a true shame to offer such poor food which is not fit for dogs but it seems to be all a useless husband is able to bring home," said Arnaluk as she offered the liver to her new family. She was blushing deeply since it was her first experience as a married woman and hostess. Nobody gave any sign that the situation was at all unusual and they all ate with great appetite. Afterward the young girls were told about Arnaluk who had won great honor by resisting her husband so heroically and showing such stubborn reluctance to get married.

Some form of marriage, like religion, is a human universal, although marriage customs vary widely. **Polygyny,** for example, was known to the Eskimo but was very rarely practiced when compared with some African or Pacific Island cultures. And although **polyandry** was not institutionalized, the much publicized Eskimo custom of wife lending, not actually very widespread, performed much the same function. Seen in its proper context, wife lending appears to be a perfectly sensible response to the demands of physical survival in an inhospitable environment. As there were so few Eskimo, and since they were at times so totally dependent upon the hospitality of others, fighting between suitors or others over women would have been terribly disruptive. For a man to lend his wife to another was an act of friendship and generosity. It was not carried out without the woman's consent. Other seemingly strange or even bizarre marriage customs, like those of the Nuer of Africa, for example, whereby a woman can legally marry another woman or even a ghost, make perfect sense when seen in the context of the belief system that surrounds them (Evans-Pritchard, 1951). In spite of the extremes of variation in what is permitted, **monogamy** is in fact everywhere the most common form of marriage, and it is the basic building block in the systems of **kinship** that have fascinated anthropologists for such a long time.

Although ethnographic short stories and novels have not been fully accepted by anthropologists as means for presenting ethnographic information, no careful analysis has ever been made of their adequacy in this respect. It may be that certain kinds of information—in this case Eskimo modesty and attitudes towards marriage—are actually better presented in this way than they are in the traditional ethnographic monograph. Generally speaking, the authenticity of Freuchen's information has not been questioned, but there is a question about the way his style of presentation may have affected it.

There are literally hundreds of books on the Eskimo. Obviously, they are not all of uniform quality, and most of them, from an ethnographic standpoint, are quite useless. Among the readable ones that also have considerable ethnographic interest are Freuchen's **Eskimo** (1931), Diamond Jenness's **The People of the Twilight** (1959), Jean L. Brigg's **Never in Anger: Portrait of an Eskimo Family** (1970) and Gontran de Poncins's **Kabloona** (1941). Two Eskimo life histories of interest are **I, Nuligak,** edited by Maurice Metayer (1966) and **Eskimo Boyhood,** by Charles Hughes (1974). A recent novel by James Houston, **The White Dawn** (1971), is based on an authentic historical occurrence and is also ethnographic. It has been made into a major motion picture.

For more basic information on the Eskimo see Knud Rasmussen's account **The People of the Polar North, a Record** (1908) and Vilhjalmur Stefansson's **My Life with the Eskimo** (1913) and **Hunters of the Great North** (1922). Also Kai Birket-Smith's, **The Eskimo** (1959), Franz Boas's **The Central Eskimo** (1964), and Richard K. Nelson's **Hunters of the Northern Ice** (1969). Asen Balikci's **The Netsilik** (1970) gives a broad ethnographic coverage and can be supplemented with the nine quite exceptional ethnographic films on the Netsilik that he directed.

The first documentary film ever made, **Nanook of the North,** by Robert J. Flaherty, is still often used by students of anthropology. It remains a unique and valuable account of Eskimo life. Freuchen's novel, **Eskimo** (1931) was also made into a film. Other films on the Eskimo include **The Wedding of Paolo** (1937) and **Angotee.**

3

Asemo

K. E. READ*

Out of the experience of anthropologists and from the attempt to overcome ethnocentrism developed the concept of **cultural relativity.** Cultural relativity holds that there is no single scale of values for all cultures and that therefore particular customs, beliefs, and practices must be judged only in the context in which they occur. This poses a terrible paradox, however, since the antidote to ethnocentrism cannot simply be unthinking approval. Even the most ardent proponents of cultural relativism did not take the position that Nazi values were acceptable in the context of Nazi Germany. To attempt to understand something does not mean you must also necessarily approve of it. This constitutes a kind of occupational hazard for anthropologists. However much they may try to be objective, fieldworkers are often repelled by some of the customs they observe and record. This is part of the experience that is referred to as **culture shock.** Most anthropologists experience culture shock, although in varying degrees of intensity. At the same time, anthropologists are often profoundly moved and permanently changed by their experiences with alien cultures so different from their own. In the following unusual and obviously subjective account Kenneth E. Read describes his per-

* Reprinted by permission of Charles Scribner's Sons from *The High Valley* by Kenneth E. Read. Copyright © 1965 Kenneth E. Read.

sonal reaction to a dramatic but terribly violent male initiation ceremony in the New Guinea Highlands.

The Gahuku-Gama, the people whom Read describes here, were totally unknown to the outside world until the early 1930s. Even when Read did his pioneer fieldwork among them, approximately twenty years later, the Gahuku-Gama had been only minimally affected by contact with Europeans. In the early 1950s there were no roads in the Highlands. Read and his informant, Makis, who is mentioned in the following account, had to walk everywhere over exceedingly rough terrain. In the early 1960s Makis was killed by a truck while walking along the Highlands Highway. The rites described below were abandoned almost as quickly as the Highlands Highway was constructed, a rate of **culture change** almost without precedent. As Read predicted, he was among the last of the handful of Europeans to observe them in their aboriginal form.

The **nama** cult, of which the ritual presented here is only one part, is a religious system featuring sacred flutes (**nama**) and a form of **ancestor worship.** The flutes represent ancestral power. As **descent** is reckoned only through males, and since they believe they all share a common ancestor, this represents an example of what anthropologists term a **patrilineal descent** system. Power is thus held by a group of male **agnates** who generally reside together on the territory of their fathers (**patrilocal residence**), constitute a **patrilineal clan,** practice clan **exogamy** (they must marry outside of their own group), and, in their turn, pass their power on to their male descendants. Much of the religious practice is directed towards maintaining the idea of male superiority and reinforcing the residential separation of the sexes. Men sleep together in a common men's house, whereas each married woman has her own house where she, her children, and her pigs spend the night. Unlike the Pygmies and the Eskimo, the New Guinea Highlanders are **horticulturalists.** Domesticated pigs are the major form of wealth and are slaughtered and consumed only on ritual occasions. They are well cared for and are fed in part from large gardens of sweet potatoes, yams, taro, beans, bananas, and a variety of other crops. This represents a way of life that survived virtually unchanged for hundreds of years and, although it has features repugnant to us, it has some desirable aspects as well.

32

For the first time in many weeks the flutes were silent that morning. The day broke in fountains of light, and clouds piled high above the mountains, leaving the whole valley open to the sky, a vast green arena waiting for the events that had been so long in the making. As I dressed, the village filled with the sounds of preparation, and Hune-hune, bringing me my breakfast, had exchanged his cotton lap-lap for a bright new male skirt in the Bena-Bena fashion, a style from the east that some Gahuku chose to wear at important ceremonies. In the street later the men put on their finest decorations, standing patiently while boys dressed their long hair or, like Makis, studying the effect of every precisely placed feather in a trade-store mirror propped between his knees. The sun flashed on mother-of-pearl that had been smeared lightly with crimson oil. Feathers fluttered on every head, shaking their colors—bright yellows and reds, peacock hues of blue and green—over skin shining like dark glass under a new application of grease. Familiar features were entirely transformed by paint or barely recognizable behind bone ornaments inserted through pierced septums. Coronets of emerald scarabs and bands of white shells circled every brow, barbaric contrasts to deep-set eyes flashing with anticipation in their wells of shadow.

Entering the street, I was hailed from a dozen different directions with an uninhibited effusiveness that urged me to share the excitement. I took a seat near Makis, moved by my reception and trying to express, by my closeness, the gratitude that always rose to my throat when I encountered this ready acceptance. Over the heads of the men, southeast of the ridge of Asarodzuha, the green trough of the valley had begun to shimmer in the morning sun, reality already succumbing to the illusions of heat. A dozen Gama settlements were identifiable by their groves of casuarinas, each standing below a column of pale blue smoke. The silence in the landscape, compared with the noisy preparations close at hand, pricked my skin with anticipation. The things I wanted to see were happening there, hidden from my eyes by distance. My mind bent toward Asemo on the morning of his manhood, wishing him more than he could possibly achieve.

The men dallied so long over their dressing that we were late in setting out for Gama, forced to maintain a pace that taxed every muscle in my body as I tried to keep up with them. In front of me, Makis had looped his long ceremonial bilum,* which he wore like a

---

* bilum—a net bag made by women and worn suspended from the forehead. Men have long capes made in the same fashion which they wear mostly on ceremonial occasions.

cloak, across his right arm, holding it high, like a woman protecting her skirts from the wet grasses of the trail.

Almost an hour passed before we reached the outskirts of the nearest Gama settlement, entering it near a new clubhouse that had been built to receive the initiates. I had expected a noisy welcome, but the village was completely silent, a double row of houses flanking a street whose exit was hidden by the twisting contours of the ridge. The men entered it boldly, knowing their destination. Groups of women standing near the houses allayed my anxiety that we might have arrived too late. They noted our presence with a few cursory greetings, not moving from their waiting positions, their eyes returning immediately toward the hidden end of the village. Many of them wore mourning, the mothers of initiates who had smeared their bodies with clay in ritual recognition of their separation from their sons, who were formally crossing over to the male division.

As we advanced, the silence seemed to gather itself into a tight coil. The eyes of the women were dark, sightless sockets in their masks of grey clay, their chalky limbs motionless, skeletal figures arranged in rigid attitudes of listening concentration. An answering response came from the men. Their pace increased to a fast trot, then suddenly, signaled by a shattering explosion of sound, they broke into a headlong run that carried us into the concealed end of the street.

The noise and movement were overwhelming. Behind us, the shrill voices of women rose in keening, ritual, stylized cries informed by genuine emotion that were like a sharp instrument stabbing into the din around me. The ululating notes of male voices locked with thumping shouts, deep drum beats expelled from distended chests counterpointed the crash of bare feet on the ground, and, rising above it all, came the cries of the flutes, which I heard at close quarters for the first time, a sound like great wings beating at the ear drums, throbbing and flapping in the hollow portions of the skull.

For several minutes utter confusion filled the street. Abandoned by the villagers of Susuroka, I tried to draw back from the engulfing sound, to impose some order on the scene in front of me. At least fifty men were in the clearing, decorated in the full panoply of war, chests and faces daubed with paint or pig's grease mixed with charcoal, some armed with shields, others with only their bows and arrows. The dark skin of their bodies was punctuated dramatically by the whiteness of shell, the yellow of the plaited bands that clasped the muscles of their arms and calves. The tossing array of plumes, parrot and bird of paradise, which fluttered like attendants over their heads, was a coruscating, swirling mass of brilliance matching their movements, swooping low as they bent from the waist, flying back again with their lifted heads, circling the space between the rows of houses. Dust rose under the rushing feet, a haze separating lower limbs from glistening torsos, and, as the minutes passed, chest and shoulders from the extended line of a throat, from faces that were almost expressionless in their ecstatic communion with an invisible force.

Asemo and his age mates were somewhere in the middle of the throng, almost certainly blinded by the dust, carried along by the press of stronger bodies, their heads, like mine, spinning with the noise and the shrilling of the flutes. Other youths had told me, laughing, of their panic during these opening minutes of their day-long ordeal, their fear of being trampled and the chilling effect of the flutes, apparently no less moving because they knew of the simple deception practiced on the women. I could only wonder with pain what Asemo felt, reaching out to him across a distance immeasurably greater than our respective years. For suddenly a barrier that had lifted briefly during the past few months had dropped between us, foreclosing any possibility we might have had of meeting each other on the same side.

For the rest of the day I carried this feeling with me, a curiously ambiguous mixture of closeness and detachment from the whole sequence of events that followed the initial eruption of sound in the Gama village. At times of group crisis I felt most alien, the outsider who became virtually invisible. But on other occasions there was a personal identification with the individuals that transcended the boundaries established by our different backgrounds, the very strength of the feelings displayed before me drawing me into the tide of a common emotion. This time it did not happen. Partly, perhaps, the reason lay in the fact that what I saw that day revolted me. At one level I could appreciate the drama of the rites, their arrogant sweep through the valley, their staging, observing them as a splendid spectacle, and beneath the physical acts I could see a more important symbolism, meanings not particular to the Gahuku context alone but drawn from the universal range of human experience. But the violence, the aggressive overstatement also laid me open to a rejection of it not uncommon while I was in the valley and the basis of my frequent need to contrive a screen between myself and this life.

Nothing could have contrasted more sharply with the periods I had spent alone with Asemo; perhaps nothing else could have served so dramatically to promote awareness of our inevitable separation. Indeed, as the events unfolded I felt the separation had been accomplished already, that I had had all that I was entitled to expect from our relationship, forced to stand aside while the stream of his own life carried him away from me.

I was not far behind the men as they burst into the arena of the valley. Released from the confinement of the trees, the flute calls and the shouts leaped toward the sky, spinning across the grasslands to the distant mountains. The forward rush of the men carried them along a path, almost too narrow to contain them, that ran between high fences of pit-pit. Those on the outskirts of the throng were pushed against the fences by the press of bodies in the center, the blows from their legs and shoulders thrashing the leaves of the cane until the entire space above our heads seemed to toss to the music, a frantic dance that followed us through the length of the gardens.

Passing the last patch of cultivated land the men changed direction abruptly, turned from the path and plunged down the side of the ridge. For an astonishing moment I stood at the place where they had disappeared. They were already far ahead of me, careening down the step slope, legs lifting to the level of their waists to force a passage through the grass that fell behind them in a lengthening wake. The whole hillside seemed to shiver under the momentum of their rush. Bright stands of crotolaria broke under their feet, scattering their yellow flowers on the trampled grass; saplings bent to the ground like ravaged derelicts. As I hesitated at the edge of the path the flute cries and the shouting were answered from other points of the valley, filling the sky with a shrill vibration. In a sudden vision I saw the clans of Gama streaming down the neighboring ridges, turning aside from the well-worn tracks, taking to the slopes and the broken ground in the same symbolic show of strength, surging irresistibly toward their meeting place at the river.

It was more than a mile away, farther by the normal paths that kept to the high ground above me. I was virtually alone, outstripped by the men, following behind them on the sound of the flutes, my feet slipping and sliding along their trail of devastation. The sun was high and hot, draining the landscape of its color, veiling the mountains in a smoky haze that obscured their shape and reduced their shadowed folds to fading bruises. As I stumbled and fell I was not aware of any feeling other than the need to reach the river. The abrasive grass, cutting my hands as I clutched it for support, and the confining wetness of my shirt were almost unnoticed as I listened to the different streams of sound converging in the distance, meeting and leaping towards a turbulent climax, a final drumming of voices, of wheeling and beating cries that tore at the roots of the mind as I reached a knoll above the water.

A scant six feet below me, the river curved around a wide gravel spit. The sun struck its surface from directly overhead, splintering painfully on the shallows, where stones kicked the water into a white flurry, sliding like a mirage across the deeper reaches near the opposite bank. A vast crowd of men, drawn from all the Gama clans, were gathered on the spit. Most of them faced the water where, above their heads, I saw what the initiates in the front ranks had been brought to see, perhaps a score of naked figures, standing or lolling in the shallows, openly displaying their genitals. Even by the normally outspoken standards of the Gahuku this ritual exhibitionism was frankly overstated, a direct and obvious demonstration of the sexual aspects of male strength, the actions of the figures in the water keyed to hooting shouts of admiration and encouragement.

My immediate reaction was neither one of surprise nor shock, having nothing to do with the men masturbating in the stream below; rather, it was as though the scene below me was totally unreal, something that might give a puzzled tug to my memory at a later date, like an unplaced name or face that causes a momentary and fruitless search through the past in an effort to locate it. All the brightness of the sky seemed to be concentrated in front of me. Distant landmarks, the mountains, the rolling sweep of grass were blurred and indistinct, the action on the spit detached from any larger context, occurring in some independent world of experience, close to me yet immensely remote.

I am not sure how long I stood on the knoll. When at last I went down to the crowded spit the naked figures had left the river and the flutes were silent momentarily. The heat was intense, rising in almost visible waves from the stones, stabbing back at my eyes from the surface of the water. Though the beach and the bend of the river were completely exposed, plainly visible from the elevated ground behind us, the air was close and stifling, heavy with sweat and grease and the cloying odor of unguents, with the biting smell of the overwrought emotions of the crowd. I remained at the edge of the throng where many of the younger men, not long past their own initiation, were watching their elders prepare for the second act of the ritual. The shouting had ceased, but voices were raised excitedly above their normal pitch, creating a general level of noise in which it was impossible to distinguish the individual commands and instructions of the clan leaders.

Gradually, purpose and direction began to emerge from the apparently disorganized movements of the crowd. Past the ranks in front of me I noticed a movement toward the river, several men stepping out until the water parted around their calves, its dark stains eating into their trailing crimson cloaks. As they turned to face the beach my eyes fell on the youth who stood between them. No older than Asemo, his head reached only to the shoulders of the men who held him firmly by the upper arms, the tightness of their grip forcing his soft flesh into folds between their fingers. Against the violence of their paint, his figure looked slighter than it was, his nakedness touchingly immature. His knees were slightly bent, as though his legs swung helplessly in the currents of the river. When he raised his head, the eyes looking toward the bank were wet with panic.

Suddenly, if only momentarily, the screen that had separated me from the action seemed to part. The noise, the smell of several hundred bodies, the dazzling light swept over me like a rush of stale air from a sealed room. Drawn involuntarily into the crowd, feeling the lick of its tension, I searched for Asemo, filled with a need to be near him, to expiate the betrayal for which I felt unreasonably guilty. Thinking I recognized Makis, I tried to push my way toward him through the crush, but was several yards from my goal when a ringing shout went up from the beach and the cries of the flutes bit into the sky above my head. I was forced back from the water as the crowd around me retreated, clearing a path along the margin of the spit.

Several men had appeared on this narrow stage in front of the initiates. One of them, a man in his early thirties, was Gapiriha of Nagamidzuha. He was above average height, very powerfully built, his skin shining like metal through rivulets of sweat and grease, the musculature revealed as sharply as the detail of an anatomical drawing. There was a striking Mayan cast to his features, the curving nose almost meeting lips that were feminine in their fullness, their sculptured lines partly hidden by the circular bone ornament hanging from his septum. Known as a "hard" man, he was given to sudden outbursts of violence, too forceful and self-assertive to care much for the opinions of others, too impatient of the subtleties of persuasion to attract and hold a following, but nevertheless a man of reputation, direct and aggressive, clearly identified with the more obvious male virtues. His chest shuddered and his eyes were intensely bright, a shine that lacked the slightest flicker of recognition, looking out from some pinnacle of personal experience, some private state of feeling and awareness that distended the veins of his neck in explosive, inarticulate shouts.

I watched him with fascination and disbelief, the combination of recognition and rejection that is sparked by any violent display of emotion. He moved out into the river and faced the crowded bank where the water swirled around his calves. He was holding two cigar-shaped objects fashioned from the razor-sharp leaves of green pit-pit. Flourishing them like a conjurer in a spotlight, raising them above the level of his shoulders, he tilted his head back and thrust the rolls of leaf into his nostrils. My flesh recoiled in shock, nerves contracting as though they were seared by the pain that must have swept through

38

his own body as his fingers sawed at the protruding ends of the wadded leaves, thrusting them rapidly up and down inside his nose. I felt sick with distaste, wanting to turn from the exhibition of self-mutilation that provoked a chorus of approving shouts from the crowd, a sound climaxed by the familiar ululating cry of accomplishment as he withdrew the bloody leaves and lowered his head toward the water. Blood gushed from his nose. His fingers, holding the instruments of purification, dripped it onto the surface of the river, where its cloudy stain divided around his legs. His knees trembled, seemed almost about to buckle under him as he bled, and when he raised his head to stagger out toward the beach his lips, his chin, and his throat ran with bright red.

Even before he reached the gravel spit the crowd's attention had returned to the river, where half-a-dozen men were following his example. As though surfeited by the excess, my initial shock dissipated into a feeling of detached revulsion, not yet connecting the events before me with Asemo. My ears rang with the clamor that rewarded the exhibition in the water. The odor of blood, warm and cloying, added a new ingredient to the acrid smell of the crowd, its presence a sharp reminder of the patterns of thought and the motives lying behind this violent mistreatment of the body. The action taking place in the river was not an isolated or infrequent occurrence, but a standardized performance by which men sought to promote their strength and vigor. For all their protestations of superiority, their perception of women was tinged with an element of envy, and in objective moments they sometimes made unfavorable comparisons between the inevitable processes of maturation in the sex they despised and the less certain, because less obvious, indexes of male development. Women's natural advantages were linked to menstruation, and the proud male sought to engineer the same effect by self-inflicted bleeding, starting at initiation. Once introduced to the practice, men who had the right concern for their health bled their noses regularly, using the wads of leaves to purify their flesh, to rid their bodies of the contaminating influence of women, and to ensure that they faced the dangers of their position in a cleansed condition, ritually protected from the hazards of aggression.

As with every event that occurred that day, notions of physical growth, of ritual pollution, and of social separation of the sexes were blended in this act of characteristic violence, and the assumption of manhood, the formal identification with the masculine side of life was sealed with the shedding of the initiates' own blood. For the crowd-rousing demonstration in the shallows of the river was designed primarily for the edification of the row of youths whose arms were pinioned by older men, a graphic, overacted prologue to their own role in the unfolding drama.

The implications for Asemo were brought home to me suddenly as the last of the blood-stained figures staggered up the gravel beach and the center of attention shifted to the row of waiting boys. My search for him, interrupted by the entrance of Gapiriha, had brought me within several paces of where he stood. Like his age mates, his arms were held by two men, Makis on one side and Bihore on the other, the contrast of their plumes and paint investing his own unadorned nakedness with almost sacrificial innocence. I recalled his elder brothers' descriptions of their feelings at this precise moment, their minds numb with the apprehension of pain, the urge to struggle and escape constrained only by the greater fear of shame. I am sure he did not recognize me. His own eyes saw nothing but the need to marshal the defenses of his body for the imminent act of violation, and he could not have been aware of the manner in which my heart rushed toward him. It was not simply the thought of his suffering that closed off my senses so that momentarily we were alone in the shimmer of light and water, facing each other across a void, the noises and the smells of the crowd nothing more than a remote intrusion beating unsuccessfully at the boundaries of recognition. Everything I had gradually learned of him in the past few months returned to me, rendered more vivid by the weeks of separation, so that I realized suddenly the gap his precipitate departure had left; and the loss stabbed the more sharply because I saw him, now, clearly projected against a screen of impersonal events whose sweep ignored the justifications for his present predicament.

I was probably the last of my kind to witness the action taking place in the river, and generations of Gahuku younger than Asemo would know it only at second hand, as an element from a past that in moments of frustration and disillusionment they might romanticize and regret. But I was seldom successful in maintaining the required clinical distance between myself and the villagers, and at this moment my relationship with Asemo imposed its own particular construction on the scene. He stood for the inarticulate aspirations of a people thrust unwillingly into the uncharted sea of time, and I was struck suddenly by a feeling of poignant futility, a compound of sympathy for those who acted as though the past still showed a viable perspective on the world ahead, and a deeper pain for those whose visions of a possible future blinded them to the externally imposed limits of reality. This was precisely where Asemo stood. The figure of his Gama sponsor concealed him from me as he received the thrust of the purifying leaves, but when the older men moved aside, his violent mission done, the bright blood flowing from Asemo's lowered head was like a hopeless offering for peace between embattled opposites.

My recollection of the day's subsequent events is curiously anticlimactic, though in fact the tension and the violence grew in intensity, building up to the wild, running chase that carried the men back to their settlements. But everything of personal importance had been said to me when Asemo's blood reddened the water, and the things he suffered after this seemed like an unnecessary reiteration, an example of the Gahuku's exhausting tendency to seek excess.

It was past midday when the initiates' first ordeal ended. The light and heat, magnified by the reflecting surfaces of stones and water, had built toward the blinding point. A dozen men moved out into the shallows, their features totally unrecognizable behind the masks of paint crusted with drying blood. The fingers of the man nearest to me worked at releasing the length of cane that circled his waist twice, above the broad, plaited band supporting his vees. Though I had often noticed this item of apparel (it was worn by some men as an everyday part of their attire), I had never ascribed any significance to it and had not thought to ask its purpose. Now I experienced a sudden apprehension as he shaped it into a long, narrow U. Leaning forward from the waist, he placed the rounded section in his mouth, straightened, tilted his head, extending the line of his neck, and fed it into his stomach. My throat contracted and my stomach heaved, compelling me to look away. When I turned to him again most of the cane had disappeared, only two small sections, the open ends of the U, protruding from the corners of his mouth.

I have no idea how long he held this grotesque stance, his straining abdomen and chest racked with involuntary shudders. Already sickened by this display, I stiffened with shock as he raised his hands, grasped the ends of the cane and sawed it rapidly up and down, drawing it almost free of his mouth at the peak of every upward stroke. The fervor of the crowd mounted to a clamorous pitch, breaking in wave upon wave of pulsing cries, the final surge matching my own relief when he dropped the cane, bent from the waist, and vomited into the river.

A new, sour smell threaded through the overheated odors of the beach. The palms of my hands were wet, and my mouth filled with the taste of nausea. I had to force myself to look when the men repeated the performance on the boys, my distaste and the urge to turn away checked by apprehension of their danger. Though it was surely less painful than the first ordeal, there was a serious risk of internal injury if the initiates struggled while they were forced to swallow the canes. Fortunately, or perhaps it had been deliberately planned, they were already too exhausted, too shocked and weak to resist, but I watched anxiously for signs of blood as their sponsors held the boys' heads between their knees. When it was over, I was giddy from the light, the noise, the acid smells, a revulsion so strong that I had to turn my back to the river.

All this time I had not seen Asemo from whom I had been separated in the interval between the two ordeals. The action had moved from the water before he came to view again, standing limply between Bihore and Makis, clearly in need of their supporting hands. Self-consciousness checked my immediate urge to go to him. I did not know what he felt, or what he was expected to feel, any more than it was possible for me to enter into and share the emotions of the older men who had bled and vomited. My sympathy probably was not expected, and I made no move, feeling more alien than ever before.

Though the flutes had ceased their shrilling and the shouts had ended, the crowd milled about the beach, clearly preparing for the final act. Older men strutted importantly near the group of sadly bedraggled boys; the agitated flourish of their red cloaks matched their rapid interchange of words and their brief, intense glances at the heights above us. For the first time in many hours the world outside the narrow beach came to mind, and following the direction of their eyes, I turned toward the ridge cresting like a pale green wave against the sky. The entire landscape seemed completely empty and devoid of life; yet I felt a faint but unmistakable premonition that this first impression was erroneous. There was something slightly ominous in the gestures of the men, signs of a new, untoward excitement that made me search the grass again. More than a mile away, farther by the paths in everyday use, the Gama settlement we had left that morning huddled below its casuarina grove, the trees blurred and bruised by the heat of mid-afternoon, their spired shapes fading into a virtually colorless sky. The intervening distance pulsed and trembled, the grasses bowed under the weight of light. There were no clumps of denser vegetation nor any shadows to offer places of concealment, and thinking of the journey home I forgot the reason for my careful scrutiny, anticipating with misgiving the toiling return to the summit of the ridge.

On the beach, the crowd was preparing to leave. Some of the younger, stronger men had lifted the initiates to their shoulders, support their dejected, limp condition seemed to need. The remainder of the company surrounded them shoulder to shoulder, a noisy corps of protectors who appeared to disregard the voluble, possibly conflicting instructions of the older leaders. No particular person was in control nor was any single command given, yet the entire body of men moved off together, jogging up the path they had avoided earlier in the day.

There was little superficial resemblance to the spectacular surge of the morning's procession. The pace was slower, the flutes silent, out of sight, and even the voices were stilled. Yet there was no mistaking the undercurrent of aggressive maleness, the concerted, rhythmic tread of naked legs, the calculated bravado of tossing plumes, the feeling of alert anticipation that pricked at the mind like the intermittent, flashing reflections of light on ornaments of polished shell. I followed close behind the throng, thankful that they had taken the easier route listening to their laboring breath, the thump of their feet, the jangle and click of their decorations, the medley of sounds superimposed like an insistent, premonitory thrill on the silence of the afternoon.

We mounted higher, now out of sight of the river as we reached the shoulder of the ridge, a point where the path widened considerably between the walls of grass. The pace increased as the forward movement met the gentler gradient of the land, but the quickening of step was also prompted by some other expectation that no one had bothered to share with me.

The confrontation came as we rounded a concealed bend in the track. A tempest of shrill cries fell on us like a rain of arrows, and hordes of women suddenly appeared among the grasses. Galvanized, the men broke into a run, lifting their voices in a thumping celebration of strength that rose and fell with their pounding legs. At that precise moment a stone hit my shoulder with a stinging blow. Startled, but trying to maintain my pace, I looked around uncomprehendingly, searching for the source of the attack and finding it the next instant when the man ahead of me, struck on the side of his neck, turned his contorted face to shout abuse at the screaming women.

In the ensuing confusion it was impossible to estimate the number of assailants. Keeping pace with the men, they ran through the grass bordering the track, stumbling and falling as it wound around their legs. The grotesque, clay-streaked figures of an earlier hour capered wildly at the edge of the group, skeletons with weirdly flailing arms and legs, but the brunt of the attack was carried by other women who were armed with a mixed bag of weapons—stones and lethal pieces of wood, an occasional axe, and even a few bows and arrows. There was no mistaking the venom in the assault. Even the men, who had known what to expect, seemed to be taken aback by it, startled by its force and the intuition that it threatened the established limits of expression. It was not the first time this thought had occurred to me. These graphic rituals of opposition spoke of deep-seated divisions in Gahuku life, not only the formal, ceremonial structure of male and female relationships, but also the avowed notions of superiority and a schism that often revealed itself in open antagonism; men held the upper hand, and they used it. Female resentment had few avenues for direct expression, though men suspected there were many indirect ones, and perhaps the superior male was aware of this on occasions when custom allowed the overt demonstration of opposed interests. As an outsider who had seen the high-handed treatment the men meted out, I could understand their concern when they faced these situations, the perceptible rise in tension correcting any tendency to regard them as a ceremonial charade; for they knew that prescribed boundaries were a poor defense against the inflammatory potential of sanctioned retaliation.

The fury of the present assault convinced me that the ritual expression of hostility and separation teetered on the edge of virtual disaster. The men had bunched together as they ran, so closely packed that they struck each other with their legs and arms. In the center of the throng the initiates, riding the shoulders of their escorts, swayed precariously from side to side, their fingers clutching the feathered hair of the head between their legs. The noise reached out to every corner of the world, the shrill cries and imprecations of the women beating against the stylized male chant that answered them in rising volume, swelling in a concert of defiance. For several minutes the two groups kept apart, an occasional stone or piece of wood hurtling from the sidelines and usually striking home, for it was almost impossible to miss the running target. The outraged shouts of those who were hit spurred the bolder women on to closer combat. Leaving the protection of the grass they darted at the flanks of the men's procession, wielding their weapons with every intent to hurt. Several victims staggered under their blows, lost their footing and their place in the crowd, and separated from their fellows, threatened on every side, took refuge in temporary flight, turning when they had reached a safe distance and hurling back their outrage in abuse. Fresh blood appeared on shoulders and legs. There was a genuine need to fear more serious injury. Neither the axes nor the arrows had been used, as far as I could see, but the pieces of wood were large enough to lay open a skull if they made direct contact, and the initial successes of the women urged them on to more heroic efforts. Undoubtedly the proper, the expected thing for the men to do was to carry on through the assault, ignoring the flying sticks and stones in a telling demonstration of strength, a graphic assertion of male values, but the women's heat had pushed the whole activity beyond the limit where it was possible, or wise, to maintain this composure. Individuals began to turn under the blows, and to follow up their shouted sense of outrage with direct action. The women held only for a moment before they sought the safety of the grass. Scattering in front of their pursuers, they were soon left behind the main body of the procession, which reached the settlement unmolested, entering the shelter of the trees as the medley of angry cries changed to the keening rise and fall of ritual anguish.

The day ended with the clans departing for their respective villages, taking their own bedraggled and exhausted boys with them. During the night the flutes cried again from every men's house where the groups of initiates had been placed for their long seclusion.

More than six weeks passed before the final act was played in the Gama village. During this time I thought often of Asemo but did not visit him in the men's house where he remained with his age mates. Instead, I followed his progress through his subsequent trials at second hand, gathering information on this period of tutelage. It would have been a simple matter to see him, even though the villagers of Susuroka, not as directly involved as the Gama, had returned to their own affairs, and I told myself I could not spare the time away from them. The truth is that I suspected seeing him would only add to my distress, sharpening that sense of his personal tragedy that had qualified his initiation. I could not close my mind to the contrast between these recent events and the motives that had led him to seek my help.

Because of this, I not only kept away from him but also had little heart for the final ceremonies in which his manhood was accepted. The pride and the tumult of praise greeting his assumption of his rightful status had overtones of sadness for me unexplainable to anyone present, and this private perception flavored the clamorous events with a peculiar bitterness.

They began before dawn, an hour conducive to moods in which we see farther than we permit ourselves at other times, and the urgent anticipation of the villagers sparked no answering response in me as we set out for Gama. The atmosphere was grey and lost, the mountains hidden by the veil of darkness, the sea of grass a silent, heavy presence bordering the track. Mists were still thick beneath the trees surrounding the Gama clubhouse where most of the men had gathered before we arrived. There was a great deal of activity but little noise, the hushed voices tuned to the hour and the stillness of the thatched house, where the initiates were being readied for their ceremonial return to life. Standing to one side, deserted by Makis who had been with me all the way from Susuroka, I shivered from the chill rising up my body from the soaked fabric of my trousers. The air had begun to stir faintly as it often does in the pause between night and day, a barely perceptible breath that shook cold splashes of water from the trees. Near me, a group of watchers hugged themselves for warmth, standing above a small fire that sputtered and smoked in the dampness.

The light increased, a gentle greying that gradually revealed the refuse of many meals littering the clearing. In the east a narrow thread of gold appeared in the sky above the mountains, counterpart to the first hint of color in the cloaks and feathered decorations of the men. Makis joined me and suggested that I go with him to the village to await the arrival of the initiates, who, garbed in the finery their kinsmen had made in the preceding weeks, were almost ready to leave the clubhouse.

It was only a short walk, but by the time we reached the street the whole world was dressed in the full panoply of dawn. Crowds of women lined one side of the avenue between the thatched houses. Every few paces, down each side of the street, ovens emitted plumes of blue smoke. The smell of aromatic greens, of blood, and of raw meat hung heavily on the air, aftermath of the vast slaughter of pigs that had taken place the previous day and harbinger of the distribution of cooked food that would close the afternoon. While Makis stopped to receive the greetings of several women in the crowd, I found a place behind them where I could look above their heads toward the entrance to the village. Almost at once a signal traveled down the line in front of me. Propped against the eaves of the house at my back, I looked to the end of the street, where the garden fences trembled in the golden light. Above the leaves of the cane, massed feathers shook their colors in the morning air as though the whole landscape had blossomed with strange flowers overnight. Knowing the Gahuku's dramatic flair, I had no doubt that the effect had been intentionally contrived, and my admiration for their showmanship increased as the procession of invisible figures delayed their entrance, winding back and forth along the garden paths while the light grew and the excitement of the women broke in a rising chorus of welcoming calls.

They entered the street when the cries had reached a peak of anticipation; the vanguard of older men trod the ground slowly and firmly, their heads high, their bows strung tight with arrows. Even at a distance I recognized the pride stretching the muscles of their calves and thighs, and I felt an answering lift as their silence erupted in the familiar, shouted celebration of accomplishment heralding the entrance of the boys, now men—changed persons, not recognizable as what they had been before.

Armed warriors walked beside them as they came down the street, stepping slowly like the others, their pace geared to the weight of the enormous headdresses that had been fashioned for them during the night, coil upon coil of bark cloth wound around their hair and projecting from the back of the head in a huge bun that strained the muscles of their necks, the whole surmounted with opossum tails and cassowary feathers. Now the women broke their lines, ran between the escorts seeking sons and brothers, feigning to mistake them in their new guise, keening and crying when they made the right identification. Darting back to the houses, they fetched lumps of fat and bamboo tubes containing pork, rubbed the youths' limbs with grease, and broke the tubes on the ground in front of their moving feet. Clouds of dust rose into the golden light, and long after the sun came up the village rang with the clamor of the welcome.

The remainder of the day was carried by on a vast volume of sound and the rushing of hundreds of feet as parties of visitors arrived to dance in the settlement. Stirring at first, the careening dance, a rush of men in the center of the street, grew stale with repetition, and I waited impatiently for it to end, restrained from leaving only by the thought that I had to record it all for future use. My personal interest had ended during the first set, when the street had been momentarily quiet and the initiates, after their welcome, had gathered for their own performance.

There were a dozen of them standing together in light that still carried the caressing glow of early morning. Bereft of their escort, they seemed uncertain and shy, no older or more experienced than the day they were carried to the river while the flutes ate at the sky above their heads. They moved unsteadily under ungainly decorations, and I failed to see the splendid, stirring change that had been apparent to their elders' eyes. But dignity touched them when they began to dance, a slow measure based on the assertive stepping of the men but held to a restrained, promenading pace by the weight they carried on their heads. For a moment I was one with the crowd of admirers, silent now, and perhaps like myself bending toward the slight figures who symbolized the promise of human life, forcing us, as we watched, to recall the hopes once held for ourselves, our own temerity in stepping out to meet the future. Asemo was in the front rank of the dancers, his legs moving in unison with his age mates, his face, like theirs, expressionless, his eyes fixed on some distant point only he could see.

The initiation of adolescents into adulthood is by no means uncommon. This is one of the **rites de passage,** like birth, marriage, and death, which in most cases is marked by a formal ritual or ceremony. Sometimes such initiations involve **scarification,** circumcision, fasting, ritual beatings, the excising of teeth, **subincision,** and other such practices. Often, as in this case, people mourn for the initiates as if they had died. Indeed, it is sometimes claimed the initiates do die and are reborn during the ceremony. Even so, most initiation rituals do not reach the extremes of violence and pain portrayed here.

As traditionally there was almost incessant fighting and raiding in the New Guinea Highlands, it would appear that male initiations were designed, at least in part, to create strong and brave warriors, an absolute necessity if the groups were to survive at all. But there are other important factors also. There were, for example, strong beliefs about the polluting qualities of menstrual blood and even of females in general. Men believed that too much exposure to women would cause them to become weak, or ill, or even to die as young men. The vomiting and bloodletting, as Read suggests, were felt to cleanse men of the influence of women and thus to keep them strong and healthy. Since wives were obtained from other groups, and since sisters married out and went away, the continuity and solidarity of males are of paramount importance. The **nama** cult is in a sense, then, a conspiracy of males designed to perpetuate male dominance. In this account, the attack on the male initiation party by the females of the community would seem to be what is called a **ritual of rebellion,** an institutionalized means whereby those in relatively powerless and inferior positions can formally rid themselves of accumulated frustration and resentment.

It must be borne in mind that not all of Gahuku-Gama life was taken up with violence, initiations, and hostility between males and females. Day-to-day life involved much cooperation between males and females as well as between all resident clansmen. There was no poverty, no crime as we know it, and there were no orphans. Although there were ritual and war leaders, it was a remarkably egalitarian and individualistic society in which people were free to do what they wished. Serious fighting between clansmen was taboo and there were some mechanisms, at least, to settle disputes when they did arise within the clan. The problem for the New Guinea Highlanders was primarily the absence of any means short of fighting for settling disputes between clans or larger groups. Morality, unfortunately, did not extend much beyond clan boundaries.

For a more straightforwardly ethnographic account of the Gahuku-Gama see Read's articles, "Nama Cult of the Central Highlands, New Guinea" (1952), "Morality and the Concept of the Person Among the Gahuku-Gama" (1955), and "Leadership and Consensus in a New Guinea Society" (1959). For information on male-female relations in this area see Meggitt's article, "Male-Female Relationships in the Highlands of Australian New Guinea" (1964); Langness's "Sexual Antagonism in the New Guinea Highlands: A Bena Bena Example" (1967); and the volume **The Ideology of Man and Woman in the New Guinea Highlands,** edited by Brown and Buchbinder (1976).

For another very readable account of the New Guinea Highlands see Peter Matthiessen's **Under the Mountain Wall: A Chronicle of Two Seasons in the Stone Age** (1962). This can be supplemented with the purely ethnographic description of the same people by Karl Heider, **The Dugum Dani** (1970).

Kiki: Ten Thousand Years in a Lifetime is a fascinating autobiography by the Papua New Guinean, Albert Maori Kiki. As the title suggests, the book deals with the almost unprecedented rapidity of change in New Guinea within the space of one man's lifetime. **The Crocodile,** by Vincent Eri (1970), is the first and only novel to date by a New Guinean. It has some ethnographic content, but is not really an ethnographic novel.

Very readable general accounts of New Guinea include **Adam with Arrows** (1954), by Colin Simpson; **The Stone Age Island** (1964), by Maslyn Williams; and **New Guinea: The Last Unknown** (1963), by Gavin Souter.

For information on other New Guinea cultures, and particularly on religion, see Ian Hogbin's **Island of Menstruating Men** (1970) and the volume edited by Peter Lawrence and Mervyn Meggitt, **Gods, Ghosts and Men in Melanesia** (1965).

Some beautiful and remarkable ethnographic films have been made in New Guinea in recent years. Chief among them are **Dead Birds,** a film on the Dugum Dani, the same people featured by Matthiessen in **Under the Mountain Wall.** There are a number of brief educational films by Karl Heider on the same people as well. **Towards Baruya Manhood** is a unique and fantastic seven-hour film on Baruya initiation rites.

4

Rain

FRANCIS HUXLEY*

It would be a great mistake to assume that all of an anthropologist's time is taken up with drama, ritual, and other interesting and exciting events. In fact, most of the fieldworker's time is taken up with ordinary everyday occurrences and with trying to keep up with the virtually never-ending task of recording field notes. Fortunately for the note-taking, but difficult for the psyche, there are often long periods when relatively little happens and, as in the following account, when the weather, too, becomes uncooperative. I suspect that most anthropologists forget these times upon returning from the field, remembering instead the more outstanding and exciting moments of fieldwork. Francis Huxley, another of the few anthropologists who have chosen to give us more personalized accounts of their work, describes here one such uneventful segment of the time he spent with the Urubu Indians of Brazil.

Huxley wrote his anecdotal book **Affable Savages** to show the more human side of the people he lived with and studied, and also to show how they spent their time: "It [the book] is . . . an attempt to show how Indians live and enjoy themselves: to show them, in fact, as subjects, not just the objects of an anthropological study" (1956:12). Although the following selection has no plot, one does get an idea of some of the characters Huxley encountered and

* From *Affable Savages* by Francis Huxley. Reprinted by permission of A D Peters & Co Ltd.

of the "flavor" of his experience. Sitting around on a rainy day listening to stories and myths is one of the activities at which anthropologists must become adept. Giving and receiving gifts, eating strange foods, and dealing with a variety of local characters are others, as are itching and scratching, and coping with insects, snakes, and the variety of other discomforts that inevitably accompany fieldwork.

The rain, which had been light, now began to fall heavily once or twice a day. One could not forget it: even when the sky cleared a little, the jungle could be heard roaring slightly with the drip of water falling from one leaf on to another. The jungle looked different as well, as I found when I made a trip to Canindé to get the rest of my stores, brought upriver by Feliciano on one of his trips. There were fungi growing by the path—I remember especially a very large *Phallus impudicus*, looking extraordinarily grotesque with a kind of umbrella in white and bridal lace growing just below its head. Ripe fruit had dropped in great numbers from the trees; the streams, dry all summer, were now full of water, and small fish and terrapins were to be found in them. Where the ground was swampy, among the roots of prickly palms, red and black land-crabs reared back on their legs and threatened us with their claws. The armadillo I had shot was now nothing but bones, and its carapace looked like a split jigsaw puzzle; and several score more rhinoceros beetles had come out of their burrows to die in the open.

The birds were nesting; pigeons in low bushes, toucans and parrots in the holes of trees. The path was crisscrossed with the tracks of tapir, and peccary, and jaguar; and from time to time the bushes would shake convulsively as a startled deer fled away from us. With so many things to see, it was a pleasant trip for everyone, except Mbeiju who was feeling ill, and who wept several times because, she said, the stones hurt her feet, and she couldn't stop falling down, and her load was too heavy—though she carried nothing but a wicker back-basket containing two hammocks, and three puppies curled up on top.

We came back some days later, having left Picher behind. He had caught *curuba*, the jungle itch; and, being cook, had already passed it on to Chico and myself. Curuba is an intolerable malady, for one can hardly stop scratching oneself, and Picher had got it so badly that his thighs were quite raw, and he could hardly walk. Sulphur clears it up, but I had none; so Chico and I tried a cure proposed by the Indians, the juice from a certain leaf and, when that didn't work, we scratched ourselves till we bled and daubed our wounds with lemon juice and gunpowder. It was a painful but effective remedy.

The rains increased; great storms darkened the jungle, with much thunder and lightning, and when the wind blew one could hear the lengthy crash of falling trees, their roots loosened by the continual rainfall. The night after we returned to the village, indeed, a large wild cashew tree suddenly fell down behind Toí's hut—'aha!' we all cried, 'aha!' and Toí, fearful that other trees might fall on to his hut, spent the rest of the night with us.

In the next week, we cut down a number of trees: some for their fruit, on which we gorged, and some to get at birds' nests. We found a dwarf parrot's nest, with five squabs which Mbeiju took home and fed with manioc pap out of her mouth; and some toucan nests, though the birds had already flown. One of the trees we cut down was a giant, falling with a roar of snapping branches and lianas: it made a great hole in the woods, for it brought seven other trees down with it, and lay in a clearing of its own making, sprigged over with epiphytes on trunk and branch and twig, a hanging garden. Its core was quite rotten, full of a strange red clay made of dead wood, dust, leaves, and other things, and there was a root in it from a plant that had established itself in a crack forty feet higher up.

Pari and Chico found a bees' nest in the tree. They were small black bees without stings, but very angry: they mobbed Pari, getting tangled in his hair and crawling into his ears and his eyes. "Aha!" cried Pari, "hahh! hah-hah!" as the bees tormented him.

"Don't shout!" said Chico sternly, "it's bad for the honey, it won't be there if you shout!" But Pari went on shouting, he said he always shouted when cutting out a bees' nest; he only wondered if he shouldn't have whittled some bits of bark into the shapes of knives and machetes, so that he could leave them by the side of the nest in exchange for the honey.

"If you take honey from shaman bees without paying," I was told—shaman bees are a particular species, but all bees have shaman powers—"then you quickly fall ill, you get awful pains, you vomit blood, you're dead. And if you're married you don't take honey. The shaman bee knows, he says to himself, 'That man's married, he's got a pretty wife; I want her!' So he takes her and she falls ill and dies. A young man, that's all right, if he's not married he can take the honey; he cuts the tree open, pulls the honey out, then he puts into the hole a machete, a knife, a mirror, a pair of scissors. He makes them out of bark and puts them in the hole. 'Ah,' says the bee, 'that man's good, he knows, he pays when he takes honey! A machete, a mirror, a knife, he pays properly!'"

Pari didn't bother about making bark knives, he just pulled the combs out and squeezed the honey into a large gourd bowl. It was a thin clear honey, very slightly sour from the pollen which had got into it, but extremely good. Chico saved the combs in which the young grubs developed, dipped them in the honey and ate them. I did too, seeing Chico's look of satisfaction: the grubs tasted of very young hazel nuts, a milky innocent taste which I thought the honey spoilt. We had them all to ourselves.

Antonio-hu told me later that in the old days they used to have a honey feast, but no one else knew anything about it. Perhaps he'd heard about it from the Tembés, where it's an important festival. They'd hang the honey up in pots, Antonio-hu said, under the rafters, and the women would sing underneath, all through the night, for several nights, while the men sat round the sides of the hut. The feast was called Irar, after a small black animal with a white face (a species of grison) that eats honey. The women would sing the Irar song, singing that Irar sits by the bees' nest putting its hand into the honey and licking it, slup slup!

After several nights of singing the honey would be taken down, mixed with water and made into a shibé. "Ah," said Antonio-hu, "when we drink the honey we don't stop till it's all gone, we get full bellies, just with honey. And then we suruk our wives, then we make children, our rankuais are all sweet. Sweet sweet sweet."

I was surprised, considering the season, that there were so few mosquitoes about, since there were lots of pools in the jungle for them to breed in. The year before, Pari said, there had been so many mosquitoes that he couldn't sleep at all, so he took his hammock into the woods and slung it between two trees. But the mosquitoes found him out every time, though he moved all round the village trying to escape them. Even a good smoky fire underneath the hammock didn't stop them: balked in their favourite direction of attack from underneath, they came at him from the top.

There are some years with plagues of mosquitoes, other years with hardly any. It was luckily one of the scarce years, and I was never troubled during the nights. The cicadas came out, however, from their burrows in the earth. Mbeiju took several home and watched with Pari as they struggled out of their larval skins. They would bulge out slowly, slightly crumpled but magically coloured in red and green, with the wings small buds of vermilion, till in a few hours their wings had expanded and their skins hardened. "Just like Maír,"* Pari would exclaim as he watched: Maír too sheds his skin.

The rains filled up the small dry creeks near the village, and

* Maír is the *culture-hero*.

54

brought fish up out of the river to spawn. Toí went with his family one day to fish a pool with poison. He cut a special kind of liana into lengths, tied them into bundles and beat them in the water with a heavy stick, so that the frothy sap came out and spread through the pool. The sap affects fishes' breathing, so that they dash wildly about near the surface, gulping in air, and they get slower and slower till they can be picked off with an arrow, or sliced with a machete.

One of the girls came home crying: she'd put her hand into a hole in the bank, after a fish that had got in there, and had been bitten on the finger by a snake. It was luckily not a poisonous one, as Paijé found out after a brief inquisition, not like the one, she told me, that had bitten her on the head years ago, and had nearly killed her. Then too she had been out beating fish-poison in a pool. She bent down under a bush and felt what she thought was an arrow pierce her scalp—"Don't shoot at me!" she yelled at her husband. "But I haven't even seen a fish to shoot at!" her husband replied: so then she found it was a snake that had bitten her, and the blood was running into her eyes from the wound. Her head swelled up as big as a water-melon, and Anakãpuka and Pari both tried to suck out the venom—they sucked and spat and sucked—and Terepik, who was pregnant at the time, tried to help but was chased away because if a pregnant woman sees someone who's been bitten by a snake her hair falls out and then her flesh falls off and she dies.

I hadn't been back from Canindé many days when I realised that Pari was getting a bore, and that the village, with its dirty and un-kempt look, depressed me. So I got most of my things together and went off to the neighbouring village, where Antonio-hu was ex-pecting me. I had already spent a few days there, and had enjoyed myself a great deal: the village, though small, was neat and hand-some, with a prosperous air about it, the clearing being full of flourishing manioc plants, seven feet high.

Antonio-hu had built a new hut against my coming. He told me that he was ashamed of his old one, ashamed that a caraí, a white man, should have to sleep in it, under a leaky thatch; so he built a new one, such as I've not seen in any other village—forty or fifty feet long, and eighteen feet wide, the top of the roof some twenty feet high. With great care he had built a table out of cut saplings for me, and a bench to go with it, where I could write: he laughed with joy when he saw how pleased I was with it.

But the village was nearly empty when we arrived: everyone had gone hunting except for a middle-aged man called Wirakangupik, who was convalescing after a bout of fever, and his wife Mirijun. Wirakangupik was the most ingratiating Indian I ever met: he had a kind of false party smile that rarely left his face, and never lost an opportunity to flatter me. "Eh, chief Arajuba!" he would call if I passed: the arajuba being a rare, completely yellow parrot much prized by the Indians for its beauty. I would retaliate by calling him chief Agouti, that rodent famous for its sexual powers; for he was the father of Saracaca, and in his youth had been as intemperate as she was. His father, interestingly enough, had been a Guajaja caught by the Urubus as a boy, and given two wives by them. I do not know if he also was a lecher, but he loved working, and passed that redeeming trait on to his son. In fact, Wirakangupik worked more than Antonio-hu did, though Antonio-hu was the chief; he and his wife more or less ran the economy of the village, getting the girls to dig up manioc and roast it when it was needed, making shibés and messes of tapioca.

Wirakangupik greeted us with his appalling smile, and gave us a shibé to drink. It began to rain again, violently: the ground flooded, and spray came drifting into the hut in misty clouds. We dug a shallow gutter around the hut below the eaves, to drain the water off, and waited for Antonio-hu and the others to come back.

They had been unlucky, killed no game, seen no tortoises, gathered no fruit. They stalked disconsolately through the rain and stood round the fire, planting their bows and arrows into the earth to dry. "I want a cigarette," Antonio-hu said brusquely, and soon I was making cigarettes for all of them. "I want sweet manioc soup," I then retorted, and Antonio-hu hurriedly set the girls to digging up a huge tuber of sweet manioc from a patch just near the hut, which was peeled and boiled down into a thin soup, to which I added some of my rice.

We sat round together, drinking it out of gourd bowls. Saracaca looked at Chico with hope in her eye; and so did her husband, lean, intellectual Alishandre, though for very different reasons: he was learning to be a shaman, like Toí, and hoped Chico would help him. Saracaca's brother was also there, with Curumiú, his bead-stealing wife, and several children, mostly girls.

Alishandre came and sat next to me in my hammock. That very morning, he said, the birds had been singing, singing so loudly that everyone thought, "It must be because Francis is coming today and bringing us beads, that's why the birds are so happy!" So I took my tin of beads out of my rucksack and shared it out. I liked giving things in Antonio-hu's village: I could see how much they liked what I gave, and they never pestered me for more, unlike Paijé who could not be satisfied.

"You're my friend," Antonio-hu said suddenly, "when you go home again you must tell everyone that we're good, tell them to come and visit us and bring us cloth, and beads, and knives, like you've done. Tomorrow I'll go hunting again, I'll kill a deer for you—that's where I'll kill it," he said, poking me in the ribs with a finger.

It stopped raining; the girls hurried into the clearing to get some more firewood, and Antonio-hu, Chico and I went down to the stream to bathe. Antonio-hu took some flour in a bowl, to make a shibé; and after he had prepared it he borrowed a tablet of soap—a scented one, my one luxury—and soaped himself white, all over. "What a good smell!" he said.

The moon came up. It was a lovely night, without a wind, the tree-trunks at the edge of the clearing standing out remarkably white; and a lively noise of frogs down by the stream.

We drank some more sweet manioc soup, rolled ourselves large cigars of tobacco and tawari bark, and then Antonio-hu and I lay down at either end of my hammock, head to foot. One lies diagonally in a hammock so as not to be bent up like a banana, and by oneself nothing could be more comfortable. Two in a hammock is companionable, but a bit squashed; still, the Indians like it, especially the young men. I've seen five in a hammock before the cord broke.

I asked him about the stars. He told me about the Milky Way, which he called the Tapir's Path: the souls of dead tapirs walk along it, eating 'fruit souls and leaf souls,' as he said. There was Grandfather Many Things, or the Pleiades, each of which was really a man dressed in his feather ornaments. Antonio-hu pointed to the east—"When Grandfather Many Things shows itself there," he said in his deep, grating voice, "it's summer." He lifted his pointing finger to the zenith: "There, the rains start! When Grandfather Many Things is there, we know it's time to plant." His finger pointed slowly to the western horizon: "The rains are over."

The Pleiades are an important constellation, which is why they are called Grandfather: the only other constellation so honoured is the Southern Cross, or Grandfather Cotton, though it does not seem to have any connection with agriculture. The Morning star is also important, being called the Mother of the Many Things, as well as the Moon's Sister; but nearly all the other stars are thought to be the eyes of animals and birds. The only two exceptions I noted were Mars, known as Macaw Egg, and Sirius, called Nenguru, a name whose etymology I did not understand.

I asked, idly enough, if they did anything when particular stars came up over the horizon for the first time every year. It was a good question. In the old days, when Macaw Eye, or Aldebaran, first showed itself, the Indians would take macaw feathers, burn them and smear the cinders on their children's foreheads; then they would take a fish-tooth and scratch their arms so that they would grow up to be strong, and good hunters of macaws. These two results mean the same thing, for the macaw is a symbol of the sun, and to shoot macaws is a symbolical way of being a hero. Then there was Deer's Eye—it was still below the horizon at the time, so that I could not identify it—that, said Alishandre, was a big star. He made a fist: "bright!" he said.

"What do you do when you see it?"

For answer, Alishandre seized hold of a young boy who was near him, held his arms and then made as though he were drawing a bow. "You *shoot* at it, you make the children aim at it, right in its eye. With a takwara, an iron-headed arrow."

"Why?"

"So they'll always kill deer," he said, reproachfully.

And he told me about Three Eyes, Orion's belt, that when it appears children wake up early in the morning when it's still dark and go bathe in the stream to become strong; and how stars are attached to the sky by a little stalk, and when the stalk breaks they fall and become shooting stars. He had come across a shooting star once in the jungle, lying on the ground; a soft jelly-like object,* he said, shining blue, and very hot.

Chico was flabbergasted. "And I had to come here to find out about all these things," he said, "all this about the stars." He was especially put out because the Tembés look down on the Urubus as being ignorant and coarse.

"You don't ask, you don't find out," I said, rubbing it in.

"That's right. No one ever asks my father so he never talks about things like that. Eh, shooting star!"

Antonio-hu rounded off the evening by telling us two long and rather boring stories about raids, full of flying arrows and slaughter; but he told them with such conviction, and in such detail, that I had good hopes of getting him to tell me a Cannibal Tale before I left. We finally got to sleep some time after midnight. I woke up shivering at four, and heard Saracaca blowing the fire up beneath Alishandre's hammock; at daybreak it was raining again.

Although magic and myth are by no means entirely absent from societies with a scientific tradition, they are much more an intimate part of daily life in small-scale nonliterate societies such as the Urubu. Some South American societies,

---

* Probably the jelly-like alga *Nostoc*, frequently—as in England—called 'star-jelly'.

in spite of their small size, have exceedingly complex series of myths and elaborate cosmologies that tie virtually all of the natural phenomena around them together into one great harmonious whole. In this account we see, for example, that bees are regarded as having **shamanistic** powers, the very same powers that Alishandre seeks to obtain. Thus they have to be paid for their honey with gifts of (imitation) objects such as machetes, mirrors, etc. The constellation of the Milky Way is associated with the tapir, an important source of food. The Pleiades, in addition to its mythological significance, is also used to mark the seasons. Deer's Eye, another star, is associated with success in hunting. The macaw is a symbol of the sun. It would be impossible to do justice to all of this here. Huxley treats it more intensively in **Affable Savages,** and there are other works that treat it in much greater detail. Among the better of these are Reichel-Dolmatof's **Amazonian Cosmos** (1968) and Levi-Strauss's **The Raw and the Cooked** (1969) and **From Honey to Ashes** (1973).

For further personal experiences with South American peoples see Levi-Strauss's **Tristes Tropiques (A World on the Wane,** 1961); Maybury-Lewis's **The Savage and the Innocent** (1965); **Jivaro: Among the Head-Shrinkers of the Amazon,** by Bertrand Flornoy (1953); **Rebel Destiny: Among the Bush Negroes of Dutch Guiana,** by Melville and Frances Herskovits; and **Through Indian Eyes: A Journey Among the Tribes of Guiana,** by Colin Henfrey (1964). Two fascinating life histories are **Yanomama: The Narrative of a White Girl Kidnapped by Amazonian Indians** (Biocca, 1970) and **Wizard of the Upper Amazon: The Story of Manuel Cordova-Rios** (Lamb, 1975).

Novels dealing with South America which have at least moderate ethnographic interest include Ciro Alegria's **Broad and Alien World** (1941), Antonio Callado's **Quarup** (1970), and Peter Matthiessen's **At Play in the Fields of the Lord** (1965).

For more serious ethnographic books of all kinds on South America, see Jules Henry, **Jungle People** (1941); **Amazon Town,** by Charles Wagley (1964); **Town and Country in Brazil,** by Marvin Harris (1971); Betty Megger's **Amazonia** (1971); Janet Siskind's **To Hunt in the Morning** (1973); **The Jivaro,** by Michael J. Harner; and **Yanomamo: The Fierce People,** by Napoleon Chagnon (1968). For an extremely detailed account of anthropological fieldwork in the area see Chagnon's more recent book **Studying the Yanomamo** (1974).

Chagnon has collaborated on a number of important ethnographic films on the Yanomamo. **The Feast** (1970) and **Man Called Bee: Studying the Yanomamo** (1974) are of particular interest here, but there are more than thirty shorter ones also available. Other films of interest on South America include **Boy of Matto Grasso, Amazon Family, Contact with a Hostile Tribe, Headhunters of Ecuador,** and **Incident in Matto Grasso.**

5

Counting coups

PETER NABOKOV*

Since the 1920s, anthropologists have increasingly employed biographical techniques to present information
about the people with whom they work. As many of the people who share their lives with us are illiterate, and thus can
describe their lives to another party only by the spoken
word, anthropologists have preferred the term **life history**
to biography or autobiography (Langness, 1965).

Two Leggings, from which the following excerpt was
taken, is quite a remarkable life history. It was compiled and
edited by Peter Nabokov of the Museum of the American
Indian from a manuscript on Two Leggings originally produced by a businessman, William Wildschut. Wildschut had
been interested in the Indians and had worked with Two Leggings on his life story between 1919 and 1923, when the
Crow warrior died at approximately eighty years of age. In
order to fully interpret many of the things recounted by
Two Leggings, Nabokov had to rely on ethnographic materials that had been collected earlier. Fortunately there is a
wealth of such information on the Crow, collected by Robert Lowie and others. Nabokov himself interviewed Amos
Two Leggings, the son of Two Leggings, as well as other sur-
vivors knowledgeable about the life of the old warrior. Out
of this he produced a life history that is not only informative, but pleasant to read. This is all the more noteworthy,
perhaps, since Two Leggings was only a minor leader and,
although he diligently and repeatedly tried, never managed

* Reprinted from Peter Nabokov, *Two Leggings: The Making of a Crow Warrior*,
with permission of Thomas Y. Crowell Co., Inc. Copyright © 1967 by Peter Nabokov.

to acquire the "medicine" that would have insured his greater success.

The Crow were not a large group compared to other Plains Indians, and they were positioned between the much larger Siouan peoples on their east and the Blackfoot on the north. Thus they were subjected to repeated attacks by raiding parties from both sides. Because of this the Crow became particularly distinguished warriors, and each Crow warrior sought diligently, and often recklessly, to surpass the deeds of past generations. It has been suggested that it was not the end of the buffalo that marked the finish of the traditional culture of the Crow, but rather the suppression of intertribal warfare. Following the career of Two Leggings, we begin to understand how this might well have been so.

On a raid the Crow novice-warrior risked his life to perform defined deeds. Two Leggings listed the four important "coups" in this order: Most praiseworthy was the striking of an enemy with a gun, bow, or riding quirt; then came the cutting of an enemy's horse from a tipi door; next, the recovery of an enemy's weapon in battle; and finally, the riding-down of an enemy.

Specific insignia advertised these honors. The winner of all four could decorate his deerskin war shirt with four beaded or porcupine-quill strips, one running from shoulder to wrist on each sleeve and one over each shoulder from front to back. Merely earning the first coup enabled a man to trail a coyote tail from one moccasin; from both if he performed the feat twice. Eagle feathers tied to a man's gun or coup display stick revealed the number of scalps he had taken. A knotted rope hanging from his horse's neck told of the cutting of an enemy's picketed mount. And the number of horses captured could be read from the stripes of white clay painted under his horse's eyes or on its flanks. From a white clay hand on those flanks one learned that the owner had ridden down an enemy.

The winter after we had made friends with the Piegans was very severe and I do not remember any war parties going out. The snow was deep and the cold so bad that several horses froze to death. We stayed close to the mountains on Red Cherry Creek, not far from the present town of Red Lodge.

At snow-melting time we moved to Arrow Creek and then our scouts reported many buffalo with thick fur in the Bighorn Valley. Sits In The Middle Of The Land gave orders to break camp and we moved through the Pine Ridge Hills. Finding great herds roaming in the valley, we easily killed enough for meat and robes.

When I had my share I could hardly wait to hear of a raid being organized. During the long cold season I had not visited the white trader for ammunition. But I had traded with the Gros Ventres for some hickory sticks and had made myself a strong bow, covering it with rattlesnake skin which I attached with glue boiled from buffalo bones. I also made arrows from chokecherry wood and straightened them with a stone arrow straightener.

After everyone had enough meat and skins, Sits In The Middle Of The Land led us back to Arrow Creek country. On our way we camped at Woody Creek and I heard of a raid to be led by Sews His Guts— once a bullet had opened his stomach until his intestines were falling out and his friends had sewn the hole with sinew and awl.

Sews His Guts let me join and early one morning twenty of us walked out of camp. I took my gun, as we hoped to stop at the trading post on the upper reaches of Big River [Fort Benton]. Sews His Guts carried his rock medicine as well as his pipe. Inside was a rock the size of a man's fist with a human face carved on it. It was a powerful medicine and had brought him through many battles.

We crossed Elk River just east of the present town of Billings. As we came up the bench north of the river we were held back by large buffalo herds. After killing some buffalo for meat we walked on to the Musselshell River, forded it, and continued north to the foothills of the Snowy Mountains. Then we began moving carefully because we were nearing Piegan country.

One day when the sun was in the middle of the sky we noticed a man on a nearby hill making smoke signals for us to come over. We could not see whether he was Piegan or a Crow from another clan. Eight men started towards him but we called them back, laid down our packs and heavy robes, and began walking in a body. Immediately men dashed out from behind rocks and bushes around the signaller, carrying muzzle-loading rifles and firing as soon as they were within range. We found cover but kept advancing. As they fell back to reload, I ran out screaming a war cry.

One hung behind and I shot him in the shoulder. Reaching back, he jerked out the arrow, broke it, and threw it on the ground. He pulled out his knife and ran at me. Jumping aside, I shot him in the breast. He also pulled out that arrow, broke it, and threw it down. I tried to keep out of his reach, yelling to get him excited. Then I shot a third arrow into his stomach. He made a growling sound, but after he broke that arrow he made signs for me to go back. I made signs that I was going to kill him. Then he made signs for me to come closer so he could fight with his knife, and I made signs that I would not.

He was almost dead and there was no reason to be afraid, so I suppose I played with him. He was my enemy and had probably killed some of my relatives. He tried to dodge my next arrow but it went into his chest and came out of his lower back. Blood ran from his mouth and nose as he walked slowly towards his friends. I shot once more. He stumbled and fell and died a moment later. Then I scalped him and tied the hair to my bow. After yelling to our men far ahead, I sang my first victory song.

Taking his warbonnet out of its rawhide case I put it on my head and danced around his body. I never thought that a Piegan might surprise me. I was only a boy and now I had my first coup. I sang and thanked the Great Above Person. I danced until the sweat ran down my body.

Eight men came back, and when they saw the Piegan they divided the rest of the scalp and joined in my singing, shooting arrows into the body. Then we ran to meet the others returning over the hill. I told of my fight but would not go back with them. After they all had shot arrows into the body they wrapped it in a robe and laid it on a rock.

The Piegans had been chased away and nobody was killed. Sews His Guts decided to return to camp, which had moved to the Bighorn Valley near the present Mission of St. Xavier.

We were singing as we walked into the village, and I held a long willow stick with my scalp tied to the end. For two days and nights the women danced the scalp dance and my name was spoken as the one who had taken revenge on the Piegans. After our celebrations we settled down to our usual life of hunting and playing games.

The Piegans must have grown very angry that season. Two other parties returned shortly after with more scalps. During the night we posted scouts to prevent their crawling into camp, but those Piegans were very clever.

Following the herds over the Little Bighorn River to the present site of Reno, we continued down river to its meeting with the Bighorn and the present site of Fort C. F. Smith. There the men hunted again to supply their families with meat and winter robes.

One night my brother and I woke to a woman's screams. Running outside, I heard her just beyond camp, yelling over and over that her mother had been killed.

Torches were lit and men were running around and jumping on horses. When I arrived at the place the woman was wailing and tearing her clothes, her mother's body beside her. Piegans had surrounded them as they left the circle of the tipis.

The daughter began pushing a knife into her forehead, and blood ran down her face. The she sliced her arms and legs. We took the knife away so she would not kill herself. Our people behaved like this when a close friend or relative died, but she did not know what she was doing.

I wanted to join the riders chasing the Piegans, but the ground was covered with snow and I wore only leggings and no moccasins. I ran back, dressed quickly, loaded my gun, and while I was looking for my horse someone excited me by yelling that we must kill Piegans. Jumping on the first horse I found, I whipped it hard to catch up. The dark-face period had passed and with dawn we could make out the Piegan tracks. My brother-in-law rode a beautiful long-winded horse, and when he noticed mine faltering he gave it to me.

They turned out to be seven men on foot. Their bullets whistled by and they fell back, trying to reload. As I was almost on top of one man he yelled and lifted his gun barrel. It caught between my left arm and body. A bullet burned a hole through my deerskin shirt. Riding over him, I grabbed the gun but could not dismount to scalp him because Piegans surrounded my horse. One swung at my head with his rifle. When I dodged, the butt struck my shoulder, almost knocking me off.

The man I had ridden down was only stunned. But as he got to his feet Bull Does Not Fall Down rode up and killed him.

I noticed the feathers attached to his hair. The other Piegans were far enough away so I dismounted and scalped him. Singing a victory song, I mounted again and waved the scalp. The six remaining Piegans were soon chased into a buffalo wallow, lying flat while we rode around them. One by one we killed them all.

Later on we built a large rock pile where this fight occurred, and it is there today. When we rode into our village we were singing and holding willow poles with Piegan scalps hanging from the ends. There was a big celebration and a dance, but I was too tired and went to bed. Then the drums woke me and I dressed to watch a woman's dance, all the girls wearing their best clothes. I thought that perhaps I should stop killing and find myself a wife and make my own house. I could still go out on raids, I told myself, but only for horses.

Then I started thinking that the time had come for me to fast for a medicine. I walked back to my tipi and lay down, trying to make up my mind. If I were to become a chief and a famous warrior, I realized that I could not think of marrying and staying at home. But it was still some time before I fasted.

On these early raids. Two Leggings has been tempting fate; he has been warring without a "medicine." Throughout literature on American Indians this word is the translation for a variety of terms meaning "imbued with sacred power," perhaps because the curative aspect makes most sense to us.

As Wildschut interpreted the word: "The Indian who is visited in his vision by a personified animal, plant, rock, or spirit, accepts his visitant as his sacred protector through life, but he never forgets that it was First Worker who first gave his sacred helper the strength to do this. This power, known among the Crows as 'maxpe' [maash-pay], and commonly translated, 'medicine,' was given in greater or lesser degree to all things."

The Crows walked in a world where anything could be brushed with this mysterious potency. Ordinary objects, if they figured in a dream, would suddenly become sacred and valuable. Anything which demonstrated the potential for determining the course of life was considered medicine. The trick came in harnessing these latent powers to one's aid, in the container of a medicine bundle, and carefully keeping at bay their harmful aspect through strict adherence to that bundle's taboos.

After the Piegans killed the woman outside camp, we moved to the part of Wyoming near the present town of Cody. It was still early in grass-growing season and on our way we stopped at the junction of the Stinking Water and the Bighorn River.

While we were there a war party returned from the Sioux country with horses. I watched the dancing in their honor and could wait no longer. I told some friends that I was going after horses, not scalps, and seven were willing to join. We needed a pipeholder so I asked Three Wolf, one of the youngest pipeholders and always ready for a raid. In a dream some nights before he had been promised horses; he said we would not have to travel far.

He chose Wolf Head, Busy Head, and myself for scouts and led us toward the southern slopes of the Bighorn Mountains. We rode up Old Baldy and before reaching the top killed a buffalo, skinned it, and built a cooking fire. This was our last meal for two days.

We had only been out for two days and did not expect enemies so close, but a scout Three Wolf had sent to an open area up the mountain returned to report people hunting in the valley on the other side.

We rode back with him and saw a large party of Utes and Cheyennes chasing a herd toward our fire. Riding deeper into the mountains, we watched from some thick pines. When the Utes and Cheyennes discovered the smoking wood they began talking and moving their arms, and soon were spreading out to find us. But a trail on rocky slopes, especially in winter, is hard to follow. They returned to the valley, where we watched their women setting up tipis in a large circle. We stayed hidden until dark and then went for our horses picketed deeper in the trees. As we mounted I told my friends that all earth creatures, the birds, and we ourselves must die sometime. Tonight we would crawl into this camp for horses and if we were all killed it was not important. But I said that if we lived our names would be praised and the women would dance.

We dismounted at the base of the mountain and crawled to a dark grove near their camp. They expected a raid and had picketed their horses within the tipi circle. Fires ringed the camp and we saw men wrapped in blankets, carrying guns, waiting for someone crazy enough to try to reach their horses.

Sometimes a guard yelled out, asking us to come and smoke. But they were afraid to leave the fires. Wolf Head whispered that we would get nothing if we just sat there, and started to crawl towards the tipis, taking only a knife and a buffalo-hair rope coiled around his waist. He dropped to his stomach and wriggled straight for a campfire where three men with guns were kneeling. Then he was gone, but we saw his plan. Between him and the fire was a bunch of sagebrush; he had crawled into their shadows. As long as none of the men in the firelight moved, he was safe.

It seemed a long time before we heard a noise behind us, thinking first that some Cheyenne had found our location. But then Wolf Head whispered, and walked in leading a fine black horse. After crawling between two tipis to cut a picket rope attached to a tipi door, he had escaped through the shadows on the other side of camp, making a wide circle back. We admired him and I told myself I would be just as brave.

When Wolf Head announced that he was going home, some younger men grew afraid the Cheyennes would discover the cut rope and left with him. Piegan [personal name], Pozash, and I changed our hiding place. But the fires threw such a bright glare we were afraid to sneak between them.

Then dawn began to show and the firelight paled. Walking along the river bank, I saw three tipis faintly outlined on the other side. I hid behind a big cottonwood and made out the forms of three horses picketed beside them. Sounds came from inside one tipi and I ran back to picket my horse near the river, took off my clothes, and laid down my gun. Then I began to wade, holding my knife, bow, and arrows over my head. But swimming made too much noise so I dressed again.

Beavers had built a dam there, forming a deep pond. I wrapped a blanket around myself and my bow and arrows so only my eyes showed. I crossed and passed between the two nearest tipis. People were talking inside and I smelled smoke.

Walking slowly up to a fine bald-faced horse I tossed my rope. The animal was nervous and snorted. I looked at the tipi door, but it was still. As I tried to rope the horse's neck better a gun went off next to my ear.

At the same moment I felt the air of the bullet the horse reared, knocking me to the ground. The man who had quietly slipped out of the tipi must have thought he had killed me. I woke to his shouts and saw men with guns running towards us. Racing to the river, I leaped from the bank to the beaver dam. When the Cheyennes started shooting from the bank I threw myself flat. Then, when they had emptied their guns, I ran the rest of the way, untied my horse and picked up my gun, and joined my friends in the trees.

They noticed the bullet holes in my leggings and blanket and were surprised I was alive. We pushed our horses higher, looking for a place to hide for a few days before trying again. But when we reached an open area we saw below a large party of Cheyennes leaving their tipis and soon heard the men in front yelling as they found our tracks. Their horses were fresh, and they quickly chased us out of the trees and up the steeper slopes.

My horse could hardly walk and by the time I reached the top it would not move. The Cheyennes were close, singing and yelling, and one called us women in our language.

I had my gun in my belt, my quiver under my left arm, and my bow ready. Piegan, Pozash, and I scattered. The man speaking Crow was Wears A Mustache, well known among us. When he called us women again, challenging us to fight, I became angry. My horse had started to walk and I just hoped it could reach some nearby woods. I turned to shoot at Wears A Mustache, but was out of breath and the arrow fell short.

I called out to Piegan, a little ahead of me, that we should die fighting rather than be killed like this. He looked back but kept riding as Pozash and I dismounted. Then Piegan dismounted and ran towards us. First I took my muzzle loader, but after one shot it would be useless so I also grabbed my bow and arrows. As I ran towards a thick pine grove I saw Pozash hit with a bullet.

One Cheyenne, holding a large feather-fringed shield, was running after me and another kneeling man shot at me, his bullet kicking up dirt between my legs. I took my gun but changed my mind. When I hit him with an arrow he limped back to his horse.

I had been running and dodging bullets but calmed down when I wounded this man. As I headed again for that pine grove another bullet just missed me. Cheyennes were running to head me off, but then I entered the trees and they seemed afraid to follow. I shot at them once with my muzzle loader, and while they ducked I ran like a deer and was soon out of sight.

By the time I made my way to the next slope I could see Cheyennes in the lower meadow. I dared them to follow me. They must have been very angry.

I had lost my horse and blanket, my moccasins were torn apart, and my leggings and shirt were in rags. But I still held my gun, bow, and arrows. Piegan appeared ahead of me and together we headed home.

That night we were caught in a rainstorm and were miserable without any blankets. There was little shelter in those mountains, and anyhow we could not stop because Cheyennes might be behind us.

After killing a buffalo the following day we ate a little meat and packed some and patched our moccasins. When we reached the Bighorn River where it enters the canyon we built a raft, tied on our clothes, and pulled it across with thongs held in our teeth. Once on the other side we felt safer and a few days later arrived in our village, still near the present town of Red Lodge. Everyone thought we had been killed since Wolf Head and his men had already come back.

After my return I began thinking over all that had happened and felt afraid. All those Cheyennes had been shooting at me and I had lived. Pozash, who had been in much less danger, was dead. I decided to fast for a vision in which I could see the Without Fire who had been my protector.

When I told Wolf Chaser and Crooked Arm about my escape they said I should stop going out. They were right and I told them I wanted to go on my first fast soon. But I would not promise to wait until I had obtained a medicine before leaving on another raid.

Wolf Chaser was afraid for me and one day gave me a medicine bundle, teaching me the songs and ceremony for opening it and handling it. I was thankful but did not feel it was very powerful. He had never been a real warrior and preferred to live in camp.

It would be somewhat misleading to characterize the sporadic fighting and raiding that went on between most American Indian tribes as warfare, as that term is more appropriately applied to the large-scale, much more formally organized hostilities that go on between nations or states. Although as Two Legging's account indicates, people were at times killed, there were elaborate rules for raiding and a well developed etiquette for making known your achievements. It was not a battle of all against all, since ties of kinship and clanship operated to prohibit raiding and killing between related groups, and there were in some cases larger political alliances between **phratries** and **tribes** as well. There was a well developed system of authority with greater and lesser chiefs, and, in some groups at least, there was a well organized police force. It is interesting to note that although all Plains groups lived under much the same conditions and exploited much the same resources, some were patrilineal, whereas others were **matrilineal.**

Even though, like so many other people, the Plains groups had trouble getting along with each other, few, if any, people have had a deeper understanding of their relationship to their environment. This cannot be said for those who came later. The history of contact between American Indians and their European conquerors is one of the vilest and most unpleasant on record, the former watching in absolute astonishment as the latter senselessly slaughtered almost everything they encountered, including the Indians themselves. Although the Indian was scarcely an innocent when it came to killing, as is clear from Two Leggings' account, there was an irreconcilable difference in attitude between Indian and European towards the world in general. This can be seen in the following statement by Chief Luther Standing Bear:

> We did not think of the great open plains, the beautiful rolling hills, and winding streams with tangled growth, as "wild." Only to the white man was nature a "wilderness" and only to him was the land "infested" with "wild" animals and "savage" people. To us it was tame. Earth was bountiful and we were surrounded with the blessings of the Great Mystery. Not until the hairy man from the east came and with brutal frenzy heaped injustices upon us and the families we loved was it "wild" for us. When the very animals of the forest began fleeing from his approach, then it was that for us the "Wild West" began. [Quoted in McLuhan, 1971]

Whereas the Indian lived in relative harmony with the environment, the white man quickly set about modifying things to suit himself. Whether his modifications were all for the better is only just now being raised as a serious question. In any event, no "medicine" was strong enough to stop the process once it was begun.

For basic information on the Crow see Robert H. Lowie, **The Crow Indians** (1956), **Religion of the Crow Indians** (1922), and **Social Life of the Crow Indians** (1912). For contrasting Plains groups see Alfred W. Bowers, **Mandan Social and Ceremonial Organization** (1950); Clyde Kluckhohn and Dorothea Leighton, **The Navaho** (1946); and Morris Opler, **An Apache Life Way** (1965). For general information on Plains Indians see Lowie's **Indians of the Plains** (1963). A fine and informative book on the fate of the buffalo, so essential to all of the Plains Indians, is Tom McHugh's **The Time of the Buffalo** (1972).

For further life histories of Plains Indians see **Lame Deer: Seeker of Visions** (Lame Deer and Richard Erdoes, 1972); **Crazy Horse, the Strange Man of the Oglalas,** by Mari Sandoz (1945); **When the Tree Flowered,** by John G. Neilardt (1951); and **Black Elk Speaks,** by the same author (1961). Another Crow life history, of a more important contemporary of Two Leggings, is **Plenty-Coups: Chief of the Crows,** by Frank B. Linderman (1962).

There are several accounts of what happened to the Plains Indians. See Merrill D. Beal, "**I Will Fight No More Forever**" (1963); Ralph K. Andrist, **The Long Death: The Last Days of the Plains Indian** (1964); Mari Sandoz, **Cheyenne Autumn** (1953); and Dee Brown's bestseller, **Bury My Heart at Wounded Knee** (1971). For some Indian statements on what happened see T. C. McLuhan's **Touch the Earth: A Self-Portrait of Indian Existence** (1971).

The literature on the American Indian in general is so large as to make adequate recommendations almost impossible. But for what remain absolutely fascinating accounts see the early work of George Catlin, **North American Indians** (1844), and the remarkable multi-volume texts and photographs by Edward S. Curtis, **The North American Indian** (1907–1930). Other general treatments are Clark Wissler's **The American Indian** (1917) and Paul Radin's **The Story of the American Indian** (1927).

An excellent novel dealing with **culture change** is Oliver LaFarge's Pulitzer Prize-winning story of the Navaho, **Laughing Boy** (1929). Bandelier's **The Delight Makers** (1890) is still entertaining and worthwhile reading, as is Ruth Underhill's **Hawk Over Whirlpools** (1940). Theodora Kroeber's unusual account, **Ishi in Two Worlds** (1961), should be read by everyone with an interest in American Indians.

One of the curious features of early **culture contact** between Europeans and Indians was the fact that in a surprising number of cases whites who were taken captive by Indians did not wish to return to white "civilization" even when given the opportunity. Conrad Richter has written an interesting novel on this theme, **The Light in the Forest** (1953), which, according to Schmaier (1960), is entirely faithful to the **ethnohistorical** sources that stimulated it. A later novel, **A Country of Strangers** (1966), is based on the same materials.

For obvious reasons, there are virtually no ethnographic films of American Indians as they were during the period narrated by Two Leggings. For a rare treat see the film **The Shadow Catcher,** which deals with the life and work of Edward S. Curtis and which includes some fairly extensive footage on the Kwakiutl of the Northwest Coast. Curtis shot the film himself and, although the story was made up, the ethnographic background, including the costumes and dancing, is quite authentic. There are many recent films on various American Indian groups. See, for example, **Washoe** (1966), **Tahtonka-Plains Indian Buffalo Culture** (1966), **Our Totem is the Raven** (1972), **Before the White Man Came** (on the Crow, 1920), **Circle of the Sun** (on the Blood Indians, Canada), **Comrades of the Desert** (Navaho), **Ishi in Two Worlds** (1967), **The Silent Enemy** (Ojibway, Canada), and **The Exiles** (about three young Indians in Los Angeles).

6

Short Kwi the hunter

ELIZABETH MARSHALL THOMAS[*]

Anthropologist-writer Elizabeth Marshall Thomas, with her father, mother, brother, and several others, crossed the Kalahari Desert in southern Africa three different times while gathering material for **The Harmless People** (1959), from which the following excerpt is taken. The purpose of their expedition was to study and to film the life and customs of the Bushmen about which little was known at that time. Their film, **The Hunters,** has been seen and appreciated by countless numbers of anthropology students.

The Bushmen are an excellent example of a type of social organization referred to as **primitive bands.** Having long ago been pushed into their desert environment, they have developed their senses and skills in quite remarkable ways. Their origins are obscure. Aspects of their language and culture, and even of their physiognomy, are strangely different from those of other people, even from those of their closest neighbors. Laurens van der Post has called them "the first people" of Africa but, of course, that is not truly known.

There are great human tragedies played out in remote places that are seldom reported by anthropologists or by anyone else. In the following touching account we become participants in such a drama. We gain an appreciation of what it is like to know that one's own survival, and sometimes that of others, depends totally on one's mind, senses, and physical skills. It is a poignant story—unusual in anthropological writing—and it is exceedingly well told.

[*] Reprinted from *The Harmless People*, by Elizabeth Marshall Thomas. Copyright © 1958, 1959 by Elizabeth Marshall Thomas. Reprinted by permission of Alfred A. Knopf, Inc.

We asked for other people, the other members of Toma's large band, and Toma told us that they were well, living far away in a mangetti forest. Naturally, Toma's family had not seen this group for some time because of the distance, but Toma said now that he would take us to see them someday soon because he believed that we would be able to help them; one man in their band, a man called Short Kwi, or sometimes Kwi the Hunter, had been bitten in the leg by a puff adder and was very badly hurt. We got the impression that he had been bitten recently and, hoping that we might draw the poison from the wound, we said that we would leave at once. But Toma said that it happened during the last rainy season, so there was no use hurrying; other Bushmen had cut the wound and had sucked the poison, saving Short Kwi's life, but his leg was so badly hurt that he couldn't use it. It had turned black, said Toma, and black liquid ran out at the wound. We thought then that there would be nothing we could do to help; but perhaps rumor had exaggerated the misfortune, and so we told Toma that we would certainly go to do what we could.

Short Kwi came from a famous family; he was the younger brother of the man who murdered Toma's father, but Short Kwi was famous in his own right, famous as a hunter. He often killed more game in a year than many other men kill in their lives, a great hunter among a hunting people. The other Bushmen told stories about him—about the time he had killed four wildebeests in a herd of many, about the time he had killed an eland, a wildebeest, and a wild pig all in one day. It was his technique of hunting to be relentless in his pursuit; therefore, if he shot an animal and suspected others to be in the vicinity he would let the wounded animal run where it would while he hunted on and shot another, and another, and when all were as good as dead he would rest, then return to pick up the trail of the one that he felt would die the soonest. He almost never lost an animal, for his eyes were sharp and he could follow a cold trail over hard ground and even over stones; he could tell from fallen leaves whether the wind or passing feet had disarranged them; and the meat that resulted from his prolific hunting was never wasted, for he would bring other hunters to help him dry it, then carry it off to a werf somewhere to share with others.

His life in the veld seemed lonely, but I doubt that it was; he had his wife, who adored him, for company in the evenings, and although she may have missed companionship more than he did, they were both shy, both quiet, and it may be that they both enjoyed their life apart. Short Kwi hunted most of the time. He would hunt on and on and when word would reach the large band of his wife's family that he had killed, the band would go out to where the animal was, dry the meat, and eat it. When there was enough meat Short Kwi would rest, would relax in the sun, would talk with his wife or make himself a new skin bag or garment, and when word would reach him that all the meat was gone he would move again. The men of his wife's family hunted too, of course, but never as successfully as he, yet his great ability set him so far apart from ordinary mortals that for once the Bushmen forgot their jealousy and agreed that he was the best hunter the Kalahari had ever known.

It is a custom among Bushman hunters to cut strips of skin from the foreheads of the antelope they kill and fashion them into bracelets which their wives wear on their arms. Short Kwi's wife and daughter wore dozens of these; their arms were covered and heavy with them. Short Kwi himself wore no ornament of any kind, nothing except a crown of badger hair which he owned for a while but later gave to Toma, the very crown that Toma's son now wore.

One day, said Toma, Short Kwi had been walking in the veld and had failed to watch where he was going. He had stepped on the tail of a puff adder, which had risen up and bitten his leg, just below the knee. It was a rare and terrible accident; in all the time we had been in the Kalahari we had known of only two people besides Short Kwi who had been harmed by snakes—a young boy bitten by a mamba who had died the day he was bitten, and a young woman who had been pulled into a waterhole by a water python and had drowned. Usually, snakes move away when you come near them, or if they don't, you can usually see them; but you can't walk with your eyes on the ground all the time, especially if you are hunting, as Short Kwi had been. His misfortune was regarded as a horrible accident and it was felt that the spirits of the dead were to blame. They had led Short Kwi down the very path the puff adder had chosen, and perhaps had even placed the snake where his foot was sure to fall. Toma and Gao Feet were very depressed to think of it. Although the talk turned to other things, Gao Feet mentioned the accident again and again; everything seemed to remind him of it. At last Toma said to us: "Perhaps you can help him hunt again. Since he was bitten his people have had no meat."

Because it was getting close to noon and the sun, now only veiled by the smoke, was burning over our heads, we decided to start our search for Short Kwi. After Toma, Toma's son, Gao Feet, and Lazy Kwi decided to go with us and the others decided to stay at home, we got on the truck and drove away, lurching over the stones at the edge of camp and out to the wild veld, to the west, where the soft wind was blowing and the horizon seemed dim because of the smoke. Ledimo, the interpreter, came too, and my brother and myself, and that night we slept in the veld, not even bothering to build a fire, but eating a few handfuls of cold food and sleeping in our blankets around the truck. The following afternoon we reached the werf of Short Kwi and his people. This werf, too, was hidden in the bushes and if the men of the band hadn't come out into the plain to meet us we might have gone by it, for Toma himself hadn't known exactly where it was. They came out because they knew it would be us they were meeting, for, they explained later, the European farmers couldn't possibly have found them there.

Six men and several young boys suddenly stepped from the bushes and appeared in front of our truck, all of them brown and naked and waving wildly to us, and the truck stopped so fast that those of us on top were nearly thrown off, and we all climbed down to greet them.

Three of the men were brothers, the brothers-in-law of Short Kwi, for their old mother had a strong hold on her family and kept them all beside her. Her sons and her daughters all lived with her; the sons at least might have been expected to live with the families of their wives, but they had never left her and they were here with her now. They stood together in front of the truck and when we climbed down they embraced us.

We went on toward the werf with these men and boys clinging to the sides of the truck and laughing loudly at those among them who were raked by thorn branches that the truck drove through, and at the edge of the werf we saw the women standing all together, waving and calling to us, and we stopped again and they too embraced us and kissed me, and the little children gravely shook my hand.

Short Kwi's mother-in-law was there with a wide and toothless smile, her face all wrinkled like a little shriveled pear, and many other people, among them the old man who had never shot a buck and whose sister had died in the forest; he now was nobody's close relative and we noticed he had lost an eye and seemed even more malevolent and sad. He greeted us distantly, but the others were enthusiastic. The little children tried to climb on me and finally someone put a baby in my arms. The baby bit me, but he meant me no harm, for when he bit I felt the sharp edge of a new tooth coming, which probably itched.

We passed through the bushes and came into the werf, where the people had obviously been living for a long time, judging by the size of the ash heaps at the fires and the depth of the nests that people had dug for themselves. Looking around, it came to us that many people whom we had expected to see were not there, Short Kwi for one, and his wife. When we asked for them, Short Kwi's brother-in-law said

76

that he would take us to see him presently. When we asked for the others who were missing—among them the man with two wives named Kushe and two daughters named Xama—we were told that these people had all been taken by the farmers and had never been seen again. We were very sad to hear it, for many of them were too old to have to do the heavy work required on the farms, and also because certain members of the families were still here and now these families were broken forever.

On our way to see Short Kwi, the brother-in-law led us to the far end of the werf, behind a clump of bushes, to the scherm where Short Kwi lived. We saw him there, sitting with his wife and little daughter by the ashes of their fire, side by side, and we caught our breath at the sight of him. He looked tiny, no bigger than a child, and his flesh had wasted away so that his pale skin stretched tightly over all his bones. His leg was hidden by a blanket, his hands were as thin and fragile as a girl's, and his eyes were huge. He looked up at us when we came and smiled wanly, wryly, and his wife and daughter looked up at us and his wife also smiled wanly, but his daughter did not smile at all. The first thing Short Kwi did was to rearrange the blanket over his foot to hide his toes, but not before we had seen them, dry and black, dead entirely like the toes of a mummy. His leg was the first thing in his mind, but this was natural; we reminded him of better days.

We sat down at his fire to talk, all of us who had come from Nama and most of the people from his werf, and his wife gave those of us from Nama a palmful of sa, the finely powdered yellow-green leaves that smell halfway between roses and sage. We crossed our faces with it, sprinkling a stripe up the bridge of our noses to our foreheads and another stripe across our cheeks. It smelled very nice, a sweet present to give to someone who has arrived from a long journey. Hours later it was still fragrant and we could smell it, faintly, for days.

We asked Short Kwi to show us his leg and as he started to unwind the blanket the Bushmen from Nama leaned forward, fascinated, but the other Bushmen did not look because they had seen it before. Short Kwi drew back the blanket and revealed a tiny, skinny stick that was his leg wrapped in some kind of rag, bound by a thong that tied the calf to the healthy thigh above, with the black foot showing below, and then he slowly and carefully unwound the thong and then the rag and opened it.

For once the people of Nama had not exaggerated a misfortune. The leg was even worse than they had described, all dead and black at the ankle, and above that, rotted away down to the bone, which was gray now, but while the foot was rotting and dry, the leg was rotting and wet and oozing a little black slime or juice. It was gangrene. A faint stench rose. Those of us who had not seen it had to look away, and Short Kwi, perceiving this, looked calmly down at the ground, at his ruined black leg, and he wrapped the rag around it again, tied his calf to his thigh with the thong, and covered it all with the blanket.

Short Kwi's wife had watched the whole thing with calmness and composure, her hands in her lap, and when the leg was covered she opened one of her hands, revealing a palmful of little white beads, which she began to drop, one by one, into a tiny bag she wore around her neck. With her head bent to see the mouth of the bag she looked very girlish and young; someone said something unusual, an unfamiliar word, and Short Kwi glanced at his wife to see if she had heard it but saw instead what she was doing, and he looked at her with such a deep look of adoration and affection that I wondered how it was she didn't feel it and look up. The word was the word for European doctor, *docteri*, which is not part of the usual vocabulary. Short Kwi's wife had not understood it and when she had finished dropping the beads into the bag she whispered to ask her husband what it meant. He answered her softly, in a masculine, affectionate way, and the other people chimed in, so for a moment everyone was speaking except Short Kwi's wife, who looked around at them all gravely, listening, and when they had finished she nodded her head. "A medicine man of Europeans." they said.

"So," said she.

We talked about the foot for a while, for although he had covered it we could still see the toes. The people of the werf described how Short Kwi was bitten and everyone claimed credit for his part in saving Short Kwi's life. One man had killed the snake, another had cut the fang punctures, and others had given advice at the time and later. The leg had swelled enormously and the medicine men had cut the swollen skin to let blood; the scars of this still showed on the healthy thigh above the blanket. All the people seemed very depressed when talking about it, though; for one reason, they ate meat less often, but also they truly admired him and did not seem to enjoy watching the disaster. Toma asked Short Kwi how he felt and Short Kwi said he thought that his leg had seemed to be getting a little better during the last few days.

It was almost evening, and we heard voices singing in the veld. Two women and a young girl were coming home from a trip for veld food. These three were also very happy to see us and the little girl kissed me but not the men, then asked for her mother, who lived at Nama and whom she had not seen for seasons, and we told her that her mother was well. The girl had been newly married and she was as pretty as she could be, with lots of beads, and with long ornaments of tsi nuts hanging beside her face. She wore a fine kaross which she had rubbed with red powder, often a sign to men that a girl is menstruating, as perhaps she was, that men may be careful not to touch her and endanger their powers to hunt. Marriage seemed to have agreed with her. She looked very happy. She was only ten, but already she had lost her childish belly, although her breasts had not yet begun to grow.

Now everyone was in the werf and people had begun to go back to their fires, leaving Short Kwi alone. When most people were gone, Short Kwi's brother-in-law squatted beside him and, taking his injured leg, began laboriously to help him move toward the veld, toward a little pathway that we had not noticed before. Short Kwi's wife had cleared the path; it led to a place in the veld where Short Kwi could urinate, and slowly, painfully, Short Kwi and his brother-in-law moved down it, the brother-in-law duckwalking, carrying the bad leg while Short Kwi—he who once could run great elands down—edged himself forward on his buttocks, using his hands to brace himself and his good leg to pull himself along.

We were not at his fire when he got back, but we could see him through the trees, inching, and then, when Short Kwi was alone with his wife and daughter, we could watch him sitting by his fire, looking idly around. He was like a wild goose with pinioned wings, squatting there before his fire, watching the sky, the veld, and other people come and go.

Those of us from Nama made a camp apart from the werf, through long grass as high as our chests, inside a little glade of thorn trees. We cleared some of the grass and built a fire, and even then the Bushmen could not stop talking about Short Kwi, although they tried to change the subject; they spoke of him creeping along on his buttocks, even this impossible without someone to help, and all because he had failed to notice an adder that was waiting in his path. Of course, the Bushmen said, he was lucky to be alive. I felt that he was luckier than they supposed, because of his wife, that quiet, gracious, gentle, pretty woman, and his grave little daughter, the image of her mother. The people felt, said Toma, that Short Kwi's wife would leave him now for a better man, but she had not and was not going to. He was, after all, the same husband, only sadder.

Later in the night we went back to talk with Short Kwi once more, to tell him that we thought he could be helped to walk again, but not that we thought his leg would have to come off, for we did not want to frighten him. Our plan was to drive him to Windhock, the capital of South-West Africa, where he could go to a hospital and perhaps be fitted with an artificial leg. We planned eventually to tell him this, but gradually. The long grass was wet with dew when we pushed through it this time, and we were drenched. Short Kwi was still sitting where we had seen him, still beside his wife, not speaking. When we asked him if he would come with us because we believed he could be helped, he smiled such a heart-breaking smile of pure happiness that we felt sickened because we knew what he thought. His wife looked at him and smiled and then they both looked up at us and their smiles faded and their faces fell and I think that when they saw us they knew we couldn't restore his leg to him.

Early in the morning when the sky became light, misty yellow—for the sun was still swallowed by smoke—we broke camp and made a comfortable bed for Short Kwi on top of the truck, then went to the werf to get him. He and his brother-in-law were just creeping back on the path from the veld, but Short Kwi's belongings were ready, tied up in bundles by his wife. We waited a long time while Short Kwi made his way toward us, sweat standing out on his forehead although the air was cool, but oddly, even his slow and painful creeping seemed graceful. It did not have the heaving awkwardness of movement that one associates with injured human beings, but rather the liquidity and co-ordination of a three-legged dog. This morning, though, he did not look at anyone and seemed more silent even than he had been before.

The men made a carriage of their arms and lifted Short Kwi to the top of the truck, and in the process one of them lost his footing so that Short Kwi was jounced, which must have hurt him although he did not show it, Bushmen being very good at concealing pain or despair. His wife climbed on to help make him comfortable and to receive their bundles, which were being handed up, and at the sight of this his baby began to cry without a sound, slow tears rolling down her checks and dropping to the ground. I lifted the baby and tried to play with her, jumping a little and smiling to make her smile, although of course I could not cheer her, and when Short Kwi's wife looked over the truck's side the baby twisted away from me and held up her arms.

When Short Kwi was ready we asked who would come with us, and most of his relatives decided to wait and join us later because one of the young boys, a child of twelve or so, had shot his first buck two days before and as the buck had still not been found, the people did not want to leave it. Toma's son himself wanted to remain because, it turned out, the buck had been shot with an arrow which he had given to another boy, who in turn had given it to the young hunter, and Toma's son, as original owner of the arrow, wanted his rightful share of the meat. When Toma said that his son could wait if he wanted but that we couldn't wait for him, his son turned to some other little boys who stood near him and began discussing the possibility of his joining the search for the animal. It was very interesting to see this conversation, these adult dealings beginning among the ten- and twelve-year-olds, these new, young hunters, these small figures of hope and strength, and we waited a long time while Toma's son rubbed his head with his tough little fingers to make up his mind. Finally he left his friends and climbed on the truck. Home was too far to walk to, he said, and he was going to forfeit. As we drove away, his friends ran after us, shouting that they would bring him his share if they were able.

We reached Nama Pan late in the afternoon. Toma and Gao Feet cleared a werf for Short Kwi, and when he was settled comfortably with his back against a tree and with soft grass and blankets arranged all around him he said softly, just to himself and anyone else who might be listening, that during the night his leg had fallen off. After he said this he began to cry, and Gao Feet slowly crouched beside him, unwound the blanket slowly, and untied the bark, then gently lifted the knee away from the calf, which remained on the ground, just like the leg of a mummy. When the calf had fallen off, Short Kwi had pushed the two pieces back together again. Short Kwi was crying and biting his hand and his wife was crying, and Toma and Gao Feet stood beside him for a minute looking, the expression on their faces as dark as night. Then they picked up the leg and carried it away to the veld, where they buried it in a hole, exactly as if it were a person, they were so sad.

Later, when we had dressed the stump, Toma and Gao Feet came back to sit with Short Kwi and talk with him. Gao Feet told about a Bantu man he had seen far in the north who had been injured in a mine accident and had been fitted with a false foot. Short Kwi could have one too, Gao said; but Toma said, almost too depressed to speak: "What does it matter? He is a cripple now."

Then the men went away and left Short Kwi to rest, and during the evening the children and young people were talking happily, but all the adults in all the werfs were too depressed and sad. Finally, one by one, the men went back again to Short Kwi, who by now had rallied and was sitting up, surely having been through the worst of it the night before, and talked to him about the antelopes he had killed and about the time he killed a wildebeest, an eland, and a wild pig all in one day.

It has been said that Bushmen abandon cripples or people who are old or sick and cannot travel. This is not true.

Far into the night, people who could not sleep sat up and talked at each other's fires. We heard the guashi being played, its long strings sounded in repetitive little songs of four or five notes which themselves were played over and over, for the guashi was being passed from hand to hand, played idly by people who just wanted something to do.

It was a warm night. The frogs in the pan were croaking and the north wind blew the cooking-fires around. Later, when the moon rose and made a blood-red fire all its own, the people began to go home, Toma and Gao Feet and their sons stopping to visit us on their way; they walked silently up to our fire from the darkness and dropped to their haunches one after the other, and sat quietly, their grave faces tilted back, hands shading their eyes. Toma's son wore the crown of badger hair, which moved in the wind a little. Presently the men and their sons stood again one at a time and walked on, as silently on their bare feet as they had come. We heard the low voices of other people who were passing, then saw fires flare up at the werfs, and much later, when the wind had died and even the frogs were silent, we knew that some of the people were dreaming, for they groaned in their sleep.

Although increasing amounts of research on the Bushmen have been undertaken in recent years, we still possess only a limited understanding of them. Enough is known, however, to demonstrate that this group cannot truly be described as "simple" or "primitive." Even in their desert environment they do not have to spend all of their time in the quest for food. In addition to being skilled hunters they are artists, dancers, and musicians. Furthermore, it cannot be assumed that the Bushmen of today are representative of our early ancestors. Since they, like all existing hunters and gatherers, inhabit very marginal areas, the Bushmen simply do not typify the "primitive bands" that followed the enormous herds of bison, antelopes, and other herd animals that were contemporaneous with earlier men. Attempts to equate existing nonliterate people with our earliest ancestors were very common until well into the twentieth century. This view is now known to be terribly oversimplified and inaccurate.

In the large-scale industrial societies so familiar to us,

the individual ordinarily counts for very little. In small hunting bands the existence of a Short Kwi or an Imenak can sometimes spell the difference between survival and disaster. An accident such as the one that befell Short Kwi threatens the well-being of the entire group.

Medical science tends to spare modern man many of the anxieties that still beset societies without advanced medical systems. Even so, such peoples do not always eagerly embrace modern medicine. First, they have medical traditions of their own in which they often believe strongly. Second, as they rather typically believe in magical causes for illness, such as **witchcraft** or **sorcery,** they often ignore medical aid even when it is available. After all, what could a European doctor know about such things? This is not to say that these people are unaware of the relationship between cause and effect. In this story, for example, the Bushmen knew that the snake had caused Short Kwi's problem. But why was Short Kwi bitten, rather than someone else?—because of the spirits of the dead. Magic has always been an interest of anthropologists. The study of non-Western medical systems, **ethnomedicine,** has become an ever-expanding area of investigation in anthropology in recent years. Such studies have shown that local systems of medicine, magical or not, are often more efficacious than they appear at first glance.

Medical problems can pose a great dilemma for the fieldworker. How could Short Kwi have reached a hospital without the transportation provided by the Marshalls? Here the decision was apparently made quickly and with few problems. But what if you are living with a large group, you have the **only** available transportation, and receive frequent demands to take people to the hospital? What if a patient absolutely refuses medical attention, although you realize that he will surely die without it? What if you have only enough medicine for yourself, and others need it too? Anthropologists very frequently face such problems and dilemmas.

For another remarkable and equally moving account of the Bushmen see **The Lost World of the Kalahari,** by Laurens van der Post (1958). The sequel to this, **Heart of the Hunter** (1961), while entertaining, is more mystical than ethnographic.

For more scholarly accounts of the Bushmen see

Khoisan Peoples of South Africa (1930), by Isaac Schapera, and **Subsistence Ecology of the Kung Bushmen,** by Richard B. Lee (1965).

The film made of the Thomas expedition, **The Hunters,** won the Robert J. Flaherty Award in 1958. Van der Post also made a film, entitled **The Lost World of the Kalahari.** Two more recent and exceptionally interesting films on the Bushmen are **Arguments About a Marriage** (1966) and **N/um Tchai** (1966), which deals with trance dancing and curing.

7

The master hunter's apprentice

DOUGLAS LOCKWOOD*

Although some people are born with keener eyesight, better hearing, or stronger legs, and thus become better hunters, warriors, or athletes than others, no one is born with the instinct to hunt, nor with a drive to work mathematical equations, play Bach, pole vault, nor to engage in any other cultural pursuit. Indeed, two of the most important characteristics of the human species are an almost total lack of anything that might be considered **instinctive** and an overwhelming dependence upon learning. In many societies there is no such thing as formal education. That is, there are no schools as such, no specialized teachers, and no fixed curriculum. Much more reliance is placed on observation and imitation than on verbal or written instructions. The following autobiographical account by an Australian aborigine offers an unusual and valuable picture of the way such an educational system works.

The book from which this selection was excerpted, **I, the Aboriginal** (1962), was written by an Australian writer, Douglas Lockwood. Although not an anthropologist, Lockwood was familiar with aboriginal customs and used

* From I, *the Aboriginal* by Douglas Lockwood. Reprinted by permission of Rigby Limited, Adelaide, South Australia.

essentially the same interviewing and recording procedures that anthropologists use. His account is based on more than a hundred hours of interviews with Waipuldanya. As a youth Waipuldanya was trained in aboriginal ways. He later became a skilled medical orderly and an unusually well educated man. In addition to telling us a great deal about the culture of Australian aborigines, Waipuldanya gives us many valuable insights into what it means to have to adjust to two cultures with conflicting and inconsistent demands, a process termed **acculturation.**

In the schoolroom I had been taught by two white women and a half-caste girl. But in the bush my teacher was to be Sam Ulagang, a manly Ngandi tribal hunter ten years my senior. He was my tutor in the tradition of the tribes because his sister, Nora Bindul, had been promised to me in marriage.

If the Alawa and the Ngandi, the Ritarrngu and the Nungubuyu had been Professors of the Art of Living in the University of the Bush, aboriginal students would always have topped the class. Academic knowledge came to us slowly. The reverse was true in those practical subjects on which our lives depended.

And yet my training as a hunter occupied half my life, and I am still learning.

My earliest recollection is of a day soon after I began to walk when my father first wrote a message for me. Didn't I say he was illiterate? Quite so, but this was a message with a difference.

I sat on a log near the camp-fire while he squatted on the ground with both legs folded in front of him.

"Now I will write for you," he said. "Learn well. Always remember. Always remember that the bush and the ground tell a story—if you can read."

He smoothed a square of sand with the back of his arm.

"What is this track?" he asked.

He clenched his fist, and with the thumb uppermost depressed his closed little finger into the sand. Around the apex made by the middle knuckle he touched a finger lightly into the sand four times.

"Dog," I said. I had often seen and identified them near our camp.

He made cat tracks with the tip of a finger, wallaby and kangaroo tracks with the ball of the hand for a pad, and the edge of the hand and little finger for toes. He made the tracks of turtles, goannas, emus, crocodiles, porcupines, birds, cattle, and horses, and told me to copy them. My cattle were calves and my horses foals because my hand was small. But that didn't matter. The exercise impressed upon me for all time the outline of their tracks.

In this way, watching and studying tracks became instinctive with me. Today I read the ground as other people read newspapers and books. The footprints of my wife, my six daughters, my brothers, and other relatives are as familiar to me as their faces. My wife's footprint was the first thing I learnt about her. At the settlement where I now live I know at least fifty people by the track they leave on the ground.

Like most aborigines, I have hypersensitive eyesight and acute hearing. The fact that a wallaby blends well with the colour of dead grass does not conceal it from me. I can see through a camouflage of leaves and point out a bird which has not moved. I can distinguish easily between natural sounds and those made by a moving animal.

It is all much simpler than eight times seven. And there are easy formulae as mathematically precise as the principle of Archimedes to help us solve the most difficult problems.

On hard ground where tracks are invisible it is still possible to follow the movement of an animal by reading the story in trampled grass and disturbed pebbles.

Grass which has been knocked down always points in the direction an animal has taken. A pebble dislodged from its bed in the ground is pushed backwards from the line of flight. The tracks of a snake might be thought to have no beginning and no end, and yet it is easily followed: at each bend the sand is forced towards its tail.

Possums and squirrels which climb gum trees leave a scratched track in the bark. Getting them down is well worth the effort; the flesh is tender, and aboriginal women prize the fur for belts and other articles of clothing.

During my schooldays I was taught the elementary usage of spears and boomerangs by boys who were several years my senior. I practised with my toy weapons until I could throw them accurately. But when I was big enough for graduation to the traditional killing weapons—the shovelnose spear thrown with a woomera, and the heavy boomerangs—my education was taken over by a professional hunter.

This was Sam Ulagang of the Ngandi. To him I owe my ability to live off the land with weapons I have made. He was a great teacher, a proud tribesman, and the most meticulous tracker I am ever likely to know.

I had thought that after a few days with Sam, or a few weeks at most, I would be bringing home my own kangaroos. I found instead that I must curb my itching impatience for many months before I was so much as allowed to follow Sam while he stalked.

At first I was relegated to the rather unedifying duty of spear-bearing. At first, did I say! Ulagang was my father's friend, the brother of my intended wife, and I expected him to treat me courteously.

"You carry the spears," he said during the first month.

"You carry the spears," he said in the second month.

In the third month he said, "Waipuldanya, you carry the spears."

I was so burdened that when we saw a kangaroo I could do nothing either to help stalk it or kill it. I was a walking arsenal, but otherwise helpless. Now I realized why tribal women, laden with weapons and camping gear, always followed at a distance behind their unfettered husbands.

In the fourth month Ulagang said, "You carry the spears. You wait and watch me closely when I go after a kangaroo."

Ah! So now I could wait and watch! Well, that was an improvement. But what did he think I had been doing all these months?

Ulagang saw a wallaby and indicated with a twist of his mouth that I was to stay behind as usual, to wait and watch every movement he made.

I wanted to learn, so I studied him well. I saw him fight impulsiveness. I saw him curb impetuosity. I saw that he watched the wind carefully, moving quickly when it blew strongly, pausing when it eased, walking always with the freshness of it in his face so that his human smells were not carried down to the animal.

In my mind's eye I mapped out the route I would have taken had I been the hunter, and was chagrined when he selected another. I looked for a reason and saw the tall grass he had deliberately avoided as an unnecessary hazard: other wallabies hiding there might have been put to flight and thus disturbed his quarry. I was beginning to appreciate the reasons for his patience.

"Waipuldanya," I told myself, "you will soon be able to hunt."

I lost sight of him behind dense scrub and trees, but I continued to observe the wallaby for another half-hour. Then it stiffened suddenly, a rigid spear-shaft bisecting it at right angles, its cloven body grotesquely skewered and ready for the grilling spit.

Ulagang walked back slowly and nonchalantly handed me the dead animal to carry, as though killing it had been so boring that he wanted to yawn.

"Next time," he promised, "you can track my tracks."

I was elated at this condescension of the Great Black Hunter. But such patronage! Such insufferable conceit!

So he thought that the son of Barnabas was a fit person to track his tracks! An Alawa, and he a mere Ngandhi!

"It is as well," I muttered, "that the Testing Time at the Corroboree Place taught me restraint. Sam would make an excellent base for a right angle."

Had I realized then that my probation was beginning rather than ending, that many weary months of watch-and-wait were still ahead, that Sam was dangling a juicy goanna just out of my reach, I may have been a truant from his school. And yet in my heart I knew that this was the best training I could have. I knew that when he was finished with me there would be little difference between his bushcraft and mine. Whether my spear-arm would be as competent was something which Sam couldn't influence, but that had been schooled since I was a small piccaninny, since the day I was big enough to throw a toy spear.

Next morning Ulagang said to me, "All right. Today we go. Today we go to the Tough and Skinny Place where the grass is rank and the trees are sparse. You can track my tracks."

Thanks, Sam, you pretentious prig. Thanks, Sam, you ostentatious oaf. Thanks, Your Majesty of the Ngandi. So I'm to be allowed to walk behind you! Maybe that's unwise for one so overstuffed with peacock-down. Maybe we'll let a little air in between your shoulder-blades so that humility can enter!

What idle nonsense! Of course it was I who was vain. It was I who needed an injection of meekness. I had speared statued goannas and thought I knew how to hunt. I had speared hypnotized fish and let the entire camp know. But had I stalked and killed an animal bigger than myself, with the odds in its favour, with a millenia of inherent alertness and cunning working for it?

What do you say, Waipuldanya?

No, Sir. Nothing like it, Sir.

All right, then. Fall in behind Sam Ulagang and see if you can learn. Sam is what you might call a demonstration teacher. There are none better, even if he is a Ngandi.

"All right," Ulagang said. "We go now. You carry my spears to the Place Where the Buffalo Wallow. There we will get brown mud to seal the man-smells to our bodies and to make us blend with the dry grass."

"And in the Green-Grass-Time?" I asked.

"You learn well," Sam said. "The Ngandi is pleased. In the Green-Grass-Time you get grey-green mud from the river bank, and moss and leaves."

We smeared ourselves with brown camouflage, oozing and fetid and vile and, it seemed, unnecessary. I remember that Ulagang had not used it when I was simply the spear-bearer.

"Why do we paint ourselves today, Sam?" I asked.

"Because you are tracking me," he said. "You will be unwary. The wallaby will see you unless you are hidden."

The great arrogant oracle again!

"Always, when you are very hungry, you will paint with mud," he said. "It is not good to increase one's hunger with a long stalk and then watch the wallaby jump away when he sees you. The trouble these days is that the Alawa are too well fed. A full belly maketh a careless man. Hunger makes the hunter."

We go . . . and we go . . . and we go . . . and we go . . . and we go. L-o-o-n-g way! Until we are close-to at the Tough and Skinny Place. Come up-wind, climb the hill, and look down.

Ah, there! And there! And there! Three-feller wallaby. Sorry, Miss Dove. I mean three wallabies. Yesterday this would have meant little more to me than that I was to stay there and observe. Today my pulse was beating faster. For now I would track the tracker, stalk the stalker, walk in the Steps of the Master Hunter.

Ulagang ignored me and watched the wallabies. They were grazing into the wind, which meant that their backs were to us. The merest shadow of a smile tripped the corners of his mouth. The wind was good. But three animals together: that was not so good. Three wallabies against one hunter. Or against two hunters? Were the odds three-to-two, or did the fact that I was there make it six-to-one on the wallabies? They had three noses to smell, six eyes to see, six ears to hear. And the speed of light in their feet.

Sam motioned with his mouth and we slipped below the brow of the hill.

"You track my tracks," he whispered. "My right foot, your right foot, same place. My left foot, your left foot, same place. I crawl, you crawl. I sneak along, you sneak along. I stop, you stop. Don't talk. Don't cough. Don't brush grass. Don't brush bush. Stay in shadow, stay in shadow, stay in shadow. The one on the right. It is nearest and we must take it. I will wound it in the leg, then you can track the blood and kill it."

Applause, please. Have a medal, Sam. Boasting again! The unconstrained ego of the man was nauseating.

Although our chance of even getting near three wallabies together seemed slim to me, Sam was so confident of approaching within spear range and then being able to hit one where he liked that he had promised me a bloodtrail and a kill.

All right, Sam. Let's go. Let me see how good you are. Let me see The Master Hunter at work.

We sneak up. We sneak . . . and we sneak . . . and we sneak . . . and we sneak. Sam's body formed a right angle at the waist. His legs were vertical, his torso was horizontal to the ground. I watched his feet, only his feet. If I was to do as he said, to step in his steps, to track his tracks, I had no time to look elsewhere.

While the breeze blew freshly, and we were still a hundred yards from the wallabies, he moved quickly, surely, and expertly. But as the range narrowed, his caution increased and speed slackened. I suppose we were still fifty yards away when Sam stopped in mid-stride: so literally with one foot poised that I was reminded of a hunting dog. And with the same foot he pointed . . . at a dry twig he had almost trodden on. His foot was an exclamation mark.

"Beware!" it said.

He avoided the twig and many others like it. I was careful to step exactly in his imprints. Anyone following may have believed that only one man was ahead.

Now we went slowly, knees bent, hugging the shadow, sighting the wallabies rarely. We stopped still, scarcely breathing, when two birds settled in a tree above us. Sam waited until they had flown off naturally before moving again. He didn't want them to give a raucous danger signal.

The next twenty yards across sparsely wooded ground took fifteen minutes. There were times when I thought that Sam would never go on. When he did take a step I noticed the animals had turned their heads away from us.

Sam's objective was a big tree only thirty feet from where they grazed. The last dozen yards to this tree was through tall grass. We inched forward on our bellies, minimizing the movement of the grass tips, dragging the spears horizontally behind us.

Arm forward, knee forward, down, wait.

Arm forward, knee forward, down, wait.

At last Sam was at the base of the tree, its large bole protecting him from discovery. Even so, his motions were still slow and deliberate. He rose to his knees, then on one foot, and finally was standing upright, flat against the tree. He trod on his spear, fitting the shaft between two toes and raising his leg until he could reach it without stooping. He repeated that to retrieve his woomera. Half an hour had passed, perhaps more, since we left the brow of the hill. In that time neither of us had spoken or made a sound. I was proud to have come through behind him without cracking a twig or rustling the grass.

Now Sam fitted the pointed end of his woomera into the base of the ten-foot steel-headed killing spear. With infinite care he edged his eye around the side of the tree, head erect, hair bound, spear-arm poised but not yet cocked. I watched from the ground, where I remained prone, missing no detail of everything this wonderful hunter did—for now I was convinced of his greatness. In my lifetime in the bush I had never been within thirty feet of any wallaby that was unaware of my presence.

Sam's arm came back and clicked. Safety catch off. He had to raise the spear in front of him, a movement the wallaby might have seen. So he did that quickly and threw mightily with the reflex action, almost in the same instant.

The woomera hissed quietly. The spear was gone. Wh-i-i-s-h! And then the dull thud of something hard striking something soft, followed by the frantic flight of two animals and the retarded struggle of another. I knew before I stood up that it was hit.

"Got 'im! Got 'im! I shouted.

Sam was unimpressed. "You brushed a bush back there," he said severely. "Next time keep away from anything that will make noise. Otherwise you'll go back to spear-bearing."

I remembered the bush, of course. I hoped that Sam hadn't noticed. But he was the teacher and missed nothing. I had a sense of momentary deflation, of youthful pique, at being thus criticized in the moment of triumph for what I thought was a creditable performance.

Fortunately there was little time for inquests. A wounded wallaby was bounding ahead, a potential feast for the camp, and it had to be caught. Now was the time when I should carry home my first kill, trying vainly not to strut, offering the traditional apportionment to my tribal relatives as it had been offered to me.

"Track it and kill it," Ulagang ordered. "I hit it in the right leg. That will happen to you often when you begin hunting alone unless your aim is true. Remember that every mile you chase a wounded animal is another mile you must walk back with the load, perhaps without water. You are taught this lesson today so that you will always throw to kill. Now go. I will follow."

I began to run, following a heavy blood trail and depressed grass which pointed like a signpost.

"Remember that you are coming back," Ulagang warned. "Conserve your energy. It may be a l-o-o-n-g way."

Nevertheless, I hurried impatiently, my itching triggerfinger pressed on the point of the woomera. As bleeding eased and wild panic ebbed the wallaby recovered some of its natural cunning, climbing from the grass country to the ironstone ridges where tracks and the blood-trail would be fainter.

I go . . . and I go . . . and I go . . . and I go.

Sam was behind me. "Keep going," he said. "This will teach you not to hurry. Perhaps you will knock-up-along-wind and have to rest soon? Perhaps you want rubbing-medicine for your tired legs?"

He was needling me, taunting at the inherent pride of every aboriginal in his physical fitness, in his ability to travel without fatigue.

We followed the trail for an hour, winding for five miles across the red-brown gravel, never once sighting the wounded animal. The day was hot and steamy. We sweated freely and were perishing for water when finally the tracks showed me that the wallaby was crawling and dying. A few minutes later I fired my first shot in anger at the slowly moving target and pierced it through the heart.

"You are about to learn why it is wise to kill close to the camp," Sam said. "You carry it home."

I put the sixty-pound carcass across my shoulders and walked six miles back to camp.

My back ached. I thirsted and hungered. My throat and mouth were dry, but I would not give in. I drank mightily when we reached the river and then walked proudly into the camp. I was now a Hunter Second Class, and anxious for the next lesson.

Ulagang took me with him for another six months, each time wounding a wallaby for me to track and kill.

I was disappointed that after the first two or three such expeditions he did not allow me to lead the stalk and throw the first spear. My sagging patience may have been exhausted except that, invariably, Sam taught me a new trick on every trip.

I remember that on one particularly hot day, with only a light breeze, he began catching and killing the small black flies that settled on his body, and indicated that I should kill those that settled on me.

I had never seen this done nor had I heard of it. I asked Sam why it was necessary.

"Today the wind is variable," he said. "Sometimes it blows from the north, sometimes from the east or the south. If flies smell a kangaroo they will leave a man and go to it. They prefer the kangaroo's smell to ours. But when the flies arrive the kangaroo will catch several in its hands and sniff them for human scent."

And that day, with a change in the breeze, our flies migrated when we were within twenty yards of a kangaroo. As they approached I watched it catch several with electric movements of its hands, smell them, and hop away to safety. The secret was out! A finely tuned sense had warned it that Man, the principal enemy, was within fly-range. That also meant within spear-range.

On the way home, our shoulders naked of game, Sam repeated the lesson. "Be careful of flies on a hot day when the wind is change-able. They can keep you hungry," he said.

Eventually my apprenticeship was ended, but only because I took direct action. I had been with Ulagang for more than a year. I thought I knew all there was to know, yet I was afraid the lessons would go on for months longer unless I was able to prove my ability.

The opportunity came during a holiday walkabout with my parents, uncles, aunts, and friends to the Sandy Place where the Hodgson River flows down into the Roper.

Barnabas Gabarla, my father, called the young men to him. "All-about go hunting for food," he said. "But be careful you don't bring back a dead Alawan. Remember that a spear which can kill a kangaroo can also kill a man."

Two boys said they would climb trees and find sugarbag. Others decided on robbing birds' nests. But to me, Hunter Second Class Waipuldanya, that was child's play. I was now Kingsize. Hadn't I killed the wounded wallabies which Ulagang set up for me? Hadn't I tracked The Master and been his spear-bearer for a year? Didn't I know how to paint my body with mud, and use the shadows, and ap-proach up-wind, and avoid the rustling grass, and not disturb the birds, and catch the flies?

All right. All right then. Let's go. Look out, all you fat and juicy wallabies. Look out, all you kangaroos. The Great Black Hunter is on the march, marching against you, matching his wits with yours be-cause you have eaten and he is hungry. Smell well today's flies. Keep your radar ears revolving and the twitching nostrils open.

Davis Mayuldjumdjumgu, a boy of ten, my cousin, came with me as weapon-carrier. Ah, yes, I now rated my own spear-bearer. I had an apprentice to train, even though I had still not hunted and killed a wallaby alone. Davis hadn't speared anything bigger than a fish.

We covered our bodies with mud and moved out to a ridge where I could watch him, and he could watch me, in case the pygmy Burg-ingin or the Stone-People, the treacherous Malanugga-nugga, should follow us. Ten-year-old boys are easily frightened in the bush, as I re-membered well.

On the brow of the hill I looked to the valley, and there, one hundred years away, saw a wallaby grazing.

"Stay here. Stand still!" I told Davis. This was the first order I had ever given, and the authority of my command surprised me.

The air was subdued, but with an unkind variable breeze flicking at the leaves and the tips of the grass. I knew before I began that the stalk ahead of me would have tested Ulagang at his best.

Caution. Caution.

Would I catch him?

Might-be, if the wind doesn't change.

Might-be, if the grass doesn't rustle.

Might-be, if the flies don't migrate.

Well, . . . might-be.

Quietly sneak-up. Quietly sneak-up.

I sneak . . . and I sneak . . . and I sneak . . .

Ah, the wind changeth!

What was it that Stanley Port had told us in Sunday School about the Lord rebuking the winds? I wished the Lord was here now to govern their constancy.

I approached to within thirty yards, crouching low over rough ground, catching flies, once freezing into an aboriginal arabesque when the wallaby looked up. I stayed there on one foot for several minutes, my right leg extended grotesquely behind me, my arms outflung, motionless while the animal perhaps wondered why it had not noticed the sculptured image before.

It was when I had reduced the range to twenty yards, with only another five to go before the moment of truth, that I saw the whirlwind coiling towards us.

A willy-willy!

Red with dust and dry leaves, convoluting prettily from a pinpoint on earth to dispersion in heaven, but menacing and ugly to the hunter.

How had Ulagang warned me about them? It sounded like one of Miss Dove's theorems: "A *willy-willy sucks the air towards it from all directions, no matter which way the breeze is blowing. If you are close enough to be in that vacuum the animal will smell you.*"

In that instant I became Hunter First Class Waipuldanya.

I picked up a small stone and tossed it lightly over the wallaby's head to fall between it and the whirlwind. The unexpected noise of the stone striking the ground startled it. The animal instinctively hopped a few yards away from the sound—towards me!—and there propped and glanced back to investigate, its eyes, its nose, and its ears all diverted from the danger behind its back.

And that was its last free act. I had shipped my woomera and spear while the stone was still in the air, careful that I didn't tap one against the other. I fired at point-blank range and the vicious blade transfixed the body.

"Got 'im! Got 'im!"

For an incredulous moment the wallaby tugged at the shaft with it almost human hands, trying frantically to remove the skewer. Then it fell forward and died.

"Yak-ai! Yak-ai!" Davis shouted from the hilltop.

My spirit exulted. My heart shouted: "You got 'im, you got 'im. And it wasn't easy. That was first-class stalking." But I remembered Ulagang's nonchalance, his "Oh, it's easy" attitude when he killed, and I repressed the urge to shout back at my young friend. Instead, I took the dead wallaby and dropped it at his feet.

"Carry that to Ulagang. Tell him about the willy-willy," I said.

"Big one," Davis said. "Fat one." There could be no sincerer tribute. He reached down to lift it to his shoulders. "Ah, heavy one," he said, remembering that the camp was two miles away. It was heavy, indeed, so we carried it between us, suspended by its big tail and the tiny hands which this time had failed to catch a fly to warn it that an expert spearman had entered the bush.

My father, my mother, and my Uncle Stanley Marbunggu were proud and surprised.

"We can depend on you now. You are a Hunter First Class," my father said.

"I grew him up," Marbunggu said.

"I grew him along here," my mother said, and patted her belly.

"I trained him," Ulagang said. "Now he is fit to look after a wife and kids. Mayuldjumdjumgu told me about the willy-willy. He told me how you threw the stone and brought the wallaby towards you. I will hunt with you, my friend."

That was the ultimate praise, to tell a younger man that you were prepared to hunt with him. Ulagang seemed proudest of them all. Except me, perhaps, for I was transcended.

Australian aborigines have played an important part in the development of social science and of psychological theory. Much of the earliest fieldwork was done among them and scholars in many disciplines have been fascinated by them since before the turn of the century. Sir James George Frazer's early work on the evolution of magic, religion, and science (1890) was influenced by what was then known about Australian aborigines. Sigmund Freud drew heavily on the Australian materials as he created psychoanalytic theory. Emile Durkheim and Herbert Spencer, the most distinguished sociologists of their day, were similarly influenced by what they read or were told about the original inhabitants of the Australian continent. As it became known that the aborigines had kinship and religious systems of great complexity, along with a technology that was relatively simple, the then prevailing views on the evolution of culture had to be drastically revised.

Like the Bushmen, many aborigines inhabited desert regions of exceedingly limited resources. But many lived in the much more fertile and productive regions along the Australian coast. Naturally, those living in the most desirable regions were the first to be driven out or, like their Tasmanian relatives to the South, the first to be exterminated entirely by European settlers. In some areas, and continuing even into the twentieth century, aborigines, like the Bushmen, were hunted with dogs and shot like animals—an example, again, of the more "civilized" behavior of Western Europeans. Wherever they lived, aborigines shared similar features of culture that linked them to each other and bound them inextricably to their sacred places, to their **totemic ancestors,** and to their ancestral past—to what they refer to as "the dreamtime." In this way the land, as well as all of the creatures with whom they shared it, was as sacred to them as it was to the American Indian, and its expropriation and exploitation were equally as traumatic and painful.

For ethnographic accounts of Australian aborigines see Spencer and Gillen's early, definitive work, **The Native Tribes of Central Australia** (1898); their book **The Arunta** (1927); Lloyd Warner's account of the Murngin, **A Black Civilization;** Mervyn Meggitt's **Desert People** (1962); Richard A. Gould's **Yiwara: Foragers of the Australian Desert** (1969); and Hart and Pilling's **The Tiwi of North Australia** (1960). More general accounts of aborigines are A. P. Elkin's **Australian Aborigines** (1938), Berndt and Berndt's **The First Australians** (1952), and Kenelm Burridge's **Encountering Aborigines** (1973).

Very readable and ethnographically informative novels about Australian aborigines include Eleanor Dark's **The Timeless Land** (1941), and **Men of the Honey Bee,** by A. E. Wells (1971). A collection of short stories by Australian writers about aborigines and culture change is **Aliens in Their Land,** edited by Louise E. Rorabacher (1968). **The Passing of the Aborigines,** by Daisy Bates (1967), is a remarkable account of an unusual woman who spent her entire life with the aborigines.

For unusual and informative films about Australian aborigines, including their complicated and painful initiation rites, see the series of films made by Norman Tindale in the 1930s (available from the Department of Anthropology, University of California, Los Angeles) and also the more recently filmed **Desert People.** See also **Djalambu** and **Men of Dream Time.**

8

Listen to the lizards

CARLOS CASTANEDA*

All men, everywhere it appears, believe that it is possible to transcend ordinary, everyday experience and to gain supernatural power of one sort or another. Just as the Indians of the plains fasted and sought visions, the New Guineans underwent painful initiation rites, and members of certain religious sects in the United States fall into trances and handle poisonous snakes, so other men in still other places have developed a wide variety of magical techniques for overcoming human limitations and helplessness. The following extraordinary account tells us the details of one such attempt.

The Yaqui Indians inhabit the dry, semidesert country of Northern Mexico around Sonora. They are a horticultural people with a highly developed ceremonial life. Their belief in **diableros**—people who practice black magic and can turn themselves into animals—is very strong. Carlos Castaneda, as a graduate student in anthropology, reportedly spent five years with such a person, a Yaqui Indian sorcerer called don Juan, learning to use and control a variety of supernatural powers, including hallucinogenic plants. His remarkable account of this experience, **The Teachings of Don Juan** (1968), from which the following excerpt is taken, became a best-seller. Much of the interest in the book stems from

Castaneda's ability to convey how the Yaqui themselves understand knowledge, and how those who wish to attain it must seek it patiently, persistently, and bravely. As is clear even from the brief passage presented here, the path they tread is not an easy one.

Sunday, April 21, 1963

On Tuesday afternoon, April 16, don Juan and I went to the hills where his *Datura** plants are. He asked me to leave him alone there, and wait for him in the car. He returned nearly three hours later carrying a package wrapped in a red cloth. As we started to drive back to his house he pointed to the bundle and said it was his last gift for me.

I asked if he meant he was not going to teach me anymore. He explained that he was referring to the fact that I had a plant fully mature and would no longer need his plants.

Late in the afternoon we sat in his room; he brought out a smoothly finished mortar and pestle. The bowl of the mortar was about six inches in diameter. He untied a large package full of small bundles, selected two of them, and placed them on a straw mat by my side; then he added four more bundles of the same size from the pack he had carried home. He said they were seeds, and I had to grind them into a fine powder. He opened the first bundle and poured some of its contents into the mortar. The seeds were dried, round and caramel yellow in color.

I began working with the pestle; after a while he corrected me. He told me to push the pestle against one side of the mortar first, and then slide it across the bottom and up against the other side. I asked what he was going to do with the powder. He did not want to talk about it.

The first batch of seeds was extremely hard to grind. It took me four hours to finish the job. My back ached because of the position in which I had been sitting. I lay down and wanted to go to sleep right there, but don Juan opened the next bag and poured some of the contents into the mortar. The seeds this time were slightly darker than the first ones, and were lumped together. The rest of the bag's contents was a sort of powder, made of very small, round, dark granules.

I wanted something to eat, but don Juan said that if I wished to learn I had to follow the rule, and the rule was that I could only drink a little water while learning the secrets of the second portion.

The third bag contained a handful of live, black, grain weevils.

* Datura—a plant of the solanaceous genus *Datura*, the plants of which have narcotic properties.

And in the last bag were some fresh white seeds, almost mushy soft, but fibrous and difficult to grind into a fine paste, as he expected me to do. After I had finished grinding the contents of the four bags, don Juan measured two cups of a greenish water, poured it into a clay pot, and put the pot on the fire. When the water was boiling he added the first batch of powdered seeds. He stirred it with a long, pointed piece of wood or bone which he carried in his leather pouch. As soon as the water boiled again he added the other substances one by one, following the same procedure. Then he added one more cup of the same water, and let the mixture simmer over a low fire.

Then he told me it was time to mash the root. He carefully extracted a long piece of *Datura* root from the bundle he had carried home. The root was about sixteen inches long. It was thick, perhaps an inch and a half in diameter. He said it was the second portion, and again he had measured the second portion himself, because it was still *his* root. He said the next time I tried the devil's weed I would have to measure my own root.

He pushed the big mortar toward me, and I proceeded to pound the root in exactly the same way he had mashed the first portion. He directed me through the same steps, and again we left the mashed root soaking in water, exposed to the night air. By that time the boiling mixture had solidified in the clay pot. Don Juan took the pot from the fire, placed it inside a hanging net, and hooked it to a beam in the middle of the room.

About eight o'clock in the morning of April 17, don Juan and I began to leach the root extract with water. It was a clear, sunny day, and don Juan interpreted the fine weather as an omen that the devil's weed liked me; he said that with me around he could remember only how bad she had been with him.

The procedure we followed in leaching the root extract was the same I had observed for the first portion. By late afternoon, after pouring out the top water for the eighth time, there was a spoonful of a yellowish substance in the bottom of the bowl.

We returned to his room where there were still two little sacks he had not touched. He opened one, slid his hand inside, and wrinkled the open end around his wrist with the other hand. He seemed to be holding something, judging by the way his hand moved inside the bag. Suddenly, with a swift movement, he peeled the bag off his hand like a glove, turning it inside out, and shoved his hand close to my face. He was holding a lizard. Its head was a few inches from my eyes. There was something strange about the lizard's mouth. I gazed at it for a moment, and then recoiled involuntarily. The lizard's mouth was sewed up with rude stitches. Don Juan ordered me to hold the lizard in my left hand. I clutched it; it wriggled against my palm. I felt nauseated. My hands began to perspire.

He took the last bag, and, repeating the same motions, he extracted another lizard. He also held it close to my face. I saw that its eyelids were sewed together. He ordered me to hold this lizard in my right hand.

By the time I had both lizards in my hands I was almost sick. I had an overpowering desire to drop them and get out of there.

"Don't squeeze them!" he said, and his voice brought me a sense of relief and direction. He asked what was wrong with me. He tried to be serious, but couldn't keep a straight face and laughed. I tried to ease my grip, but my hands were sweating so profusely that the lizards began to wriggle out of them. Their sharp little claws scratched my hands, producing an incredible feeling of disgust and nausea. I closed my eyes and clenched my teeth. One of the lizards was already sliding onto my wrist; all it needed was to yank its head from between my fingers to be free. I had a peculiar sensation of physical despair, of supreme discomfort. I growled at don Juan, between my teeth, to take the damn things off me. My head shook involuntarily. He looked at me curiously. I growled like a bear, shaking my body. He dropped the lizards into their bags and began to laugh. I wanted to laugh also, but my stomach was upset. I lay down.

I explained to him that what had affected me was the sensation of their claws on my palms; he said there were lots of things that could drive a man mad, especially if he did not have the resolution, the purpose, required for learning; but when a man had a clear, unbending intent, feelings were in no way a hindrance, for he was capable of controlling them.

Don Juan waited awhile and then, going through the same motions, handed me the lizards again. He told me to hold their heads up and rub them softly against my temples, as I asked them anything I wanted to know.

I did not understand at first what he wanted me to do. He told me again to ask the lizards about anything I could not find out for myself. He gave me a whole series of examples: I could find out about persons I did not see ordinarily, or about objects that were lost, or about places I had not seen. Then I realized he was talking about *divination*. I got very excited. My heart began to pound. I felt that I was losing my breath.

He warned me not to ask about personal matters this first time; he said I should think rather of something that had nothing to do with me. I had to think fast and clearly because there would be no way of reversing my thoughts.

102

I tried frantically to think of something I wanted to know. Don Juan urged me on imperiously, and I was astonished to realize I could think of nothing I wanted to "ask" the lizards.

After a painfully long wait I thought of something. Some time earlier a large number of books had been stolen from a reading room. It was not a personal matter, and yet I was interested in it. I had no preconceived ideas about the identity of the person, or persons, who had taken the books. I rubbed the lizards against my temples, asking them who the thief was.

After awhile don Juan put the lizards inside their bags, and said that there were no deep secrets about the root and the paste. The paste was made to give direction; the root made things clear. But the real mystery was the lizards. They were the secret of the whole sorcery of the second portion, he said. I asked whether they were a special kind of lizard. He said they were. They had to come from the area of one's own plant; they had to be one's friends. And to have lizards as friends, he said, required a long period of grooming. One had to develop a strong friendship with them by giving them food and speaking kind words to them.

I asked why their friendship was so important. He said the lizards would allow themselves to be caught only if they knew the man, and whoever took the devil's weed seriously had to treat the lizards seriously. He said that, as a rule, the lizards should be caught after the paste and the root had been prepared. They should be caught in the late afternoon. If one was not on intimate terms with the lizards, he said, days could be spent trying to catch them without success; and the paste lasts only one day. He then gave me a long series of instructions concerning the procedure to follow after the lizards had been caught.

"Once you have caught the lizards, put them in separate bags. Then take the first one and talk to her. Apologize for hurting her, and beg her to help you. And with a wooden needle sew up her mouth. Use the fibers of agave and one of the thorns of a choya to do the sewing. Draw the stitches tight. Then tell the other lizard the same things and sew her eyelids together. By the time night begins to fall you will be ready. Take the lizard with the sewed-up mouth and explain to her the matter you want to know about. Ask her to go and see for you; tell her you had to sew up her mouth so she would hurry back to you and not talk to anyone else. Let her scramble in the paste after you have rubbed it on her head; then put her on the ground. If she goes in the direction of your good fortune, the sorcery will be successful and easy. If she goes in the opposite direction, it will be unsuccessful. If the lizard moves toward you (south), you can expect more than ordinary good luck; but if she moves away from you (north), the sorcery will be terribly difficult. You may even die! So if she moves away from you, that is a good time to quit. At this point you can make the decision to quit. If you do, you will lose your capacity to command the lizards, but that is better than losing your life. On the other hand, you may decide to go ahead with the sorcery in spite of my warning. If you do, the next step is to take the other lizard and tell her to listen to her sister's story, and then describe it to you."

"But how can the lizard with the sewed-up mouth tell me what she sees? Wasn't her mouth closed to prevent her from talking?"

"Sewing up her mouth prevents her from telling her story to strangers. People say lizards are talkative; they will stop anywhere to talk. Anyway, the next step is to smear the paste on the back of her head, and then rub her head against your right temple, keeping the paste away from the center of your forehead. At the beginning of your learning it is a good idea to tie the lizard by its middle to your right shoulder with a string. Then you won't lose her or injure her. But as you progress and become more familiar with the power of the devil's weed, the lizards learn to obey your commands and will stay perched on your shoulder. After you have smeared the paste on your right temple with the lizard, dip the fingers of both hands into the gruel; first rub it on both temples and then spread it all over both sides of your head. The paste dries very fast, and can be applied as many times as necessary. Begin every time by using the lizard's head first and then your fingers. Sooner or later the lizard that went to see comes back and tells her sister all about her journey, and the blind lizard describes it to you as though you were her kind. When the sorcery is finished, put the lizard down and let her go, but don't watch where she goes. Dig a deep hole with your bare hands and bury everything you used in it."

About 6:00 P.M. don Juan scooped the root extract out of the bowl onto a flat piece of shale; there was less than a teaspoon of a yellowish starch. He put half of it into a cup and added some yellowish water. He rotated the cup in his hand to dissolve the substance. He handed me the cup and told me to drink the mixture. It was tasteless, but it left a slightly bitter flavor in my mouth. The water was too hot and that annoyed me. My heart began pounding fast, but soon I was relaxed again.

Don Juan got the other bowl with the paste. The paste looked solid, and had a glossy surface. I tried to poke the crust with my finger, but don Juan jumped toward me and pushed my hand away from the bowl. He became very annoyed; he said it was very thoughtless of me to try that, and if I really wanted to learn there was no need to be careless. This was power, he said, pointing to the paste, and nobody could tell what kind of power it really was. It was bad enough that we had to tamper with it for our own purposes—a thing we cannot help doing because we are men, he said—but we should at least treat it with the proper respect. The mixture looked like oatmeal. Apparently it had enough starch to give it that consistency. He asked me to get the bags with the lizards. He took the lizard with the sewed-up mouth and carefully handed it over to me. He made me take it with my left hand and told me to get some of the paste with my finger and rub it on the lizard's head and then put the lizard into the pot and hold it there until the paste covered its entire body.

Then he told me to remove the lizard from the pot. He picked up the pot and led me to a rocky area not too far from his house. He pointed to a large rock and told me to sit in front of it, as if it were my *Datura* plant, and, holding the lizard in front of my face, to explain to her again what I wanted to know, and beg her to go and find the answer for me. He advised me to tell the lizard I was sorry I had to cause her discomfort, and to promise her I would be kind to all lizards in return. And then he told me to hold her between the third and fourth fingers of my left hand, where he had once made a cut, and to dance around the rock doing exactly what I had done when I replanted the root of the devil's weed; he asked me if I remembered all I had done at that time. I said I did. He emphasized that everything had to be just the same, and if I did not remember I had to wait until everything was clear in my mind. He warned me with great urgency that if I acted too quickly, without deliberation, I was going to get hurt. His last instruction was that I was to place the lizard with the sewed-up mouth on the ground and watch where she went, so that I could determine the outcome of the experience. He said I was not to take my eyes away from the lizard, even for an instant, because it was a common trick of lizards to distract one and then dash away.

It was not quite dark yet. Don Juan looked at the sky. "I will leave you alone," he said, and walked away.

I followed all his instructions and then placed the lizard on the ground. The lizard stood motionless where I had put it. Then it looked at me, and ran to the rocks toward the east and disappeared among them.

I sat on the ground in front of the rock, as though I were facing my plant. A profound sadness overtook me. I wondered about the lizard with its sewed-up mouth. I thought of its strange journey and of how it looked at me before it ran away. It was a weird thought, an annoying projection. In my own way I too was a lizard, undergoing another strange journey. My fate was, perhaps, only to see; at that moment I felt that I would never be able to tell what I had seen. It was very dark by then. I could hardly see the rocks in front of me. I thought of don Juan's words: "The twilight is the crack between the worlds."

After long hesitation I began to follow the steps prescribed. The paste, though it looked like oatmeal, did not feel like oatmeal. It was very smooth and cold. It had a peculiar, pungent smell. It produced a sensation of coolness on the skin and dried quickly. I rubbed my temples eleven times, without noticing any effect. I tried very carefully to take account of any change in perception or mood, for I did not even know what to anticipate. As a matter of fact, I could not conceive the nature of the experience, and kept on searching for clues.

The paste had dried up and scaled off my temples. I was about to rub some more of it on when I realized I was sitting on my heels in Japanese fashion. I had been sitting cross-legged and did not recall changing positions. It took some time to realize fully that I was sitting on the floor in a sort of cloister with high arches. I thought they were brick arches, but upon examining them I saw they were stone.

This transition was very difficult. It came so suddenly that I was not ready to follow. My perception of the elements of the vision was diffused, as if I were dreaming. Yet the components did not change. They remained steady, and I could stop alongside any one of them and actually examine it. The vision was not so clear or so real as one induced by peyote. It had a misty character, an intensely pleasing pastel quality.

I wondered whether I could get up or not, and the next thing I noticed was that I had moved. I was at the top of a stairway and H., a friend of mine, was standing at the bottom. Her eyes were feverish. There was a mad glare in them. She laughed aloud and with such intensity that she was terrifying. She began coming up the stairs. I wanted to run away or take cover, because "she'd been off her rocker once." That was the thought that came to my mind. I hid behind a column and she went by me without looking. "She's going on a long trip now," was another thought that occurred to me then; and finally the last thought I remembered was, "She laughs every time she's ready to crack up."

Suddenly the scene became very clear; it was no longer like a dream. It was like an ordinary scene, but I seemed to be looking at it through window glass. I tried to touch a column but all I sensed was that I couldn't move; yet I knew I could stay as long as I wanted, viewing the scene. I was in it and yet I was not part of it.

I experienced a barrage of rational thoughts and arguments. I was, so far as I could judge, in an ordinary state of sober consciousness. Every element belonged in the realm of my normal processes. And yet I knew it was not an ordinary state.

The scene changed abruptly. It was nighttime. I was in the hall of a building. The darkness inside the building made me aware that in the earlier scene the sunlight had been beautifully clear. Yet it had been so commonplace that I did not notice it at the time. As I looked further into the new vision I saw a young man coming out of a room carrying a large knapsack on his shoulders. I didn't know who he was, although I had seen him once or twice. He walked by me and went down the stairs. By then I had forgotten my apprehension, my rational dilemmas. "Who's that guy?" I thought. "Why did I see him?"

The scene changed again and I was watching the young man deface books; he glued some of the pages together, erased markings, and so on. Then I saw him arranging the books neatly in a wooden crate. There was a pile of crates. They were not in his room, but in a storage place. Other images came to my mind, but they were not clear. The scene became foggy. I had a sensation of spinning.

Don Juan shook me by the shoulders and I woke up. He helped me to stand and we walked back to his house. It had been three and a half hours from the moment I began rubbing the paste on my temples to the time I woke up, but the visionary state could not have lasted more than ten minutes. I had no ill effects whatsoever. I was just hungry and sleepy.

Thursday, April 18, 1963

Don Juan asked me last night to describe my recent experience, but I was too sleepy to talk about it. I could not concentrate. Today, as soon as I woke up, he asked me again.

"Who told you this girl H. had been off her rocker?" he asked when I finished my story.

"Nobody. It was just one of the thoughts I had."

"Do you think they were your thoughts?"

I told him they were my thoughts, although I had no reason to think that H. had been sick. They were strange thoughts. They seemed to pop up in my mind from nowhere. He looked at me inquisitively. I asked him if he did not believe me; he laughed and said that it was my routine to be careless with my acts.

"What did I do wrong, don Juan?"

"You should have listened to the lizards."

"How should I have listened?"

"The little lizard on your shoulder was describing to you everything her sister was seeing. She was talking to you. She was telling you everything, and you paid no attention. Instead, you believed the lizard's words were your own thoughts."

"But they *were* my own thoughts, don Juan."

"They were not. That is the nature of this sorcery. Actually, the vision is to be listened to, rather than looked at. The same thing happened to me. I was about to warn you when I remembered my benefactor had not warned me."

"Was your experience like mine, don Juan?"

"No. Mine was a hellish journey. I nearly died."

"Why was it hellish?"

"Maybe because the devil's weed did not like me, or because I was not clear about what I wanted to ask. Like you yesterday. You must have had that girl in mind when you asked the question about the books."

"I can't remember it."

"The lizards are never wrong; they take every thought as a question. The lizard came back and told you things about H. no one will ever be able to understand, because not even you know what your thoughts were."

"How about the other vision I had?"

"Your thoughts must have been steady when you asked that question. And that is the way this sorcery should be conducted, with clarity."

"Do you mean the vision of the girl is not to be taken seriously?"

"How can it be taken seriously if you don't know what questions the little lizards were answering?"

"Would it be more clear to the lizard if one asked only one question?"

"Yes, that would be clearer. If you could hold one thought steadily."

"But what would happen, don Juan, if the one question was not a simple one?"

"As long as your thought is steady, and does not go into other things, it is clear to the little lizards, and then their answer is clear to you."

"Can one ask more questions of the lizards as one goes along in the vision?"

"No. The vision is to look at whatever the lizards are telling you. That is why I said it is a vision to hear more than a vision to see. That is why I asked you to deal with impersonal matters. Usually, when the question is about people, your longing to touch them or talk to them is too strong, and the lizard will stop talking and the sorcery will be dispelled. You should know much more than you do now before trying to see things that concern you personally. Next time you must listen carefully. I am sure the lizards told you many, many things, but you were not listening."

Friday, April 19, 1963

"What were all the things I ground for the paste, don Juan?"

"Seeds of devil's weed and the weevils that live off the seeds. The measure is one handful of each." He cupped his right hand to show me how much.

I asked him what would happen if one element was used by itself, without the others. He said that such a procedure would only antagonize the devil's weed and the lizards. "You must not antagonize the lizards," he said, "for the next day, during the late afternoon, you must return to the site of your plant. Speak to all lizards and ask the two that helped you in the sorcery to come out again. Search all over until it is quite dark. If you can't find them, you must try it once more the next day. If you are strong you will find both of them, and then you have to eat them, right there. And you will be endowed forever with the capacity to see the unknown. You will never need to catch lizards again to practice this sorcery. They will live inside you from then on."

"What do I do if I find only one of them?"

"If you find only one of them you must let her go at the end of your search. If you find her the first day, don't keep her, hoping you will catch the other one the next day. That will only spoil your friendship with them."

"What happens if I can't find them at all?"

"I think that would be the best thing for you. It implies that you must catch two lizards every time you want their help, but it also implies that you are free."

"What do you mean, free?"

"Free from being the slave of the devil's weed. If the lizards are to live inside you, the devil's weed will never let you go."

"Is that bad?"

"Of course it is bad. She will cut you off from everything else. You will have to spend your life grooming her as an ally. She is possessive. Once she dominates you, there is only one way to go—her way."

"What if I find that the lizards are dead?"

"If you find one or both of them dead, you must not attempt to do this sorcery for some time. Lay off for a while.

"I think this is all I need to tell you; what I have told you is the rule. Whenever you practice this sorcery by yourself, you must follow all the steps I have described while you sit in front of your plant. One more thing. You must not eat or drink until the sorcery is finished."

There has been considerable controversy over whether or not **The Teachings of Don Juan** and the other three books by Castaneda that followed are authentic. This stems in part from the fact that the details of don Juan's life have never been made clear—nor, for that matter, have the details of Castaneda's life. It has been suggested that don Juan may not actually exist and that Castaneda simply fabricated his information. Whether the account is completely authentic or not, it still represents one of the most comprehensive and convincing descriptions we have of a non-Western theory of knowledge. It cannot be Castaneda's considerable skill as a writer alone that enabled him to achieve such a high degree of verisimilitude. Until the facts of the matter become known, and until the relationship between "novelistic" and more traditional anthropological writings is more fully explored, it would be unwise to simply dismiss **The Teachings of Don Juan** as without anthropological merit.

Questions of authenticity aside for the moment, Castaneda's attempt to present the Yaqui view of reality rather than his own, represents what is known in anthropology as an **emic** approach. As such, it is an extreme example of what anthropologists have always attempted to do—to provide the native's point of view rather than the anthropologist's. Much of the emphasis on spending long periods of time in the field and learning the local language derives from just this goal. This method contrasts with an **etic** view, the view imposed on the data by the investigator.

Castaneda's work raises two further issues in anthropology. First, what is the fieldworker's obligation to his informants? Should he, as in this case, refuse to reveal their true identity or whereabouts? Or must he, as scientific work demands, reveal the information so that others could, if they wished, attempt to replicate and verify his findings? In this particular case there is little doubt that don Juan's life would have been profoundly disrupted had his anonymity not been protected.

A second point has to do with the style of anthropological writing. **The Teachings of Don Juan** is a first person account of fieldwork, and in that sense it is similar to **The High Valley** and **The Forest People.** But whereas Read and Turnbull chose the style to convey something of the subjective fieldwork experience and of the people they met, Castaneda was virtually forced to use it by the nature of the attempt and by the situation itself. The book could not have been as powerful had this not been the case. It thus demonstrates the usefulness of what has been termed "the personal approach to fieldwork" (Honigman, 1976) as opposed to the more objective, impersonal, scientific approach.

The Teachings of Don Juan is the first book of four, the others being **A Separate Reality: Further Conversations with Don Juan** (1971), **Journey to Ixtlan** (1972), and **Tales of Power** (1974). All should ideally be read in the order in which they appeared, but each can be read for itself. Taken together they give a comprehensive account of the conflict between two systems of values and beliefs. Curiously, they tell us little about Yaqui Indian culture as such. For information on this point see **Pascua, A Yaqui Village in Arizona** (1940) and **Potam, A Yaqui Village in Sonora** (1954), both by Edward H. Spicer. See also **The Yaqui Gold** (1943) by Edward D. Laughlin and **Yaqui Gold** by Thomas Sewell (1963). For interesting life histories see **The Tall Candle: A Personal Chronicle of a Yaqui Indian** by Rosalio Moises, Jane Holden Kelley and William Carry Holden (1971), and **Four Yaqui Women** by Jane Holden Kelley (n.d.).

There are some quite remarkable films that deal with magico-religious experiences in various parts of the world. Of particular relevance here is **To Find our Life: The Peyote Hunt of the Huichals of Mexico** (1969). **N/um Tchai** (1966) deals with trance and curing among the Bushmen. **Pocomania . . . A Little Madness** deals with trance in a secret Jamaican cult. **Trance and Dance in Bali,** an early film by Margaret Mead and Gregory Bateson, remains a classic. **Ma' Bugi': Trance of the Toraja** (1974), a more recent film made in the Toraja highlands of Sulawesi (Celebes) Island, Indonesia, is most informative on trance ritual. **Holy Ghost People** (1967), on Appalachian snake handlers, is outstanding. For films dealing with shamanism see **Pomo Shaman** (1964), **Himalayan Shaman of Northern Nepal** (1967), and the BBC film on African curses, **The Witch Doctor.**

9

Amara

ELENORE SMITH BOWEN*

The Tiv of Nigeria represent a type of culture quite different from those we have seen up to now. They reside in **compounds** of from five to over a hundred persons, and they engage in **subsistence farming.** They represent what anthropologists call a **segmentary lineage system,** a society made up of autonomous lineages which oppose one another for certain activities, but which occasionally join with other lineages to create still larger units when required for other functions. This lineage structure constitutes the Tiv's political system as well, since there are neither chiefs nor political officials of any kind. There are, of course, men who have more prestige and influence than others. These men are leaders largely by virtue of having a following within their lineages, and they become influential primarily because of their personal qualities. Law, too, is maintained through the lineage system; groups of lineage elders meet to resolve difficulties as they arise. However, as the following account will show, strong-willed men sometimes refuse to acknowledge such authority.

Although this selection focuses on a witchcraft accusation, it illuminates other aspects of Tiv culture as well. It is an unusual account, originally written under a pseudonym by a well-known anthropologist, Laura Bohannan. Although

*From *Return to Laughter*, copyright 1954 by Laura Bohannan. Reprinted by permission of Doubleday & Company, Inc.

in her introduction to the book from which the selection is taken, **Return to Laughter,** the author insists that it is a **fictional** account, and although the book has been referred to as a novel, it has been widely adopted by anthropologists for classroom use. It raises questions similar but not identical to those raised by **The Teachings of Don Juan,** questions about the respective natures of fiction and anthropology. It is interesting to note, however, that Bohannan originally felt she had to write this type of book under a pseudonym, and that she was criticized by some of her peers even then.

Sunday brought a message with my early morning coffee: Amara had been in labor all night; I was to come at once with medicine. Yabo's peremptory voice was audible even through Sunday's rendition. "As soon as I've had my coffee," I told Sunday. He had already told the messenger that I could not possibly come until the sun was there: Sunday's outstretched arm pointed to the second row of horizontal roof ties—ten o'clock. "Where is the sun now?" I inquired, gulping coffee. My alarm clock had broken; my hut remained quite dark until ten. Sunday's arm went to a spot halfway up the wall—about seven-thirty. Sunday, having observed that being hurried through my coffee upset my temper for the day, took pains to protect himself by protecting me during that crucial time. His having mentioned the matter so early struck me more as a proof that he shared the general fear of Yabo than as any recognition of my well-known fondness for Amara.

There was, actually, no point in hurrying. I knew nothing of midwifery, could not possibly do anything to help Amara. Nevertheless, I skimped my coffee and set off hastily. I made my way over the muddy path as quickly as I could, and I soon found myself behind Udama, who was walking at a more leisurely pace. With her was a massive woman with a large goiter and a husky voice. Udama explained her presence. "Yabo's senior wife has summoned all the midwives. This case is too much for her."

At Yabo's instructions, Amara had been carried out of the hut and placed under the shade of a tree in the yard. The breeze, he said, would refresh her; here, too, there would be space for all the midwives, and they would be able to see the better. Already about a dozen women had gathered around her. I recognized the senior women of Yabo's homestead and a middle-aged woman who was Amara's co-wife. She had appeared, with their husband, as soon as word had reached them.

I looked at the assembled midwives. Yabo's senior wife had indeed sent far and wide. One old crone, bent almost double and shaking with age, lived four miles away. "You have come far, my mother," I congratulated her, for I had occasionally seen her on the path, tottering, clutching at her stick, always balancing on her head a small calabash that quivered and slid as the old woman trembled, and yet miraculously never fell off.

Udama's husky companion pushed her way into the midst of the clustered experts. Amara was lying back in a sloping wooden chair, head lolling, eyes shut. Her co-wife supported her. The midwives argued, loudly and volubly, asking Yabo's senior wife for details, interrupting her replies and unanimous only in their disapproval of her treatment.

Yabo, with a sheaf of herbs in his hand, appeared at my elbow. Shouting down the midwives, he demanded my medicine. "I have none," I spoke loudly and to them all. "In our country also childbirth is the affair of old experienced women, or of doctors." Only Amara's kin seemed disappointed. The old women looked rather relieved that they were to remain in charge. They resumed their consultations.

Meanwhile Yabo crushed the herbs into a pot, poured water over them and told one of his wives to put it on the fire to boil. As I jotted down the names of the ingredients, he added that this was medicine associated with some magic most commonly involved in difficult childbirth; there was little use in performing the ceremony without positive diagnosis from the diviner, but there could be no harm in administering the medicine and it might help.

The midwives had reached an agreement: not an agreement on any one course of treatment, but that each of them was to apply her own remedies. One of them had begun to massage Amara with cruelly stiff fingers whose touch made Amara whimper. Several others had scattered into the bush to gather roots, leaves and grasses from which they would prepare those medicines they had found most efficacious. Soon the homestead was full of bustle. The old women commandeered pots, mortars and pestles, and the palette-like slabs of smooth, dark stone on which one grinds snuff and medicine.

I wandered about from one to the other. I tried to put my whole attention on herbal recipes. It distressed me to watch Amara. One woman prepared an oleaginous mess that was to be smeared on Amara's abdomen; it would gradually soak in and strengthen her muscles. Another produced an oily application to grease and make easy the "path of the child." Most of them were preparing medicine for Amara to drink: some were to induce violent labor pains; others would give the mother strength for her ordeal. The shaky old crone was boiling three kinds of bark and lots of pepper into a thick reddish mess with a nauseating odor; this was the most important of their medicines, for it was associated with the only magic controlled by women and would assist Amara far more than these other, purely secular doses.

As they finished their medicines, each midwife poured her brew down Amara's throat. After about the fourth gourdful, Amara complained that she felt sick. Her protest produced only yet another draught which would, they assured her, settle her stomach. Whenever their unfortunate victim closed her lips and would not swallow, they began to shout. "Drink, my child. It is medicine. Drink." They gave her no peace until all the potions were finished.

Udama drew me from Amara's side. "It will take time for the medicine to walk through her body to the place it must do its work. Come, Redwoman." She drew me into Yabo's reception hut. The other midwives followed, leaving Amara under the care of her co-wife. Inside were Yabo, Amara's husband, her father Lam, all the men of the homestead, and Yabo's younger full brother Yilabo who had built a separate homestead years ago after a bitter quarrel with Yabo. They were in earnest consultation. It was time to visit a diviner. Lam and Amara's husband wished to set off at once. The others advised waiting until the midwives thought it necessary.

Soon there was a call from Amara's co-wife: "The medicine has begun its work." Again the midwives gathered around Amara, encouraging her, massaging, pouring still more messes down her throat, hopeful and confident. The hours passed. Amara, exhausted, could not respond to their shouts. She seemed to withdraw from her body, and her body from its task, until there was only an inert mass slipping from our hold.

Udama gravely walked to the reception hut. Standing erect outside, she called to Yabo, "The matter is too great for us. It has become your affair."

Lam and Amara's husband at once came out. Without a word, they reached for the spears they had leaned against the thatch of the reception hut. Without a word, they set off for the diviner.

Udama turned to me. Soberly she said, "Go eat your food, Redwoman. Then return. Nothing will happen while you are gone, for there is nothing we can do. There is magic in this, perhaps witchcraft. The world was so created that, as the field brings forth its fruit, so does a woman bear her children. Only evil willed by man can prevent it. Unless the elders seek out this evil and remove it, no medicine can help her."

I stood over Amara. She tried to smile at me. She was very ill. I was convinced these women could not help her. She would die. She was my friend, but my epitaph for her would be impersonal observations scribbled in my notebook, her memory preserved in an anthropologist's file: "Death (in childbirth) / Cause: witchcraft / Case of Amara." A lecture from the past reproached me. "The anthropologist cannot, like the chemist or biologist, arrange controlled experiments. Like the astronomer, he can only observe. But unlike the astronomer, his mere presence produces changes in the data he is trying to observe. He himself is a disturbing influence which he must endeavor to keep to the minimum. His claim to science must therefore rest on a meticulous accuracy of observation and on a cool, objective approach to his data."

A cool, objective approach to Amara's death?

One can, perhaps, be cool when dealing with questionnaires or when interviewing strangers. But what is one to do when one can collect one's data only by forming personal friendships? It is hard enough to think of a friend as a case history. Was I to stand aloof, observing the course of events? There could be no professional hesitation. I might otherwise never see the ceremonies connected with death in childbirth.

I marched over to Yabo. "Do you wish Amara to live?" Yabo grunted his willingness to hear me out.

"There are doctors who can save both her life and the life of her child. They have stronger medicines than yours to bring forth the child. If those fail, they know how to reach up into the womb. They even know how to cut open the living body, bring forth the child and then heal the mother. I will send a messenger on a bicycle to the hospital and another for a truck. I will pay carriers to carry Amara up to the road and on it, until the truck meets them. I will write a paper to the hospital, asking them to give her the best medicine and telling them that I will pay. I have always spoken truth to you, Yabo, and I speak truth now. Give my friend Amara to me, that she and her child may live."

Yabo spoke more kindly than I had ever heard him speak, but with unmovable determination. "You are Amara's friend and your heart wishes her well. I am grateful. I will even believe what you say of your doctors. But can your doctors remove the magic? Can your people deal with our witches? These things I can do, but they can not. Unless these things are done, my brother's child will die. Amara stays here."

I argued with him, passionately. The ceremonies could be performed for Amara, even in her absence, on a cloth she often wore. The magic would be less powerful, but surely it would suffice to ward off evil until her return, especially if she could have our medicine meanwhile. It would cost them nothing in effort or money.

Yabo grew no less firm, but far less patient. Nothing I could say moved him. I was only making a nuisance of myself. When I would not stop, Yabo simply ceased to listen and forced me to recognize his refusal by starting a loud conversation with his brother Yilabo.

Defeated, I sat on by Amara all that day, forced to watch her in pain and steadily growing weaker. I heard the diviner's report, saw the messengers dispatched to bring back experts in that magic which Yabo himself could not perform. I watched Yabo sacrifice chickens, make ritual motions and anoint Amara with sacrifical blood as he mumbled the magical invocations. Yabo, like Undu's father, was doing his best. But it could not help and they would not allow me to help. In silence and in bitterness, at nightfall, I left.

I returned the next day at sunrise. The midwives had not returned, but Yilabo's wives had come and all the women of Yabo's homestead sat in the reception hut, waiting. They sat around Amara, who lay there on a plank bed. She was alive, little more. Her co-wife supported her head in her lap. Their husband had gone to summon his age set to defend him if he were accused of killing his wife, and to support him when he accused others. For the diviner had discovered that four men had reason to bewitch Amara: her father Lam, her two uncles Yabo and Yilabo, and her husband. With this report before them, the elders must themselves identify the witch and settle the disputes and grudges which had driven the witch to this action.

During the early morning, the ritual specialists Yabo had summoned arrived, one after the other. Jovial, some of them, like hearty country doctors; they made their jokes and radiated confidence as they slit the throats of chickens and daubed mud, blood and feathers on the ritual symbols and on Amara's navel. Most of them were dignified old men, clad in ragged togas, who probed seriously and thoroughly into the findings of the diviner and muttered their incantations gravely. All of them, the ritual finished, prescribed the herbal remedies associated with the ceremonies they had performed and supervised the mixture.

Each time her co-wife raised Amara's head. Each time Yabo held the potion to her lips. Each time they called to Amara, as to someone far away, until she opened her eyes and weakly swallowed the medicine. Each time they had to call louder and longer to make her hear. And each of the elders, his task finished, took the spear he had leaned against the entrance and left the homestead. I marveled, for usually elders gather where there is serious illness and enjoy nothing more than magical consultations.

Yabo's eldest son entered the reception hut. "They refuse."

"They can't refuse!" Yilabo was a thin, excitable man, as highly strung as his brother Yabo, but without Yabo's stamina or intelligence.

"Oh, my father," Yabo's son began formally, to dissociate himself from any responsibility for the message he brought, "the elders all say you have refused their advice in the past. Therefore they will not come to advise and assist you now." He dodged out quickly, away from Yabo's condemnation of the elders as timid evil-wishing fools, weak-kneed followers of that smiling villain Kako. Yabo cursed his son as a bungling, easily intimidated idiot while Yilabo's high-pitched voice scolded Yabo for the contempt which had alienated the elders. The women stirred uneasily; who now would protect Amara from her closest relatives, from those who should protect her life but had the power to cause her death? They muttered secretly among themselves.

Yabo was the first to pull himself together. He rose, dominating the reception hut, his feet red with camwood in the sunlight that slanted through the door, his face and body gloomy in the dim light within. "There are four of us who might have willed this thing. When Amara's husband returns, we shall all be here. Then we ourselves shall discuss it. I, Yabo, forbid Amara's death. I am stronger than all of you, and I forbid it. The elders' refusal is therefore of no importance. Nevertheless," he added, "they shall repent their insult to me."

Perhaps none of us looked convinced. Yabo, a shrewd man though one not usually concerned with the comfort of his guests, sent his women off to prepare food. He ordered Lam to prepare some medicine which he Yabo had held in reserve. Then he engaged Yilabo in an enumeration of the magic they possessed, to see if any possibly helpful ceremony had been left unperformed.

Thus it was that when Amara's husband arrived with his age mates, they found a feast ready for them. They may have come to accuse. They found themselves eating greedily. While they gorged themselves on porridge dipped in a chicken and sesame sauce, Yabo skillfully told him of the iniquitous behavior of the elders who had refused to come, of his own unceasing surveillance and care, of the medicine Lam would soon have ready for his daughter, of the rite Yilabo would then perform. Amara, he said, was merely sleeping; let her gather strength; there was nothing to worry about.

When the women removed the empty pots and calabashes, Yabo divided some kola nuts and passed pipes among the young men. Replete, they sat back quite contentedly to see what would be done. Only Amara's husband was still tense and suspicious. Yabo radiated good will and confidence as he inspected Lam's medicine.

But Amara would not respond to her father's voice when he called her to wake and drink medicine. "She is not sleeping, yet my child does not hear." There was dread in his voice.

"Don't whisper then," Yabo snorted. He shoved Lam aside, shook Amara and slapped her face as he roared in her ear, "Amara, Amara, drink!" He roused her. As they lifted her head, Yabo held the calabash to her lips and spoke almost coaxingly as he poured the liquid into her mouth, little by little.

Yabo's senior wife stood over them, watching Amara narrowly. "She may still live," the old woman snapped, "if you men will only discuss matters now and quickly. If you delay, she will not have the strength to bear her child."

The confidence so carefully established by Yabo had already vanished.

"It is you"—Amara's husband pointed at Yabo in accusation—"it is you who are my wife's guardian. There is rancor in your heart because you covet more bridewealth than we agreed upon. The court would not take my wife from me; therefore in anger and jealousy you have bewitched her so that seeing her sick to death I would pay you more."

During his jumbled, vehement indictment his age mates cried out their backing: "Hear, hear." "That's right." "He is speaking truth." And when he finished, one of them jumped up to shout, "Leave our age mate's wife alone. We will not allow it."

Yabo admitted that he wanted more money, but he denied that he was bewitching Amara. "You," he accused her husband, "you are killing the child in her womb, for you wish to make her ill and thus make me drop my claim." His counteraccusation was brilliant. There was only one way for Amara's husband to clear himself of all suspicion: if he admitted that he owed yet more money for Amara's bridewealth, then he also proved that he had not yet purchased the power to bewitch the child she carried. Either way, Yabo won.

Accusation and counteraccusation. The men shouted, threatened, denied and attacked. Whenever they paused, the women urged, "Agree, agree that our daughter may live!" "Agree, that your wife and mine may live."

Amara might yet be saved, if only they would settle all the grudges between them, all their possible motives for bewitching her. Witchcraft comes from the heart, sometimes involuntarily; it can cease only when the witch's heart is freed of all hate and rancor. Has the witch a just motive? Remove it, quickly. A witch can, indeed, be forced to desist. The use of physical force is dangerous in these colo-

120

nial days. It took a man like Ihugh to threaten it and convince the witches that he would use it, irrespective of the consequences. No one here would dare. And only the elders, sitting together and with unanimous consent, can wield enough witchcraft to fight fire with fire successfully. But the elders had refused to come.

Only the women were wholly free from suspicion. They were singleminded in their determination that Amara must be saved. Even if the witch's cause were just, let him abandon it that Amara might live. But although any one of the suspects—father, husband, uncles—would gladly have sacrificed his interests for her life, each knew that sacrifice would be in vain, for each one of them knew he was innocent of wishing her death.

Yabo knew he was not killing Amara. Why, then, should he forgo his claim to more bridewealth for her? It might be a motive, but he knew he was not the guilty one. As long as he persisted, however, the others, who also knew themselves innocent, suspected him, indignantly denied his counteraccusations, and just as firmly refused to cede any ground.

The women pleaded, forcing the men to look at Amara's motionless figure. Time after time, looking at her, one of them would suddenly yield. Yabo lowered his first price. Amara's husband paid it then and there. Together they performed the brief ritual of reconciliation, drinking water and spraying it from their mouths. Lam admitted that he had grudged Yabo's taking his daughter as marriage ward at a time when he was wifeless and without means of getting another wife. Yabo ceded one of his marriage wards to Lam. Yabo admitted that he had resented Lam's behavior over Atakpa's elopement. Yilabo and Yabo again went into the old quarrel that had caused them to live apart. Again their anger flared. Again the women intervened. Again those who loved her looked at Amara. Again each sacrificed his own interests that she might live. And yet again they made some compromise and were ritually reconciled.

Still Amara was no better. "You are speaking with double tongues," the women accused. "There is something else. Settle it, and dispel your hate, or Amara will die."

They were at a standstill. There were no evident motives. If there actually were no other cause, then Amara was being killed to satisfy that dreadful lust which takes possession of some witches: the desire to kill and eat the victim's body.

The ability to bewitch is a dangerous one, but it is a common human faculty and, like any other weapon, it can be used for many purposes. A good man uses witchcraft only as a last resort, and then not to kill. But there are witches who enjoy being feared, who delight in killing, and who hunger for human flesh. Such men are feared and hated. They walk alone.

Everyone turned to stare at Yabo. Here was the man. It was written in their eyes.

Yabo saw it. He turned on his full brother Yilabo with quick reproach. "How can our niece recover when you delay the ceremony?"

We had all forgotten the ceremony, and, having forgotten, felt guilty, abashed and relieved all at once. While Yilabo got ready the herbs and magical apparatus, Yabo, with apparent irrelevance, began a rambling discussion of family history, recounting the wives and children, sisters and marriage wards of two generations past. Once again he had broken the mounting tension; thinking this the only purpose behind his leisurely discourse, I gave all my attention to Yilabo's ritual performance.

Yilabo, however, was listening to Yabo. Even while he made the magical gestures, he would interrupt with his own comments and opinions. By the time he had finished and was squeezing the juice of some plants into a calabash of water, he was arguing stubbornly with Yabo. "No, you are mistaken. She was not his ward, but his uncle's."

Amara's husband and his age mates were beginning to follow their comments with interest. Lam offered his version, but was promptly squelched by both brothers. "You, you are just a youngster."

"Perhaps," retorted Lam, "but Amara is my daughter."

Yilabo, always excitable, made angry, nervous gestures. The wet herbs were still in his hand; Amara and I were sprayed with bitter water. "Do you not see what Yabo is doing? He wishes you to believe what he says so you will not think he has any cause for envying me that wife I inherited from our father. He has always been jealous of me for that. That is why he is bewitching your daughter."

There was a rising mutter from the age set. "Yes, it is Amara's relatives who are bewitching her." "It is jealousy over women."

Amara's husband sprang to his feet. He pointed at Yabo and shouted, "I ask you, I demand of you, what bitterness is in your heart?"

Yabo waited for silence. Then he leaned back in his chair and asked aloud, "Why should I bewitch my own ward Amara out of hate for Yilabo? What is she to him? Nothing." He pointed his pipe stem at Yilabo. "It is you who are jealous of me because I am the eldest and had the largest part of the inheritance. It is you who are bewitching Amara."

Yilabo dropped the calabash. His body trembled and his face was drawn with rage. "It is you, you!" Again he accused Yabo. Again Yabo twisted every accusation to his own advantage.

It had to be one of those two. Amara's husband had cleared himself. Lam was too weak a character to be seriously suspected. Yabo or Yilabo, which? We were utterly absorbed in the duel between those two. Only Amara lay unconscious of the fight for her life.

Yabo kept a deadly composure; every word struck home. Yilabo lashed out wildly, without plan. He was no match for Yabo. Yabo did not stir from his chair. He was shouting, overriding Yilabo's defense, invulnerable to his attacks—yet his very superiority was a proof that he possessed the greater power of witchcraft.

Yilabo had been pushed past coherent argument. He screamed random accusations at Yabo, attributing every misfortune that had ever befallen him to Yabo's malice. Constantly he repeated, "It is you, you who are killing Amara. You! *You!*" Yilabo stood over Yabo, his whole being shaken by his desperate passion.

I too had begun to tremble. Here it was no comfort that witches were only people. Therein lay the tragedy. These men were torn with anguish, striving to save the life of one they loved. Amara could yet live, if they could only force a confession from the witch. Each knew himself innocent. Each therefore knew the other guilty. I knew them both innocent. I watched while each strove to break the other, to force his confession, to save Amara. I knew they could not. Their battle was the more terrible to me because it was in vain and fought against shadows.

They were frantic now; if the witch did not desist soon, now, it would be too late.

Again Yabo accused, with deadly effect. Ashen, trembling, Yilabo mouthed words we could not bear. We cried out. Yilabo's dagger flashed from its sheath as he sprang on his brother below him, defenseless in his chair.

Somehow Yilabo's wife had him by the wrist, Yabo slid away from danger. Yilabo's knees gave under him as he stared at the dagger. Slowly his hand opened. He watched it, as though it were not his hand, not his doing, not his wish. He looked on while his wife took the weapon from him.

"Your own brother." A chilly whisper. "Your own brother, who nursed you when you were a child. You would have killed your own brother."

There was no motion in the reception hut, no sound but Yilabo's harsh breathing. The moment of realization is infinite.

Amara's husband rose, slowly. Deliberately he loosened his toga from his shoulders. Deliberately he twisted the cloth and coiled it about his waist in sign of war, or mourning. We stared without comprehension. Then, suddenly afraid, we looked at Amara. The woman by her answered us, "She still lives."

"She will die," and her husband's voice spoke more of war than of mourning. "One of you two is killing her. Have we not witnessed that brother would kill brother? What evil, then, is beyond you? She is my wife. I do not consent. Confess! Or my age mates and I will force you both to the ordeal."

"So be it." Yilabo smiled. "My chicken will drink poison, but it will live to prove my innocence. Then if Yabo will not cease, you may beat him and rub pepper in his eyes."

"So be it." With a terrible glance at his brother, Yabo too assumed the dress of war and mourning.

But they were afraid. They wanted to delay, to get witnesses, elders. They stood in the yard arguing, refusing to start.

Amara's husband turned to his age mates in passionate appeal. "They are killing my wife! Make them go !" The young men closed on the two elders.

Yabo raised his spear. "You dare?" he roared. "You dare!"

I screamed as they rushed upon him, then sobbed as I saw the tumultous crowd jostle and drag the two old men out of the homestead and down the path toward the ordeal master.

My knees were shaking. I was afraid to go with them. I forced myself out on the path to follow them. Amara's husband was coming back. He saw me. "Let my age mates take care of it. You come back with me and keep watch by my wife. She will die. Help me guard her body. He will kill her. I cannot prevent it. But he will have killed her in vain. He shall not eat her body."

It was dark inside the reception hut, and very quiet. The women still kept watch over Amara. Her co-wife still sat with her.

The man stood looking down upon his dying wife. A man must never call his wife by her name. He may never touch her in public. This man knelt beside his wife. "Child of Lam."

She did not stir.

Tentatively, he laid his hand on her forehead. "Amara, Amara." Perhaps he thought she heard, for he added bravely, "Nothing at all will happen to you, Amara, my wife." He clasped her hand in his.

We sat on, waiting in silence for Amara to die.

Beliefs about witchcraft are widespread, although by no means universal. Even people who do not engage in witchcraft accusations do not completely lack the traits of greed, ambition, suspicion, ignorance, and jealousy which underly such actions. The McCarthy hearings of the 1950s and the subsequent activities of the House UnAmerican Committee have often been defined as the **functional equivalent** of witch hunting. It is a reasonable comparison. Sorcery, too, is easily regarded as a functional equivalent of witchcraft although there are some societies in which both witchcraft and sorcery exist.

Bohannan's account is an example of a painful type of personal conflict experienced by anthropolgists in the field. It is hardly possible to stand idly by and watch friends and acquaintances die for lack of the medical attention that might well save them. The story also illustrates, however, the extreme helplessness of the outsider in the face of a strongly held contrary system of belief. The conflict between traditional and Western medical systems is never more agonizingly apparent than when underlying interpersonal factors, such as conflicts between **kinsmen,** complicate what would otherwise be a straightforward and perhaps basically simple medical problem.

The tragedy of such a belief system is also made clear by Bohannan. Although each of the protagonists knows that he is innocent, the system, in which all believe unquestioningly, decrees that guilt must be assigned. Thus, as is so dramatically portrayed, the innocent suffer while those equally innocent, but presumed guilty, stand quarreling until it is too late. Such belief systems are not easily relinquished, since they are intimately linked to so many other aspects of culture.

An even more dramatic presentation of the meaning and consequences of witchcraft accusations can be found in Hilda Kuper's remarkable play **A Witch in My heart** (1970). The definitive anthropological studies of the subject are E. E. Evans-Pritchard's **Witchcraft, Oracles and Magic Among the Azande** (1958) and Clyde Kluckohn's **Navajo Witchcraft** (1944). For accounts of witchcraft in our own culture see George Lyman Kittredge's **Witchcraft in Old New England** (1929) and Marvin Harris's recent **Cows, Pigs, Wars and Witches** (1975).

More academic and detailed ethnographic materials on the Tiv can be found in Paul Bohannan's **Tiv Farm and Settlement** (1954) and **Judgment and Justice Among the Tiv** (1957). For a description of the Tiv political system see

Laura Bohannan, "The Political System of the Tiv" (1958). The classic account of a segmentary lineage system is **The Nuer,** by E. E. Evans-Pritchard (1940).

Ethnographic novels on Africa include Hilda Kuper's **Bite of Hunger** (1965), John Gay's **Red Dust in the Green Leaves** (1973), Harper Martin's **Nongalazi of the Bemba** (1965) and R. S. Rattray's, **The Leopard Priestess** (1935). For some short ethnographic sketches of the Didinga see **People of the Small Arrow,** by J. H. Driberg (1930).

There are far too many novels by Africans to mention here, but for a few of some ethnographic interest see **Things Fall Apart** (1959), **No Longer at Ease** (1961), and other novels by Chinua Achebe; Camara Laye's **The African Child** (1954); **Mission to Kala,** by Mongo Beti (1958); and **A Walk in the Night and Other Short Stories** by Alex LaGuma (1967).

Some ethnographic films on various African peoples include **Hadza, The Food Quest of a Hunting-Gathering Tribe of Tanzania** (1966), **A Day Among the Berbers** (1947), **Kabylia** (also on the Berbers, 1947), **Himba Wedding** (on a Bantu group), **Touareg** (a **nomadic** group of the Sahara, 1940), and **The Cows of Dolo Ken Paye: Resolving Conflict Among the Kpelle.**

10

The younger brother

ROBERT B. EKVALL*

Tibet is to most of us a mysterious and romantic place. It is perhaps even more so now, as it has been closed to the outside world since it was taken over by the Chinese in 1949. Robert Ekvall, a missionary-turned-anthropologist, is one of the few remaining American scholars to have spent much time there. Among his many writings on Tibet is his ethnographic novel, **Tents Against the Sky** (1954), from which this excerpt has been taken. The story has to do with a group of tent-dwelling nomadic **pastoralists** at the very beginning of the Chinese takeover. Dorje Rinchen, the youngest son of a wealthy and powerful family, has previously entered a lamasery and has taken the vows of monkhood. But, since the lamaseries, along with everything else, are threatened by the Chinese, and as Dorje Rinchen has fallen in love with Lhamo Mtso, a woman from a rival group, he renounces his vows and returns to live in his parents' camp, which is now controlled by his elder brother. His story gives a glimpse of yet another remarkable way of life. At the same time it illustrates some very fundamental and universal human motives and desires.

Tents Against the Sky is an excellent example of an ethnographic novel. Such writing poses many problems that are significantly more difficult than those faced by the ordinary anthropologist or by the ordinary writer. Most novels are both written and read by members of the same culture. Thus a great many assumptions about the cultural back-

* Reprinted with the permission of Farrar, Straus & Giroux, Inc. from *Tents Against the Sky* by Robert B. Ekvall, Copyright 1955.

ground are readily understood by all concerned. The ethnographic novelist cannot assume that his readers will be familiar with the culture he is writing about—but at the same
time he must avoid didacticism or his story will lag. He must
tell a good story, but educate at the same time. Ekvall suc-
ceeds at this better than most. As we follow the story of
Dorje Rinchen we learn much about Tibet.

The people of the Shami tribe had little fear that the Chinese troops,
even if they ever should get to Lhamo, would come on through the
mountains to the great plain. Even so, those in Jatsang's tent and the
other tribesmen waited for news as though their own fate were in that
uncertain balance. If the lamasery were destroyed it would be their
loss, for it belonged to them as it did to a dozen other tribes.

Ahway thought of the lamasery in only an incidental way. Most
of all she wondered what her younger son was doing.

Milk pail in her hand, she stood at the tent door staring across
the encampment towards a break in the ring of black tents, where the
Lhamo trail came in. Riders zigzagged purposefully through the dusk,
cutting across straying colts or heading back wandering cattle.

If, as it was rumoured, the monks were riding the trails armed like
laymen prepared to discard their vows, she wished Dorje Rinchen
were at home and riding from the encampment as a layman wearing
the dzakwa and carrying a rifle. For the sake of the lamasery, she had
given her son. Now it might be that he had broken his vows and for
the sake of the lamasery. As so often, she wished he could have stayed
at home, by this time bringing another daughter-in-law into the tent.
Such thoughts stirred in her mind as she mended the fire, gave instructions to Wochuck about a strayed calf, and then went back to the
lines where the milch cows waited. The darkness came quickly and in
that blackness the milking must be finished.

She was not alone at her task. Two servant-girls as well as Wochuck worked quickly along the tether-lines, milking, tethering cows
and calves, and stopping now and again to drive straying horses and
oxen to where the men were hobbling and tying them in separate
groups. The milking of even as many cows as belonged to the wealthy
family of Jatsang was finally finished and the workers began to gather
within the tent which, dark and monstrous against the sky, yet leaked
flashes of light along the smoke-vent in the roof and through the flapping curtain that served as door. As the light failed outside so it
seemed to grow in the tent. Ahway turned to fill the kettle on the edge
of the ashpit with milk tea and then set out bowl, butter-box, and
tsamba for her husband.

Dorje Rinchen's father had aged considerably since the time when he had taken the little boy monk to watch the sheep. While his bowl of tea was being prepared he reached for his prayer-wheel and started it spinning. His face—grave, handsome, lined with the marks of strife and of winter on the way—had a listening preoccupation with the burden of his petitions, as though he waited for an answer in the faint hum from the spinning cylinder.

"A good, big chanting service on the twenty-fifth of the next moon will be just right, just right," he said. The first whine of the prayer-wheel seemed to echo the last two words a third time, but Ahway had already linked them to something in her own thoughts.

"That being so, this time we might as well have Dorje Rinchen to do the chanting. That is, if he can leave the lamasery. Unless . . . unless the Chinese have come. Hell-bent Chinese—the wretched ones!"

Ahway was seeing Dorje Rinchen, red robes and all, sitting by the fire with the sacred volume in his lap, calling up blessing from the pages upon the tent and all its inmates. And it would be nice to have him home for a day or two, at least. If only the unpredictable Chinese would stay away.

Comfort dawned in the face of the old man when he thought of Dorje Rinchen: a good monk, so everyone said, and apt at praying. There would be more reassurance in the measured intonations of Dorje Rinchen's rich baritone, not yet too husky from long chanting sessions in the cold, than in the thin whine of the spinning prayer-wheel, But the old man spoke again, uneasily.

"He is too handsome to have about in a tent family for very long." The remark was not intended to reach the ears of the two servant-girls and his daughter-in-law, occupied with the churning and other tasks in the part of the tent on the other side of the fire from where the two sat.

"Yes," answered Ahway. "Too bad he should be the handsome one when he is only a monk. We have good sons: monk and layman. Duggur is a brave son among the best, a good trader who never loses. The women, too, like him well."

A giggle rose from the other side of the tent and Ahway smiled.

The flap of the tent was pushed back now and Duggur came in, followed by the manservant of the tent. All the chores were done. Later the two would find their sleeping places on the edge of the encampment and then the night's rest would be broken by intermittent watchfulness. In face and figure he was the son of his parents, but of a sterner pattern, and his ownership and control of the tent, and the members that made up the social unit it sheltered, was so complete that he could be casual and unassertive as he jested with the three younger women.

When the rhythm of Duggur's hurried eating slowed to the more leisurely tea-drinking, he set his stamp of approval on the plans his father and mother had made for Dorje Rinchen. He was quite willing that wealth should go to his younger brother. Indeed, he added suggestions of his own about new furs and a brocade jacket for the monk. When the real right of choice and decision was his, he had no objection to giving Dorje Rinchen the best of everything. A monk missed so much of life; his younger brother was to be pitied. For all his grim mouth and ready jesting, religion to him was yet a fearsome thing with threatening terrors. Though his thoughts softened as his eyes crossed the face of his wife and he thought of what Dorje Rinchen missed, there was no feeling of superiority in his attitude towards his younger brother. Dorje Rinchen was a monk and therefore set apart.

"Have him come soon," Duggur said. "We can well pay for many chanting services. The grace of the Perfections bless us! Someone told me today that the Chinese had turned back. I wondered whether that is really true. I hope so. Dorje Rinchen knows how to chant, but does he know about fighting? I wonder!" He laughed at the thought and stretched his powerful arms.

"Sleep," said Duggur stretching himself and speaking to his wife. "Come on, bring the zho so that we can drink and then make ready our sleeping places. I hope the curds are set thick and smooth tonight. If so . . ."

But everyone had stopped short to listen. Somewhere on the edge of the camp, dogs barked and rushed. A matchlock banged and the shouting rose; the peculiar wolf-howl cadence of the Tibetan yell rising high above the canine hysteria of forty mastiffs.

"Jatsang, Jatsang, someone coming—someone coming!"

Duggur shouted in reply, "This way; we're waiting."

A white horse broke into the long lane of light that poured through the dark from the open tent. Then Duggur was helping his younger brother from his horse and together they turned into the tent, where the women's voices gave a shrill, confused welcome. Even the stick handle of the old man's prayer-wheel poised motionless and the cylinder slowed to a squeaking stop.

Duggur took the short carbine from his brother's hands and waited while he took his sword from his girdle. Jatsang had risen to give him his old place of honour, but Dorje Rinchen appeared not to have seen him and took a place next to his brother in front of the fire.

"All is saved at Lhamo," he said. "The Chinese have turned back and all is safe."

The others scarcely heard what he said. The prayer-wheel stood like a startled question mark in the old man's hands. Ahways eyes widened under her startled brows and even Duggur's grim face went slack with surprise as he stared. Dorje Rinchen had slipped his shoulders out of the pulu cloak and they showed bare and oddly light in colour where the close-fitting monk's vest had kept them from exposure to wind and sun. Whatever the story behind this change, Dorje Rinchen was no longer the monk, but only the second son of the tent of Jatsang, sitting by his family's fire. "All is saved at Lhamo," he had said, but all was not saved.

Ahway, her voice thick with conflicting emotions, spoke first. "That pulu cloak alone is too thin for the cold of the great plain even in summer-time. We must find you a dzakwa." There were always compensations. The forbidden dream of years was changing to reality. She would now see Dorje Rinchen, handsome and desirable, in the dzakwa trimmed with leopard fur. "We'll get out those extra sheepskins tomorrow and start work."

Faint giggles of excitement came from where the three younger women drank their tea at the side of the fire reserved for the servants and womenfolk of the tent, but they faded when Duggur scowled.

"Until then, wear my new light summer one," he said to Dorje Rinchen. "It will fit you nicely. For sleeping and riding you will need one without delay. You come just when we badly need one more to help with the herds."

"Whose gun is that you are carrying?" It was the query of one layman to another, equals in a way they had not been since before that time when a small boy, clad in red robes, had sat somewhat apart from the others in the group around the fire.

The circle now moved to make room for Dorje Rinchen. As it shifted, so did his family's attitude towards him. He had become part of the gathering about the fire, but, though its light flickered from face to face, it was quenched, too, by shadows that leaped from the tent walls. The prayer-wheel remained silent in the slack fingers of the old man. The signs of strife and winter on the way deepened in his wistful face.

Dorje Rinchen had come out today as a shepherd, but he knew his companions still thought of him as a monk. In a single night one might cease being a monk, but only after many days did one achieve full status as a layman completely adept in all the skills of nomad life.

It was on this identical point that he had once tended a fire and watched the sheep with his father and, as on that day, the sheep were scattering like a dissolving white cloud on the green meadow below him.

His companions—shepherds all, for the sheep of the encampment were being pastured in one flock—had ridden off to do some preliminary scouting before settling down for the day. It was Dorje Rinchen's task to make the fire at the camp site and at least he had the tea boiling before they arrived, even if they did not think him capable enough to ride with them.

He had resolutely forsworn the ease and softness of a monk's position. He had put on the dzakwa with zest and wore a sword as inevitably as he put on his boots, yet always, in those concerns of daily living, his brother was one step ahead of him. It was not altogether a matter of untrained muscles, but rather that his instinctive reaction to the movement of a falling load, a plunging horse, a charging dog, or a runaway ox was always a split second behind the hair-trigger co-ordination of his brother's big body. The difference lessened day by day until is was scarcely perceptible to an onlooker, but Dorje Rinchen knew it still existed and so, too, did his big brother. But, if doing could bring it about, Dorje Rinchen was determined to do, and unconsciously began to ape his brother's ways of eating and drinking in serious haste and to emulate his sublime unconcern with the state of the weather and the place where he would sleep. As the days went by his brother had responded, bit by bit putting more and more of the responsibility for tent concerns and the care of livestock upon him.

Dorje Rinchen fingered the rifle beside him. The famous Bora was now his. For years his brother had carried another rifle and, when Dorje Rinchen returned, his father had suddenly decided to relinquish the Bora. It seemed to the old man that the count of the prayers his son would no longer say must be made good by prayer-wheel and beads. If so, he would shoot no more. He was past that time of life. Now he must think of the life hereafter and renounce the firing of a gun. Only Dorje Rinchen knew that, among his things brought from Aku Lobzong's cloister, there had come the gift of a hundred Bora cartridges as a present from the old monk to the one who had lived with him as an acolyte. Dorje Rinchen had secretly practised and found that he did very well indeed. He had the natural gifts: eyesight and co-ordination.

For Dorje Rinchen, riding with sword in belt and rifle across the saddle-bow was an adventure in which the layman was riding away from the monk. He had broken one vow; now there was a yearning to take his place among the others by bearing part in a killing. He found that he had not been brooding over his sins. Religion, for the time, was put aside by more active thoughts; nor did he feel guilty that he spent many hours of each day thinking of Llamo Mtso. He pictured her as part of a group of girls among the Samtsa and himself as with her. Yet he was aware, too, of the women in the tent, of their giggles and their open admiration.

Dorje Rinchen's companions arrived too late to see the guilty haste with which he put aside the gun and turned to the kettle. While they drank tea and ate with the calculated slowness men force upon themselves when time is empty, the scouts told of the large flock of gazelle they had sighted not far away. Two of the men, in their early twenties and eager to start out on the hunt, carried only matchlocks. The third, a neighbour of Jatsang and somewhat older than the others, had a rifle and an additional sense of caution.

"One of us should stay to watch the sheep," he said. "He need only signal if there is any danger and we can all get back. But the one who stays should have a rifle. I suppose that's you, Dorje Rinchen. Anyhow, you wouldn't want to have a part in the killing, would you?"

Dorje Rinchen still wasn't so sure about that, but he didn't want to be left by the fire a second time. "You have a rifle too," he countered. "Why don't you stay? I'll go and try a cartridge or two in mine. That is, unless you really want to fire your rifle," he added slyly.

One of the younger fellows chuckled, making no attempt to hide his amusement. "If the old man shot a single cartridge from his belt he would spend eight incarnations regretting it. Come along with us, Dorje Rinchen. You can be sure we'll teach you how to use up some cartridges. That is one thing we know how to do."

To the others it was merely an incidental bit of fun. Inclination whipped Dorje Rinchen on to the adventure, but though deep-rooted inhibitions still tugged intermittently at the reins he could not halt the ride. In the distance, white and yellow against the green grass, the gazelle dared him on. They were wary and experienced and they kept well away from any inequality of ground that would give cover to a hunter. After several unsuccessful attempts to stalk, the hunters decided to try a drive and, as Dorje Rinchen still insisted he wished to use up ammunition, he was placed at a likely point. Together the three rode to the chosen spot and Dorje Rinchen, keeping behind the other two, dropped from his horse into a tiny hollow behind the debris from a marmot hole, trying to make himself as inconspicuous as possible.

The sound of their hoofbeats became a muffled rhythm and then faded into the vague hum that filled his ears. Between the blades of grass he could see his companions as they moved casually across the plain. Heat waves began to rise and the drive took an odd unreality as riders and game swam in the waters of the phantom lake, or loomed in strange distortion on the unstable horizon. Training his rifle in the

133

direction from which he assumed the game would come, he dug the prongs of the forked rest firmly into the turf. The sun beat down and sweat dripped from his forehead into his eyes. Three feet above him the cool steppe breeze swept over pockets of heat like the one in which he lay. As he watched, the drive seemed without point and fruitless, his companions riding listlessly towards gazelle that refused to run in a straight line in any direction, but raced in a changing orbit round the riders, held to an arc by the power of curiosity, yet equally repelled by fear. His effort to watch through the grass and yet keep hidden caused cramps in his neck. Finally, he lay with his ear to the ground, content only to listen.

The turf under his ear was a sounding-board transmitting strange murmurs blended into a low-pitched hum, varied with the faint squeaks and underground rumblings of the marmots. A cautious look through the grass failed to give him even a momentary glimpse of the game. Again he put his ear to the ground while his thoughts reverted to his life as a monk. The cloisters and chanting-halls of Lhamo, the great central square itself—all came to mind, and he saw himself in scene after scene. Faintly the temple drums began to beat and to the sound the courtyard began to fill with dancers. He remembered Trinlan's dark face in the crowd and then his first sight of Trinlan's sister. It had all happened to the beating of the drums. Suddenly he realized that the ground under his ear pulsed with sharp staccato strokes that stopped at intervals for a moment or two, only to recommence with a mounting crescendo, rolling faster than the cadence of the wildest dance. Cautiously he turned his head so that he could see the sights of the rifle; his fingers moved to the trigger guard. The thudding ceased and he found the sights squarely in line with what appeared to be the leader of a flock of gazelle whose movement, on the circumference of an ever-shifting circle, had brought them within range.

All thoughts of the lamasery vanished. Dorje Rinchen was filled with hot eagerness. More intensely alive than he had been since the night he had spent with Lhamo Mtso, his whole body stiffened with the effort of holding his breath, and then his finger lightly tightened in the trigger.

The gazelle appeared to fall in two, one part remaining on the ground while the other plunged away. Far beyond, a puff of dust exploded. The faint screech of a ricocheting bullet mingled with the sudden tattoo beaten out by tiny hooves as the gazelle stretched themselves in a panicky burst of speed. Dorje Rinchen had come to his feet and started forward before he realized that what he had thought was one gazelle was really two; one now a motionless blur of

134

white and yellow, and one that rose and fell as it tried to run, but was dead by the time he reached it.

His companions suddenly appeared close at hand, but Dorje Rinchen did not wait for their help. He drew his knife nonchalantly. He set about dressing the carcasses. This was the first time he had killed, but not the first, by many times, that he had butchered. He was well on with the job when the others arrived. Little was said, although there was some satisfied chuckling and swearing as the two bucks were skinned and dressed.

Much had changed for Dorje Rinchen in the short time taken up by the hunt. He had deliberately broken the last link of the monkish vow. Although it had not been legally binding since he had left the lamasery, it had exercised its power and threatened its penalties. Now, with a new sense of freedom, he lifted his head arrogantly as he gave directions to his two companions. Their manner, too, had changed in a way that gratified him. Dorje Rinchen was convinced that his friends would never again send him alone to build the fire while they rode armed and ready. Even now they deferred to him, and one of them flatteringly asked for the empty cartridge. Dorje Rinchen offered it readily enough, but with a faint hint of patronage in his gesture.

According to Tibetan custom, the meat was divided into four equal parts, but the two skins went to Dorje Rinchen as the owner of the gun that made the kill. The boiled livers and hearts, relished slowly throughout the rest of the day, seemed hardly more savoury to Dorje Rinchen than his mother's pleasure when he unpacked his saddle-bags by the evening fire in the tent. Ahway exclaimed, "Ah—good meat. We are just out of every bit. It will do for stew tonight."

The old man cautioned her, "Be careful about the blood and hair. Don't drop them near the fire lest the serpent devils smell the odour of scorching life and come to curse us."

Duggur grinned appreciatively. "Two gazelle? How did they get them with matchlocks?" He stared as Dorje Rinchen drew out the two skins. That would mean only one thing. "Or did you lend your rifle?" he asked, still incredulous.

"Both in one shot. I used only one cartridge," said Dorje Rinchen. "It was somewhat far, but I was well placed and waiting while the others drove the flock in my direction."

"When you fell from the priesthood, you fell well! Not like some I know. By the sacred magic, what good shooting!"

The prayer-wheel in the hands of his father began a new protest as it spun to the ceaseless mutter of the old man's praying. Dorje Rinchen, second son in the house of Jatsang and recently turned wanlog, did not heed it. At last there were no traces of merriment in his brother's face. Then his sister-in-law spoke:

"Give me the empty shell. It will make a good needle-case. You will give it to me, won't you?"

Dorje Rinchen had no shell to give. His triumph was complete.

3

Autumn came and the frequent rainstorms changed to snow with a shift of the wind. On clear mornings the frost lay heavy on the grasses. Green marshland and the purple waves of grass bloom took on the shade seen through amber glasses. It was time to harvest the hay before the creeping russet reached the grass roots and all the rich flavour vanished.

The tents moved to sites only a short day's journey from the winter quarters so that the annual harvest of hay might be gathered in. Although grazing lands were held communally, each tent had its own ranges, and all arrangements connected with the haymaking were made within each family group. The cattle and horses must get along throughout the winter as best they could on the winter-killed standing hay of the plain and mountain slopes.

Dorje Rinchen lived with most of his family in a temporary encampment among the hay. The old man and two servants had stayed behind in the main camp to get along with the herds as best they might. Duggur patrolled the area with a rifle across his saddle, on the alert against enemies or thieves. At this time of the year the poorer folk from the farmer tribes in the valleys as far away as six or seven days' journey came to the land of the tents to earn high wages and enjoy the more varied fare of the nomads.

Dorje Rinchen spent the first two days of the haying season riding to find workers. Most of these were women who bargained shrewdly for wages of butter, sheep, and wool. The family had old friends who came year after year, but more labourers were always needed.

Because the family of Jatsang was wealthy—Ahway was known as a good provider who killed many sheep and provided generous portions of fresh butter with the tea—Dorje Rinchen had no trouble in persuading workers to follow him back to camp. His rare but compelling smile had its own part in winning workers for the Jatsang haying. Girls from the land of the farms were quite frankly aware of the opportunities the occasion offered: one might become the mistress in a black tent. Such possibilities, when enhanced by the sight of Dorje

136

Rinchen sitting his horse with grace, his shoulders bare and brown in the sunshine, made decision all the easier.

"We have more workers than we've ever had before," Duggur commented as he drank tea and told the news of the home camp. "Dorje must have promised all the girls something special to get so many. We'll have more hay than ever before. But we need it: we have more horses."

"If only the skies stay clear and we have no snow," Ahway said as she finished the count of the hay on her rosary and found it more than it ever had been. Dorje Rinchen nodded, though his eyes were glazed with sleep. All four were groggy with weariness.

"If only it doesn't snow and we have to waste too many days," repeated Ahway so decisively that Wochuck, whose head had been drooping dangerously near the fire sat up with a jerk, muttering sleepily, "One day wouldn't be bad: just one day to rest a little."

"Just one day is all right," Duggur said. "It is when it rains and snows for days that the haying is ruined. Ah yes, one day would give Dorje a chance to get to know the girls he persuaded to work for us. If it snows I'm going to spend the day in camp, too. Who are they, Dorje?" Duggur wiped his huge face and grinned, relishing his younger brother's confusion.

"Doka doesn't know girls are about. You shouldn't bother him about them. He is still a monk," said Wochuck. She was fighting sleep as she spoke, but her slightly pop-eyed stare probed suddenly and insistently at Dorje Rinchen's reserve. "He watches well at night. So far we have lost no cattle as we did last year. A good thing it is for the tent of Jatsang."

Duggur's keen glance encompassed his wife and Dorje Rinchen with a certain knowingness. "Ah, then I can sleep well at night," he said. "If I only can keep warm, all alone as I am." Wochuck's habitually stolid expression changed. She swore cheerfully in response as she got up to get Duggur's horse. He was already licking his bowl clean before putting it inside the folds of his cloak. After he had mounted and ridden off, Wochuck stood watching until she saw him pull his horse to a stop among the haymakers, but she looked even more intently at Dorje Rinchen as she turned back to the fire.

That night the moon had a strange halo. Dawn beat its tardy way through a thickly falling curtain of snow. They were all at breakfast when Duggur, bigger than ever in a snow-draped raincoat that covered himself, his rifle, and most of his horse, rode almost into the tent before dismounting to join them. With his coming the meal took on an added degree of festivity. For all the wet snow in the air, underfoot, and eventually in everything, the day was a lark for the hired hands. They had food, the rudiments of shelter, and leisure for whatever might come. They could patch their clothes and boots, or sleep as much as they wished. The four members of the family of Jatsang accepted the snow as all such inevitable misfortunes must be accepted; in a determination to make the best of it. They could distribute fireside and food tasks among the others and relax into pleasantly personal existence.

Duggur, however, suggested more than mere passive comfort as he mixed humour and the giving of orders with his hurried eating. He intended to spend the day in camp. His servant was dispatched, armed with rifle and raincoat, to ride guard over the herds. It was to be a day of feasting, for Duggur had brought flour and rice from the home camp. Under his expert direction, a sheep was killed and made into coils of sausage seasoned with garlic. Generous quantities of fresh mutton-fat sauce laced with red pepper were put on the coals to simmer. One day was one day. They might as well have a good time.

The tent filled with smoke, the odour of cooking food, the smell of wet, drying leather. Duggur openly focused his attentions on one of the girls from the farm country. The pert haymaker had no scruples. Quite evidently opportunity had come her way. Her demureness became provocative. The prospect of life in a black tent was becoming a possibility and her eyes were bright. The others, occupied with their own private concerns, paid little attention to what was going on. Even Wochuck's sultry good humor remained unshaken.

Dorje Rinchen, deep in the thoughts that came with leisure, paid little attention until he began to realize that Duggur was not content to leave him alone, but was manoeuvring him into a kind of participation. Dorje Rinchen also became increasingly aware of Wochuck and her steady gaze that found him wherever he was. In the somewhat heady atmosphere of the tent, Dorje Rinchen found his pulse pounding with desire. The clearing afternoon sky and a rising wind definitely limited the vacation to a single day. Duggur shivered. "It will be cold tonight, Doka. Much too cold for comfort when one sleeps on the edge of the hay. Only one thing will keep you warm—just one thing." With a quick, unexpected lunge, his big hand deftly lifted the thong of beads and bits of lapis lazuli from the neck of the little haymaker. She squealed and made a half-hearted attempt to recover her property, but Duggur pushed her away and laughed.

"There's just one thing to keep you warm." He held the necklace high. "A string of beads like this has a certain magic. You don't think so, Doka? You don't know. No; you don't know!"

Again Duggur's big hand moved swiftly towards Wochuck. She let fly a stream of curses, but made no attempt to regain her prized string of coral and turquoises. Duggur pressed the bauble into Dorje Richen's hand. "Here! Take this with you tonight and see if the magic won't work for you too?" His laughter filled the tent and his audience shouted. Even Dorje Rinchen knew the significance of the play; knew that the accepted way for a girl to regain her property was to go and reclaim it when nightfall had come and sleeping-places were being made up. Though he had not personally snatched Wochuck's necklace he felt sure she would expect to claim her property in the time-honoured way. The string of beads in his hand gave fresh significance to Wochuck's stare from across the fire. His pulses hammered.

It was near sunset when the two brothers finally walked to the edge of the camp to plan for the morrow's hay-cutting, and only then did Duggur amplify his action with words.

"There is no need for the tent of Jatsang to have more than one wife," he said. "We can well share alike. Having only one wife will ensure the interests of the tent when the mother gets too old. Wochuck likes you. As for Yogmo, the little baggage from the valley," a note of amusement thickened with emotion rose in his voice, "maybe she'll make a good servant for a while if we need one more. But she needn't think of having a tent of her own and so split Jatsang into two tents. Don't forget the magic of the beads, Doka, you wanlog!" Laughing, he rode off to look after the cattle.

Out on the cold plain Dorje Rinchen could think more clearly than in the charged atmosphere around the camp-fire. Very clearly he realized that something more than a casual affair was implicit in his decision. If Wochuck claimed her beads in the traditional manner, he would have tacitly placed his approval on his brother's plans. All day he had been thinking of Lhamo Mtso as part of the group in the haying camp. He pictured himself travelling the expanse of plain and mountain barrier to find her among the Samtsa hay-makers. He knew Lhamo Mtso's place would not be easy as the wife of the younger son of Jatsang, but obviously it would be much harder if Wochuck came to him that night. His thoughts raced ahead to the coming days and months; fastening on the idea of a tent—the "tent of Dorje Rinchen," not the "tent of Jatsang." Against the afterglow, the sod walls of the winter encampment and the haystacks lay dark in shadow. Somewhere among those shadows he could stake a claim: perhaps even a share of hay, a part of the wealth of his father's tent, his mother's affection, and his brother's goodwill. It was his old intentness and exactly at this point the seeds of worldly ambition were sown along with his loyalty to love. No. In time a black tent would be his; his and Lhamo Mtso's. Tonight he must meet Wochuck with his decision.

As he made his way towards the camp, the rustle of dried-out grass and the squeak of snow under his heels reminded Dorje Rinchen that the boots he wore had been resoled by Wochuck. She had laughed oddly when she gave them to him. "Some day you will do something for me, no?" she had said. He found Wochuck at the edge of the encampment. Dorje Rinchen did not look forward to the burst of profanity he expected would explode when she heard his explanation. Instead, he had the greatest surprise in a day of enlightenment. Wochuck was silent for some time. Then she questioned him in half-amused sympathy. "Your flesh longs for her, doesn't it? Well, keep her warm in your heart. I wonder you have stayed away from her so long."

"I wonder that I have," thought Dorje Rinchen as he made up his bed on the edge of the hayfield. When the haying was done he would ride to Samtsa.

Disagreements between brothers are common, of course; but in cultures that recognize **primogeniture** such disagreements, when they become serious, can lead to the formation of new groups. In segmentary lineage systems, for example, new lineage groups are most often created when one of a pair or of a number of brothers departs to establish his own household. The moment for this decision has arrived for Dorje Rinchen. His choice—to "ride to Samtsa"— hints at the outcome of his part of the story. A less ambitious, less talented, and less determined younger brother might well have been content to share his elder brother's tent and the proposed polyandrous marriage. Among other things, this story illustrates the relationship of personality to the operation of social and cultural systems, and it suggests a constant interplay between them. No people are merely "slaves of custom" as was often thought in the past, nor are smaller scale or nonliterate societies as homogeneous as was once believed. The problem for the anthropologist as well as for the writer of fiction is to somehow infer from the acts of individuals the regularities and universals of social and cultural life.

New lineages do not become totally independent and autonomous. They continue to recognize a common ancestor, and the grazing lands, farm lands, or whatever else they possess as a **corporate group** has usually been ceded to them by the original lineage or clan. Thus they have much in common, and when threatened by some outside interest or force they join in mutual defense of their territories and possessions. Even when there is serious friction between groups (in Dorje Rinchen and his brother's case there is not), the rival parties very often must join forces or perish. Individual animosities and internal bickering must be suppressed, at least temporarily, in the interest of the group. It is in these cases that councils of elders, or some other recognized adjudicating authority, become crucial and that **jural equality** must give way to moral and legal considerations.

Robert B. Ekvall's other writings on Tibet include many scientific articles, a series of sketches and reminiscences entitled **Tibetan Sky Lines** (1952), and a more scholarly book, **Fields on the Hoof** (1968). For another informative book on Tibet see **Tibet,** by Thubten Figme Norbu and Colin M. Turnbull (1968).

For information on nearby Nepal see **The Himalayan Woman: A Study of Limbu Women in Marriage and Divorce,** by Rex and Shirley Jones (1976). **The Sherpas of Nepal** (1964) and **Himalayan Traders** (1975), by Christoph von Fürer-Haimendorf.

Films of interest for the general area include **Tibetan Traders, Himalayan Farmer** (1967), and **Gurka Country** (1967), which deals directly with aspects of fieldwork.

11

Tan A-hong

MARGERY WOLF[*]

Among those who find themselves living in unusual places for relatively long periods of time are the spouses of anthropologists. Although not many of these marriage partners are, strictly speaking, anthropologists, some of them have given us remarkably fine and ethnographically sound accounts. Perhaps one of the finest ethnographic books written in recent years is **The House of Lim** (1968), the story of a Taiwanese farm family. The author, Margery Wolf, is the wife of Arthur Wolf, an anthropologist specializing in Chinese culture. It is interesting to note that the goals she set herself were "to present a case study for the social scientist interested in the strains inherent to the form of the family considered ideal in China, to provide another account of village life for those with a more general interest in China, and to tell a good story" (1968:ix). Anthropologists, of course, ordinarily make no attempt whatsoever to tell a story—despite the fact that life itself has a plot. At least one anthropologist has pointed this out although, it appears, to little avail:

> **Jungle People** has a plot because the life of the Kaingang has one. Yet, since behavioral science views life as plotless, **Jungle People** violates an underlying premise. Moreover, in the behavioral sciences, to state that life not only has a plot but

* Margery Wolf, *The House of Lim*, © 1968, pp. 99–114. Reprinted by permission of Prentice-Hall, Inc., Englewood Cliffs, New Jersey.

must be described as if it did is like spitting in church. [Henry, 1964:xvii]

The story that Wolf tells, then, is not fiction, but rather the chronicle of events, good and bad, exciting and mundane, that occur in one large **extended family** group. It demonstrates, perhaps better than any other recent book, that it is possible to write ethnographic accounts that are at once important, readable, interesting, and free of anthropological jargon.

Except on the coldest days and for a few hours each night, the doors of the houses in Peihotien are never closed. A closed door in the daytime would arouse concern or suspicion and would surely bring a group of neighbors to inquire as to what the trouble might be. Few strangers come to Peihotien and when they do, they nearly always send one of the swarming children to run ahead and announce to Mr. Lim or Mr. Ong that he has a visitor. A neighbor looking for Mr. Lim or Mr. Ong simply walks into the house calling his name, and if Mr. Lim or Mr. Ong does not answer, he walks on out again. An intimate friend or relative walks into the house even more casually, wandering through the passageways until he finds someone, courteously coughing before pushing aside the curtains of a bedroom door in his search. Until I became familiar with the faces of the intimates of the Lim family and with the villagers who dropped in there frequently, I had the uncomfortable sensation that the narrow passageways of our house were thoroughfares at least as public as the lanes outside. The situation was even more confusing to me as a newcomer because the number of people actually living in the house varied from week to week. During the harvest season, gangs of workmen came up from the south to cut the rice and stayed in the house for the three or four days it took to harvest the Lim fields. When Lim A-bok strained his back, a young relative lived in the house and helped with the field work. At least twice an old woman distantly related through Lim Han-ci's wife stayed in the house for several weeks while the Lims tried to patch up her quarrel with her daughter. Other relatives came to stay for a few nights or a few months.

When Tan A-hong appeared with her five-year-old daughter, I had become so used to the stream of visitors that I didn't even bother to ask who she was for a week or so. I knew, of course, her surname, but when I casually asked A-bok's giddy wife if she was a relative; I dismissed the confused yes-and-no of her answer as just one more sample of A-ki's disorderly thoughts. However, as Tan A-hong's visit lengthened, we noticed that she consistently used kinship terms when addressing the Lims. She was visited frequently by an unusually attractive young woman who was introduced as her daughter and who was treated by the Lims as a much beloved family member. It did not take many questions to discover that Tan A-hong was the adopted daughter Lim Han-ci had given to another family when his own daughter was returned by her foster family. Tan A-hong remained in our house for several months and when one of the small village houses owned by the Lims became vacant, she moved into it, becoming a resident of Peihotien.

By Taiwanese standards, Lim Han-ci had been generous in his treatment of Tan A-hong. Since she was "only an adopted daughter," he would have been justified in selling her to the highest bidder when he found he no longer had reason to keep her and could no longer afford to keep her. The highest bidders in those days were dealers who bought attractive female children to raise as prostitutes, wealthy families who wanted slaves, or prostitutes who adopted daughters to raise in their profession as support for their own old age. Instead of this, Lim Han-ci arranged for A-hong's future in the way he would have arranged the future of a daughter born to him: he found a family who wished to adopt a girl as their son's future wife. A-hong was not sweet-tempered, even as a girl. The family who adopted her evidently had second thoughts about marrying her to their son. She was married out of the family. At least A-hong claims that her exit from the Tan family was by way of a respectable marriage, but the facts of her subsequent career and her retention of the Tan surname cast some doubt on this. The marriage, if it existed, was brief, for Tan A-hong soon moved to southern Taiwan where she earned her living as a prostitute. It was at this time that she further altered her name to include the character for phoenix (hong) which is often found in the professional names of women who follow her calling.

Legally and socially, the obligations of the Lims toward A-hong ceased when she entered the family of Tan. Even though she had been an adopted daughter in the Lim house for ten years, she had been sent with all propriety to the home of her future husband. If she left that family as a respectable bride, she should have brought her troubles back to them, or even to her natal family if she knew their whereabouts. Instead, A-hong always brought her problems home to the Lims. A quarrel with the man who was currently supporting her was grounds for a week's vacation at the Lim's. If she had trouble finding a new "friend," she stayed for awhile with the Lims. Her eldest daughter, Chun-ieng, spent as much of her childhood under the care of Lim Han-ci's wife and Lim A-pou as she did with her mother.

Why Tan A-hong felt she could make such demands on the family, and why they allowed it, is a puzzle, but she continues to do so to this day.

Chun-ieng was born during the war. Many children were sent into the country during those years to protect them from the American bombings and so Chun-ieng, of course, was sent to the Lims. A-hong's second child was a son. When he was five or six, A-hong was living with a man, apparently not his father, in Tainan. They quarreled one evening and in a fit of temper she ran out, leaving him with the boy. She stayed away for nearly two weeks, during which time the boy contracted measles. A-hong's gentleman friend did his best at an unfamiliar job, but when A-hong recovered her good humor and returned, her son was dead. Sometime later she adopted a daughter who succumbed to a similar disease before she was old enough to walk. Finally, in A-hong's fortieth year, when her fading looks had forced her to work in the least desirable brothels of Tainan, she gave birth to her daughter, Chai-ngo.

When I met Tan A-hong, it was as hard to believe that she was only forty-five as it was to believe that she had once been a very pretty woman. She is quite short, fine boned, with delicate wrists and ankles, but now her back is stooped and her shoulders hunched, perhaps, as many people suggest, from the long hours she spends at the gambling tables. Her face is beautifully proportioned with a small, thin nose, high cheek bones, fairly large eyes and a fine wide brow. But now, her cheeks are sunken and lined, and her high cheek bones suggest too strongly the skeleton that lies beneath the sallow, muddy skin. Her hair is no longer thick, but it is still unusually fine in texture. She combs it so rarely that its quality goes unnoticed. She dresses in the fashion of the poorest village wife, sloppily and with not a few greasy spots on her skirt—but the sweater she throws over her shoulders is often imported. Her voice is shrill or gives that impression because she is nearly always scolding or complaining about something, but one can imagine that it was once a light feminine soprano.

Tan A-hong had not had any permanent "friends" for some time before Chai-ngo was born, and after her birth she found it more and more difficult to make a living. Chun-ieng was sent out to work. She was nineteen when I first met her and had been working as a prostitute for four years. To me she seemed more like a sophisticated American teenager than the timid giggling village girls her age. She was considerably less curious about us than were her contemporaries in the village, but far less hesitant about satisfying her curiosity. The village girls went into paroxysms of shyness if I asked them a question, but Chun-ieng howled at my accent and then good-humoredly tried to answer my questions. I rarely saw her interacting with anyone her own age in the village, but she joins the games of small children with an abandon and glee that would bring blushes of shame to the cheeks of her stodgy peers. The childish pleasure she finds in cooking, in feeding the family's dog, or in watching a newly hatched flock of ducks is both unaffected and pathetic. When she is in the village, Chun-ieng dresses soberly and wears little or no make-up, but she is undeniably different from the other girls her age. Her upright bearing, her poise in conversation, and even her smooth, pale skin are out of place in the muddy lanes and the coarse brick farmhouses. She is tall, unlike her mother, but her bones have the same delicacy. Her face is long and thin, giving her high cheekbones the drama that her mother's lack. Her eyes are a bit too small, but she shapes her eyebrows carefully to minimize the defect. She doesn't cut her fine black hair, nor allow it to be frizzed by cheap permanents. Often in the village she pulls it back into a pony tail, giving her an innocent Alice-in-Wonderland look. She loves to gossip and has great skill in spinning a simple anecdote into an intriguing story. Without slipping into vulgarity, she can entertain the rather staid women of the Lim household with endless stories about her work—she can even keep Lim A-pou sitting for awhile. There is always more laughter in the house when Chun-ieng is home.

Prostitutes in Peihotien occupy a rather ambiguous position, resembling in no way the status forced on a prostitute, retired or active, in an American small town. They are considered "more interesting" than other women of their age and income, but judgments about their morality or respectability are not based on their profession. Too many village girls have had to "go out to work" to support aging parents or young siblings. In recent years, there has only been one girl in the area who entered a brothel by choice, lured by the fine clothes and exciting life. More commonly, women become prostitutes because they were raised for that purpose, or because their family is desperately in need of the income. The villagers are not inclined to think of these girls as martyrs since Chinese children are expected to make great sacrifices for their parents, but they are not likely to criticize them either. On the contrary, most villagers assume a girl has amply repaid the debt she owes her parents for raising her when she obeys their command to become a prostitute—repaid it more fully than the daughter who remains at home can ever hope to. Parents can nearly always count on the support of village opinion in deciding the future of their daughter unless that daughter has supported the family for several years by prostitution. By giving up her youth, the young prostitute has gained a certain amount of control over her future. In the village her respectability depends upon how careful she is to walk within the paths of traditional morality when she is home for a few days each month, how compliant she is in turning over the majority of her earnings to her parents, and how cautious she is with village males. A prostitute who carries on professional activities within the village is in deep trouble. If her relatives are not aware of her indiscretion, they will be told, and that is usually enough. It is a small community.

No one in the Lim family tried to conceal from us Tan A-hong's former occupation or the source of Chun-ieng's present earnings. They are not callous about Chun-ieng's fate, but they also see her soft fingers resting next to their scarred, calloused hands, her delicate silk dresses hanging beside their coarse, shapeless working clothes, her closed bedroom door when they come in after three hours of early morning weeding in the fields. About her future they feel pity, but the life of a woman in a farm family is not easy either. In Chun-ieng's difficulties with her mother, however, she has the family's complete sympathy. They may chide her occasionally, or remind her of her mother's seniority, but their words lack conviction. Tan A-hong's outrageous behavior toward her daughter would challenge the beliefs of the most adamant proponent of filial piety. In all fairness, I must admit at this point to a strong prejudice against Tan A-hong. I could find in her no redeeming qualities. Her life has been hard and full of frustrations, but it was a way of life she chose in preference to that of marriage. She did not allow her daughter that choice.

Tan A-hong's latest return to Peihotien was primarily at her daughter's urging. To bring her mother north, Chun-ieng gave up a good, secure income in one of the best houses in Tainan and complicated a personal love affair that mattered a great deal to her. Her motives need little explanation: A-hong, as with many women her age and, in particular, women who have been prostitutes, is a habitual gambler. She gambles as long as she can find money and players. When she runs out of money, she sells anything at hand, borrows from anyone foolish enough to loan, and begs from those who refuse loans. Chun-ieng's beauty and vivacious personality provided her with a very good income, but her mother was spending the majority of it in the expensive twenty-four-hour gambling houses of Tainan. Chun-ieng had trouble meeting ordinary living expenses. So, she persuaded her mother to sell her small house, invested as much of the money as she could get away from her into gold (the landless person's only insurance against inflation), and moved her to Peihotien. While Chun-ieng went on to Taipei to find work, her mother searched out the small gambling dens of Hotien.

Their status as guests in the Lim house had no effect on the quarrels between A-hong and Chun-ieng. They were loud and bitter. One night when Chun-ieng returned from Taipei after an absence of a week, she was greeted with the news that her mother had lost over NT$700 in two nights of gambling—nearly a week's income for Chun-ieng and almost a month's income for the average family. Chun-ieng tactlessly demanded that her mother turn over the remainder of the money she had received from the sale of the house. A-hong, of course, refused. "This is my money. Why should I give it to you? Sure, I gamble, but what about you? Don't you ever gamble? You say you want to buy gold with it! Huh! You just want to spend it. You have your own money if you want to buy gold, and you already have plenty of gold hidden away, too. I want to keep my money. Maybe I'll buy some gold, too."

Chun-ieng answered her wearily, "All right, I'm not going to argue with you. I'm too tired. I just wanted to say something about it so that people would know I tried and would not blame me."

Although A-hong expects her daughter to provide for her as for a child, she resents being treated as a child. Chun-ieng's words angered her. "How can you be so shameless. I know what you are telling people—you are telling them I lost lots of money in Tainan and then sold your clothes and your gold to get more. You are shameless. You know how little money you gave me. You didn't give me all the money you earned so I had to take it. Aren't you ashamed to tell all those lies?"

This touched a sore spot in Chun-ieng. She wants very much to be considered a proper filial daughter and her mother accused her of withholding her earnings, a most unfilial act. Chun-ieng answered defensively, "There was nothing I could do. You are too fond of gambling. I can't turn all of the money over to you."

A-hong knows her adversary well. She decided to take advantage of the wound she had inflicted by putting a few more things before the public. (Most quarrels in China take place by preference before an audience and the attention of the combatants is directed as much to the effect of their words on the observers as upon each other.) With lip-curling malice, A-hong continued, "Ah, you are right. I like to gamble. And what is my dutiful daughter going to do about it? You, of course, never gamble, do you? You don't remember the time in Tainan when you lost all of the money you had earned for two days, and I had to come and tell you not to gamble any more? Do you remember what you said to your mother that day? You said you didn't care. You told me you could just go with any of the guests when you had no more money. You told your mother that you had no reason to save money and that there were women as old as me working there."

Chun-ieng looked tired and depressed. When she didn't answer, her mother tried to goad her into a response. "Well, I'm old now. I don't care if people laugh at me, but if you keep saying all those things, you know who people will be laughing at. At a shameless daughter!"

Chun-ieng got up to leave the room, but at the door she paused long enough to say, "You speak as though I enjoyed working in that place. Is that why you wouldn't let me come home, even when I begged?"

A few days later another argument on the same subject ended with A-hong threatening her daughter with a cleaver. Chun-ieng with a sincerity that frightened all of us, stood her ground and encouraged her mother. "Kill me. I truly don't care. Just kill me and be done with it." Lim A-pou pushed the girl out of the room.

Tan A-hong often accuses the Lims of conspiring with and pampering her daughter. Her accusations are not unjustified. The Lims keep Chun-ieng's secrets, hide her money, and even find time in their busy schedule to do her laundry when she is in the village. One day when the women were washing clothes at the river, I overheard the following exchange between A-bok's wife, A-ki, Iu Mui-mue (another adopted daughter of the Lim family), and a neighbor.

The neighbor asked, "Isn't that Chun-ieng's blouse?" A-ki nodded. The next question was inevitable. "Does she pay you for that?"

A-ki answered diffidently, "No, I only wash a few things for her when she is here."

Iu Mui-mue laughed and said, jealously, "She doesn't pay you, but she bought your baby an outfit that cost over a hundred dollars."

A-ki giggled and said, "That is why we say we are going to give her my daughter to be her adopted daughter."

Mui-mue responded, scornfully amused, "Adopted daughter! Yes, you'll give her to Chun-ieng now, but when she gets older, you'll want her back."

A-ki, still giggling, said, "That's just what Chun-ieng said the other day. She said, 'Oh, I'll adopt you now, little girl, and feed you, and when you get old enough to earn some money, you will give it all to your mother and not to me. No sense feeding you!' I told her she was the same way. Mother [A-pou] fed her when she was little, but now when she makes money, she gives it all to her own mother."

Mui-mue retorted, "She gives money to Lim A-pou, too."

A-ki was quite indignant. "She only gives her a few dollars now and then—nothing like she gives her mother."

Mui-mue countered that easily. "Well, A-hong has nobody to eat with [no family], so of course she has to give her more money."

A-ki began to worry that she had said too much. "Chun-ieng treats her mother very well. She buys her the best food and lots of nice clothes and gives her money to gamble with. She treats her very well."

The neighbor, one of A-hong's gambling companions, disagreed. "Hah! How good is that. I always hear her scolding her mother. She tries to restrain her at every turn."

A-ki bristled in defense of her friend. "That is because the mother doesn't have any sense. If her mother took care of the home and didn't gamble all the time, I'm sure Chun-ieng would give her all of the money to take care of."

The continuous quarrel between A-hong and her daughter over money reached a climax several months later. It was only then I learned of the future Chun-ieng longed for and of the secret she and the Lim family had kept from her mother. While working in Tainan, Chun-ieng met the second son of a wealthy industrialist. Their mutual attraction deepened into a more serious interest, and the young man wanted to marry her. Many young prostitutes who have not yet compromised their future by a series of abortions, illegitimate children, or the adoption of young girls as support for their old age, marry into quite respectable families. There seems to be some notion among peasant families that a young woman who has had this kind of experience is less likely to succumb to temptation after marriage. Chun-ieng's young man, however, came from the upper classes and her welcome into his family might not be as warm. Moreover, they also had to wait until his older brother, then serving his term in the army, was married, it being bad form for a younger brother to marry before an elder. When Chun-ieng's lover was sent by his father to supervise a logging operation in central Taiwan, they decided upon a compromise. Chun-ieng would come and live with him there until such time as they could be married properly. Tan A-hong knew nothing of these plans, although she knew her daughter was fond of the young man. She herself was attracted by his reputed wealth, but the possibility of her daughter marrying anyone was something she refused to think about. Chun-ieng married would not only make a considerable dent in A-hong's income, but would also deprive her of her authority over the girl. No matter what agreements are reached at the time of marriage, a young women's loyalty necessarily shifts to her husband. Besides, Chun-ieng was still approaching the peak of her earning power as a prostitute. Her youth and high spirits had brought her a good income until now, and A-hong's practiced eyes recognized that her daughter's appeal was based on a handsomeness that would not fade as had her own but might with training turn Chun-ieng into the cool, sophisticated companion of the very wealthy. Whether or not Chun-ieng's talents are up to her mother's ambitions is hard to say, but with this possibility in mind, A-hong was not likely to smile upon a promise of marriage, even from the son of a wealthy industrialist.

I never found out how Tan A-hong discovered the young people's plans, but it was probably through an intercepted letter. After telling the Lim family about her daughter's deceit, A-hong set out for Taipei to confront Chun-ieng in the wine house where she worked. Lim A-pou, fearing a serious outcome, accompanied her. When mother and daughter met, there was a violent scene. Chun-ieng tried to explain that she had been putting gold away for her mother's support and that she and her lover planned to send her a generous allowance, but A-hong was too angry, and perhaps too frightened, to pay any attention. She slapped Chun-ieng repeatedly, accused her of vile deeds, and told her to "go die." Chun-ieng ran out of the room, promising her mother that she would kill herself at once. Lim A-pou, who must have seemed wildly incongruous in this setting, sent A-hong away and searched the building for Chun-ieng. The girl was not to be found, so A-pou rushed back to the village to consult with Lim Chieng-cua. A young woman's threat of suicide is not taken lightly on Taiwan—their alternatives are too few. As soon as he heard A-pou's description of the encounter, Lim Chieng-cua hurried to Tapu where he phoned relatives and friends in Taipei to organize a search.

Thus began a long tense afternoon of waiting. Tan A-hong sat in A-pou's bedroom, her mood varying between remorse and fury at the "thankless girl." In the midst of this anxious suspense, Li Guat-ngo, Lim A-pou's adopted daughter and Chun-ieng's childhood playmate, arrived to pay a visit to her family and in particular to Chun-ieng. Li Guat-ngo is now the wife of a moderately prosperous shopkeeper; she has two children, good humor, and a tendency to speak her mind.

She listened with concern to her foster mother's account of the morning's events, casting looks of utter disgust at Tan A-hong. When A-hong began a tirade of complaints against Chun-ieng, Guat-ngo refused to listen. "Do you want her to die? What if she does kill herself? What will you do then? She has been very good to you. You must have a very bad heart to talk this way."

Angered, Tan A-hong answered, "I have a bad heart? You wait until your children get older and treat you like she treats me. Then you'll know what I'm talking about."

Guat-ngo: "If my daughter is like her, I will consider myself very fortunate. Don't be so black-hearted. She is twenty years old now. If she wants to get married, she can do it, and you can't do anything about it. You can't get any more money from her then, can you?"

A-hong: "That's good! Let her just try and run away from me. Get married? Let her try! If she is going to die, it is going to be in one of two ways—either she'll die on the road [i.e. homeless, friendless, impoverished] or she'll die by my hand!"

Guat-ngo was shocked. She stared at the older woman, speechless. Finally, she said, "You are not a mother at all. You never fed her. That must be why you can say these terrible things. Now she earns lots of money for you to gamble and eat and buy pretty clothes. Isn't that enough? You had better think that's enough."

A-hong: "That's right! I never fed her, indeed! It was war-time then and I had to search all over to find powdered milk for her, and when I found it, I had to pay to mail it all the way home here. I was going to hire someone to take care of her, but A-pou's mother wanted her so I sent her home. And how do you know she gives me so much money? Are you her go-between? What do you know about it? What do you know about anything?"

By this time, A-hong was shrieking. Her shrill voice could be heard all over the house. "I'm well over forty years old. I don't have her by my side, but I'm still alive. I'm not freezing or starving. I want her to die on the road! I want her to die by my hands! I want her to die." A-hong added as an afterthought—the afterthought that so often makes Taiwanese women's quarrels so ludicrous: "I can get a job as a cook for someone."

Guat-ngo was not to be silenced by histrionics. She returned to her scolding. "Yes, you sent a lot of powdered milk home for your daughter! Why was it then that poor grandmother was up late every night grinding rice to make gruel for her? You never fed her. She had no milk to drink. No wonder you don't care if she dies."

A-hong: "You were just a child. What do you know about it? You say I never took care of her. She is over twenty years old and in all of that time I never took care of her? You don't know anything about it. All the people in this family side with her. They always say she is right. That is why she treats me so badly now. They let her do whatever she wanted to do."

Lim A-pou had been keeping out of the argument and trying by hand signals to get her daughter to drop it. When Tan A-hong began to criticize the family, however, she looked very stern and said, "Be careful of your words. My mother and father treated her like a grandchild. They are dead now, but I am not. You never thanked them for taking care of her for you, and you had better not criticize them either."

Guat-ngo: "And what do you mean I don't know anything about

it? I was nine years old when she came here, and I often carried her on my back. When she was little she often fainted, and she often had convulsions. Did *you* know that? Did *you* ever take care of her when she was sick?"

Lim A-pou recovered her calm face, but was still stern looking. "Your daughter is your daughter," she said. "No matter how bad, she is still your daughter, and no matter how bad you are, you are still her mother. You must not keep saying you want her to die. She buys nice things to feed you and nice clothes for you to wear, and she does this only for you. You are the only one she gives things to, except the children now and then. If you want to treat her badly, we cannot stop you, but because I took care of her when she was little, I have a right to say some things. If you want to be someone's servant, you won't find it such a bad job. Anybody can be a servant. You had better take a look at yourself first, though. Are you healthy enough for that?" Tan A-hong suffers from asthma and is extremely thin, both conditions exacerbated by her all night gambling and chain smoking.

A-hong: "My bad health is her fault, too. When my youngest daughter was born, it was winter and Chun-ieng refused to wash or cook for me so I had to get up and do it myself. My bad health is all due to her. She refused to help me. I want her to die. If she won't treat me like a mother. I won't treat her like a daughter."

Guat-ngo: "You just think it over. There may be some daughters who treat their mothers better than Chun-ieng treats you, but if my daughter treats me as well, I will say that I have great good fortune."

A-pou: "Your lot in life compares better with rich people than with mine. I have two sons, but even sons can't buy clothes for me. You only have a daughter, but look what a pretty sweater she bought you."

A-hong threw the sweater on the floor and said, "Pretty sweater! I may be over forty, but I don't need that wretch to feed me. She never has fed me."

Guat-ngo laughed at the absurdity of this statement. "If she has never fed you, where do you get all the money to eat? If she never gives you any money, where do you get all the money for this?" She made gambling motions with her hands. "Just where do you get your pretty clothes and fine white rice?"

Tan A-hong grew hysterical and began screaming curses at the younger woman, threatening to hit her. A-pou made her daughter leave the room. This calmed A-hong somewhat, but she continued her complaints and again began to accuse the Lims, in particular Lim Han-ci and his wife, of teaching her daughter to disobey her.

Lim Chieng-cua, who had returned from Tapu part way through the quarrel, was sitting in the next room, trying to ignore the angry voices. When A-hong spoke of his parents, he stalked into the bed-room and, very red in the face, demanded, "Has anyone asked you for money in all the time you have lived here and eaten here? Nobody wants to hear your noise. You are not right, but you think you are very smart. I have scolded your daughter several times for not being more polite to you, even though I knew she was in the right and you deserved whatever harsh words she gave you. There are several peo-ple here who are not relatives who can tell you that this is true. It is only a mother who can decide whether a girl is good or bad, but I want you to listen to this. She is not as bad as you are trying to make people believe."

Lim Chieng-cua's anger subsided when A-hong began to cry. He continued scolding her, however, sounding very much like a school-master reading lessons. "I have heard mothers say that they wanted their daughters to die, but I have never heard a real mother say this. It was always a foster mother or a stepmother. Why is it that you talk this way? You think it over for awhile. You tell us she only left you a few dollars for the whole week. You never tell her the truth, so she never knows whether you really need money or not. If you really need money you can just tell her how much you need and she will give it to you. Why must you keep pushing the girl all the time? You are her mother. She knows she has to take care of you."

A-hong, sobbing, said, "You didn't see her yesterday. You don't know what her face looks like when I ask her for money."

"I do know," Lim Chieng-cua rejoined. "I have seen that expres-sion, and it is one of the things I have scolded her about. But, if you never lied to her, if you always treated her like your own daughter and not an adopted daughter, she wouldn't be that way. She doesn't know whether you really need money or not. You have lost every dollar you got from selling your house now. Sure, that was your own money to do with as you wished, but you think about that, too. She is getting older and she is going to take care of you after she's married, but she won't be able to give you so much money to gamble with. Married or not, she won't be able to make this much money in a few more years. If you had another NT$10,000 to gamble with, you wouldn't be in this mood today."

As he left the room, Lim Chieng-cua added: "It is a rule that a child *must* be good to his parents, but parents have to treat their chil-dren decently, too. That is also a rule. You can do many things to your children, but there is a point beyond which you cannot go. You have already gone too far. You must stop pushing her. If she is dead, your next daughter is too young to be of any use to you. What will you do?"

Tan A-hong, crying quietly, went home.

Late that evening, Lim Chieng-cua was summoned to Tapu to receive a telephone call. One of the children was sent to tell A-hong. She was a pitiful sight as she walked into the house. Her anger was gone and her terror reduced her to listing absurd reasons as to why Chun-ieng would not kill herself. When Lim Chieng-cua returned, he told the assembled group that Chun-ieng had been found and was in good health. He didn't even look at Tan A-hong and retired at once to his bedroom.

Chun-ieng returned to Peihotien late the next day, and I'm afraid the villagers were rather disappointed by her appearance. She should have looked wan and dejected, but instead she looked happier than I have ever seen her. She amiably satisfied the curiosity of her neighbors, saving the details of her adventure for the family. Her skill in story-telling did not suffer even when the story was at her own expense. After running out of the winehouse, she bought some poison and went to a hotel. She gave us a humorous description of the delighted, if bewildered, pedi-cab driver to whom she gave the last of her money. Just as she was about to take the pills, she heard someone in the hotel being called to the telephone and decided she should phone her lover in Tainan so that he wouldn't think she had killed herself because of something he had done. The connection was, of course, bad, so the boyfriend made her promise to wait until he could get to Taipei to talk with her. She then spent an entertaining hour trying to locate some relatives who would come and pay her hotel bill.

The source of Chun-ieng's unexpected happiness was revealed more slowly. Tan A-hong's complaints about her daughter were not completely groundless. Chun-ieng often answered her angry words with scorn and disrespect. She did not trust her mother and sometimes treated her honest need for money with disdain—understandable perhaps, but not behavior expected of a dutiful daughter. Unfortunately, Chun-ieng *was* a dutiful daughter. The anguish which prompted her toward suicide was as much the result of her own self-blame as of her mother's imprecations. Lim A-pou told me many months later that this was not the first time Chun-ieng had contemplated leaving her mother (always with adequate financial provision), but each time she had felt sorry for the older woman and returned. The interview that took place with her lover when he arrived from Tainan seemed to provide another solution. He generously proposed that she give up her plan of joining him, but also give up her work in the winehouse. He would send her a weekly allowance (the sum of which caused many round eyes) and visit her as often as possible until the day when they could be married. After their marriage, they would decide what to do about her mother. This was indeed a fairy-tale ending if it had been in fact the ending.

We had the pleasure of Chun-ieng's presence around the village for several months. Her boyfriend visited fairly regularly and she occasionally went to see him. Needless to say, each of her trips was preceded by anxious ill-temper on the part of Tan A-hong, but Chun-ieng always returned at the appointed time. Their quarrels were either less frequent or less violent because they came to my attention only rarely during those months. After awhile, though, I began to see more of Chun-ieng in the Lim house, often in tears, and I heard more of Tan A-hong's gambling debts. It wasn't long before Chun-ieng started disappearing from the village for two or three days at a time. I asked the family about her absences and received noncommittal answers until finally Lim A-pou admitted that she had returned to work. When I asked what would happen if her boyfriend unexpectedly turned up, Lim A-pou told me sadly, "We are supposed to tell him she has gone to work as a hostess in a coffee shop and we don't know where it is." Whether her lover discovered her deception or whether Chun-ieng herself finally gave up hope, I never found out, but after a few more months his visits to the village ceased, and Chun-ieng spent most of her time in Taipei. The Lims had little to say on the subject, but I don't think I only imagined that Tan A-hong came to the house considerably less often than was her wont. Perhaps she was just busier at her gambling.

During the last few months of my stay with the Lims, I noticed Lim A-pou make several trips out of the village dressed in her formal dark clothing. I asked A-ki where her mother-in-law was going, but got only a sad shake of the head. Then one day Lim A-pou returned with Chun-ieng, accompanied by a pretty though very frightened four-year-old girl. At Chun-ieng's request, Lim A-pou had found her a daughter to adopt. Chun-ieng stayed home from work for several days, spending all her time with the child, trying to coax a smile or a few words from her frightened lips. She played games with her, told her stories, bought her candy, and changed her clothes half a dozen times a day. Before Chun-ieng returned to work, the glazed look in her foster daughter's eyes was gone, but she looked terrified whenever Chun-ieng left the room. When Chun-ieng returned to Taipei, this second abandonment seemed too great for her daughter to bear. Day after day the child sat in the guest hall, her tiny body pulled up to occupy the smallest amount of space in the wicker chair, her eyes dully resting on the floor. The busy adults tried to lure her into activity and even the children treated her with special consideration, but nothing seemed to have any effect. When ordered to eat, she ate, but as soon as possible she would crawl back into the chair. She never cried and as far as I know never spoke. Her grief totally engulfed her. I am still haunted by that tiny figure of silent despair crouching in the shadows of the empty guest hall. Her despair was to me, and from their sad faces, to the Lims as well, a symbol of Chun-ieng's despair. Chun-ieng had at last accepted her mother's profession and turned her back on dreams of a normal life.

Social systems are often broken down into **statuses** and **roles** for analytical and comparative purposes. Because prostitution and gambling are not universals (although widespread), in some social systems neither prostitute nor gambler has an assigned status. The definition of the roles of prostitute and gambler and attitudes towards these roles vary greatly even among those societies that recognize them. It is obvious from Wolf's account that Taiwanese attitudes and beliefs about such customs are remarkably different from ours. As we know, it is not necessary to condone such customs in order to understand them. In this particular case it is necessary to consider some basic Chinese attitudes—their tradition of favoring sons above daughters, their beliefs about adoption, and their system of ancestor worship, which demands of children virtually absolute respect for their parents and elders. And all of this within the context of a highly developed economic system that allows for staggering differences between rich and poor. If Chinese attitudes are difficult for us to comprehend, consider for a moment how difficult it must be for the Chinese to understand: (1) adoption laws that can make it virtually impossible to find homes for many orphans, (2) laws that make gambling a crime in one geographical area but permit it in another (or make one form of gambling legal, but not another), and (3) laws against prostitution that are either not enforced at all or that are enforced against the prostitutes but not against their customers. Cultures ordinarily "make sense," but they are not always perfectly consistent.

A similar book about a Chinese family, described as a "sociological novel," is **The Golden Wing** by Lin Yueh-Hwa (1947), a Chinese who trained in anthropology at Harvard University and who then returned to China. Although **The Golden Wing** is well worth reading it tends to suffer from too much "sociologizing"—certainly not a flaw in **The House of Lim.** A more traditional anthropological study of China, also by a Chinese who lived there, is Martin C. Yang's, **A Chinese Village** (1945). For an informative and readable life history see Ida Pruitt's **A Daughter of Han** (1945). There is also Pearl Buck's incomparable novel of China, **The Good Earth** (1931). As Western anthropologists have not been allowed on the Chinese mainland for many years, there are no recent accounts. The books mentioned here, although allowing us glimpses of an absolutely fascinating way of life, cannot be taken as representative of contemporary mainland China.

For politically neutral films on China see **China: Portrait of the Land** (1968), **China's Villages in Change** (1967), and **China's Industrial Revolution** (1967). See also **China: A Hole in the Bamboo Curtain** (1973) which, although informative, is somewhat biased against both China and socialism. **Eight or Nine in the Morning** (1973), an excellent introduction to Chinese educational policies, compares Chinese and American views of the relation of the individual to society. **Misunderstanding China** (1972) is an excellent description of the way racist views and other erroneous concepts originate and are perpetuated.

For other fine ethnographic books by the wives of anthropologists see Elizabeth Warnock Fernea's **Guests of the Sheik** (1967) and Pat Ritzenthaler's **The Fon of Bafut** (1966). For somewhat lighter but still very interesting reading there is Sheila Solomon Klass on Trinidad, **Everyone in this House Makes Babies** (1964). There is also an amusing (but unfortunately patronizing) book on Morocco by Jane Kramer, **Honor to the Bride Like the Pigeon that Guards its Grain Under the Clove Tree** (1970).

12

The sweeper

MULK RAJ ANAND *

As most novels are read by members of the same culture as those who write them, the cultural background
against which the action takes place can be assumed to be understood by the reader without any difficulty. The anthropologist's problem of cross-cultural communication, which is
far more than merely a question of translation, does not ordinarily arise. However, this vexing problem does exist, as mentioned previously, in the very special case of books written
by local authors for broader consumption—African writers,
for example, writing about Africa, but in English, for an English-
speaking audience. Quite often the authors of such works
have as one of their expressed purposes the communication of knowledge about their own culture. This
raises another troublesome question: can a person who is a
member of the culture describe and interpret that culture as
well as or better than an outsider? It has often been
claimed by the subjects of anthropological investigations,
and by others as well, that anthropologists do not, or even
cannot, properly understand them—and thus must necessarily misrepresent them. Consider what E. M. Forster has to
say about this in his preface to **Untouchable,** the book from
which this selection was taken:

> **Untouchable** could only have been written by an Indian who ob-
> served from the outside. No European, however sympathetic,
> could have created the character of Bakha, because he would

* From *Untouchable* by Mulk Raj Anand, published by the Bodley Head, London, 1933.

not have known enough about his troubles. And no Untouchable could have written the book, because he would have been involved in indignation and self-pity. Mr. Anand stands in the ideal position. By caste he is a Kshatriya, and he might have been expected to inherit the pollution-complex. But as a child he played with the children of the sweepers attached to an Indian regiment, he grew to be fond of them, and to understand a tragedy which he did not share. [1933:v–vii]

This would suggest that the ideal person to write a novel (or an ethnography) would be a member of the culture, but one not personally involved with the situation or custom he or she was reporting, a kind of compromise, as it were, between an insider and an outsider. Perhaps this might be so, but it has not often been attempted.

Anthropologists argue that it is impossible to remain objective when writing about one's own culture. In any event, the very existence of the discipline of cultural anthropology is based on the assumption that other cultures, no matter how esoteric, can be understood by outsiders, provided they stay long enough, learn the language, and participate in the lives of those they study. It can also be argued that without the broad knowledge of a great variety of cultures that comes from studying anthropology, it is impossible to understand any culture, including one's own.

India, and the phenomenon of **caste** that is so much a part of Indian culture, have fascinated students of anthropology for a long time. No anthropological account, however, gives quite the intimate and personal picture we get from Anand.

His uncle at the British barracks had told him when he first expressed the wish to be a sahib that he would have to go to school if he wanted to be one. And he had wept and cried to be allowed to go to school. But then his father had told him that schools were meant for the babus, not for the lowly sweepers. He hadn't quite understood the reason for that then. Later at the British barracks he realized why his father had not sent him to school. He was a sweeper's son and could never be a babu. Later still he realized that there was no school which would admit him because the parents of the other children would not allow their sons to be contaminated by the touch of the low-caste man's sons. How absurd, he thought, that was, since most of the Hindu children touched him willingly at hockey and wouldn't mind having him at school with them. But the masters wouldn't teach the outcastes, lest their fingers which guided the students across the text should touch the leaves of the outcastes' books and they be polluted. These old Hindus were cruel. He was a sweeper, he knew, but he could not consciously accept that fact. He had begun to work at the latrines at the age of six and resigned himself to the hereditary life of the craft, but he dreamed of becoming a sahib. Several times he had felt the impulse to study on his own. Life at the Tommies' barracks had fired his imagination. And he often sat in his spare time and tried to feel how it felt to read. Recently he had actually gone and bought a first primer of English. But his self-education hadn't proceeded beyond the alphabet. Today as he stood in the sun looking at the eager little boy dragging his brother to school, a sudden impulse came on him to ask the babu's son to teach him.

'Babu ji,' he said, addressing the elder boy, 'in what class are you now?'

'In the fifth class,' the boy answered.

'Surely now you know enough to teach.'

'Han,' the boy replied.

'Then, do you think it will be too much trouble for you to give me a lesson a day?' Seeing the boy hesitate, he added, 'I shall pay you for it.'

He spoke in a faint, faltering voice, and his humility increased in depth and sincerity with every syllable.

The babu's sons didn't get much pocket-money. Their parents were thrifty, and considered, perhaps rightly, that a child should not eat irregularly, as the low-caste boys did, buying things in the bazaar. The elder boy had developed a strong materialistic instinct, hoarding the stray pice or two he received from anyone.

'Very well,' he said, 'I will. But the . . .' He wanted to change the topic, to make his suppressed desire for money less obvious. Bakha knew from his glance what he meant.

'I will pay you an anna per lesson.'

The babu's son smiled a hypocritical smile which seemed queer in so young a person. And he signified his assent, adding as an after-thought the conventional money-lover's phrase. 'Oh, the money doesn't matter.'

'Shall we begin this afternoon?' pleaded Bakha.

'Han,' the boy agreed, and was inclined to stand to talk and ce-ment the bond with pleasant words, but his brother was now very peevish and tugged at his sleeve, not only because he thought they were late for school, but also because he hated the idea of his brother becoming rich, was jealous of the money he would be earning.

'Come,' shouted the little one, 'the sun is almost overhead! We will be beaten for being late at school.'

Bakha divined the nature of the child's anger and tried to placate him by offering a bribe.

'You will also teach me, won't you, little brother? I will give you a pice a day.'

Bakha knew this would appease the boy's jealousy and obviate any chance of his telling upon his elder brother for spite. He knew if the little one told his mother that his elder brother was teaching a sweeper to read, she would fly into a rage and turn the poor boy out of the house. He knew her to be a pious Hindu lady.

The little one was too flurried to appreciate the value of the bribe. He looked towards school and was obsessed by the lateness of the hour. He pulled at the lower edge of his brother's tunic and dragged him away.

Bakha saw them depart. He felt elated at the prospect of the lesson he was to take in the afternoon and proceeded to go.

'Stop, O *Babu!* Now you are going to be a very big man,' shouted Ram Charan ironically. 'You won't even talk to us.'

'You are mad,' answered Bakha jovially. 'I must go, the sun is "coming on." And I have to clean the temple approach, and the courtyard.'

'Acha, let me show you my madness at hockey today.'

'Acha,' Bakha said as he headed towards the gates of the town, his basket under one arm, his broom under the other, and in his heart a song as happy as the sunshine.

Tan-nana-nan-tan, rang the bells of a bullock-cart behind him as, like other pedestrians, he was walking in the middle of the road. He jumped aside, dragging his boots in the dust, where, thanks to the vagaries of the Municipal Committee, the pavement should have been but was not. The fine particles of dust that flew to his face as he walked, and the creaking of the cart-wheels in the deep ruts, seemed to give him an intense pleasure. Near the gates of the town were a number of stalls at which fuel was sold to those who came to burn their dead in the cremation ground a little way off. A funeral procession had stopped at one of these. They were carrying a corpse on an open stretcher. The body lay swathed in a red cloth painted with golden stars. Bakha stared at it and felt for a moment the grim fear of death, a fear akin to the terror of meeting a snake or a theif. Then he assured himself by thinking: 'Mother said, it is lucky to see a dead body when one is out in the streets.' And he walked on, past the little fruit-stalls where dirtily clad Muhammadans with clean-shaven heads and henna-dyed beards cut sugar-cane into pieces, which lay in heaps before them, past the Hindu stallkeepers, who sold sweetmeats from round iron trays balanced on little cane stools, till he came to the betel-leaf shop, where, surrounded by three large mirrors and lithographs of Hindu deities and beautiful European women, sat a dirty turbanned boy, smearing the green, heart-shaped betel leaves with red and white paint. A number of packets of 'Red-Lamp' and 'Scissors' cigarettes were arranged in boxes on his right and whole rows of biris, native tobacco, rolled in leaf on his left. From the reflection of his face in the looking-glass, which he shyly noticed, Bakha's eyes travelled to the cigarettes. He halted suddenly and, facing the shopkeeper with great humility, joined his hands and begged to know where he could put a coin to pay for a packet of 'Red-Lamp.' The shopkeeper pointed to a spot on the board near him. Bakha put his anna there. The betel-leaf-seller dashed some water over it from the jug with which he sprinkled the betel leaves now and again. Having thus purified it he picked up the nickel piece and threw it into the counter. Then he flung a packet of 'Red-Lamp' cigarettes at Bakha, as a butcher might throw a bone to an insistent dog sniffing round the corner of his shop.

Bakha picked up the packet and moved away. Then he opened it and took out a cigarette. He recalled that he had forgotten to buy a box of matches. He was too modest to go back, as though some deep instinct told him that as a sweeper-lad he should show himself in people's presences as little as possible. For a sweeper, a menial, to be seen smoking constituted an offence before the Lord. Bakha knew that it was considered a presumption on the part of the poor to smoke like the rich people. But he wanted to smoke all the same. Only he felt he should do so unobserved while he carried his broom and basket. He caught sight of a Muhammadan who was puffing at a big hubble-bubble sitting on a mattress spread on the dust at one of the many open-air barbers' stalls that gaudily flanked the way.

'Mian ji, will you oblige me with a piece of coal from your clay fire-pot?' he appealed.

'Bend down to it and light your cigarette, if that is what you want to do with the piece of coal,' replied the barber.

Bakha, not used to taking such liberties with anybody, even with the Muhammadans whom the Hindus considered outcastes and who were, therefore, much nearer him, felt somewhat embarrassed, but he bent down and lit his cigarette. He felt a happy, carefree man as he sauntered along, drawing the smoke and breathing it out through his nostrils. The coils of smoke rose slowly before his eyes and dissolved, but he was intent on the little white roll of tobacco which was becoming smaller every moment as its dark grey and red outer end smouldered away.

Passing through the huge brick-built gate of the town into the main street, he was engulfed in a sea of colour. Nearly a month had passed since he was last in the city, so little leisure did his job at the latrines allow him, and he couldn't help being swept away by the sensations that crowded in on him from every side. He followed the curves of the winding, irregular streets lined on each side with shops, covered with canvas or jute awnings and topped by projecting domed balconies. He became deeply engrossed in the things that were displayed for sale, and in the various people who thronged around them. His first sensation of the bazaar was of its smell, a pleasant aroma oozing from so many unpleasant things, drains, grains, fresh and decaying vegetables, spices, men and women and asafœtida. Then it was the kaleidoscope of colours, the red, the orange, the purple of the fruit in the tiers of baskets which were arranged around the Peshawari fruit-seller, dressed in a blue silk turban, a scarlet velvet waistcoat, embroidered with gold, a long white tunic and trousers; the gory red of the mutton hanging beside the butcher who was himself busy mincing meat on a log of wood, while his assistants roasted it on skewers over a charcoal fire, or fried it in the black iron pan; the pale-blond colour of the wheat shop; and the rainbow hues of the sweetmeat stall, not to speak of the various shades of turbans and skirts, from the deep black of the widows to the green, the pink, the mauve and the fawn of the newly-wedded brides, and all the tints of the shifting, changing crowd, from the Brahmin's white to the grasscutter's coffee and the Pathan's swarthy brown.

Bakha felt confused, lost for a while. Then he looked steadily from the multi-coloured, jostling crowd to the beautifully arranged shops. There was the inquisitiveness of the child in his stare, absorbed here in the skill of a woodcutter and there in the manipulation of a sewingmachine by a tailor. 'Wonderful! Wonderful!' his soul seemed to say, in response to the sights familiar to him and yet new. He caught the eye of Ganesh Nath, the bania, a sharp-tongued, mean little man, in view of whose pyramids of basketsfull of flour, native sugar, dried chillies, peas and wheat he had sat begging for the gift of a tiny piece of salt and a smear of clarified butter. He withdrew his gaze immediately, because there had recently been a quarrel between the bania and his father on account of the compound interest Ganesh had demanded for the money Lakha had borrowed on the mortgage of his wife's trinkets to pay for her funeral. That was an unpleasant thing! He resisted the memory and drifted in his unconscious happiness towards the cloth shop where a big-bellied lalla, Hindu gentleman, clad in an immaculately white loose muslin shirt and loin-cloth, was busy writing in curious hieroglyphics on a scroll book bound in ochrecoloured canvas, while his assistants unrolled bundles of Mill-made cloth one after another, for inspection by an old couple from a village, talking incessantly the while of the 'tintint' and 'matchint,' just to impress the rustics into buying. Bakha was attracted by the woollen cloths that flanked the corners of the shop. That was the kind of cloth of which the sahibs' suits were made; the other cloth that he had seen lying before the yokels he could imagine turning soon into tunics and tehmets. All that was beneath his notice. But the woollen cloth, so glossy and fine, so expensive-looking! Not that he had any intention of buying, or any hope of wearing a kot-patloon suit; he felt for the money in his pocket to see if he had enough to pay an instalment on the purchase of cloth. There were only eight annas there. He remembered that he had promised to pay the babu's son for the English lesson.

He crossed the street to where the Bengali sweetmeat-seller's shop was. His mouth began to water for the burfi, the sugar candy that lay covered with silver paper on a tray near the dirtily-clad, fat confectioner. 'Eight annas in my pocket,' he said to himself, 'dare I buy some sweets? If my father comes to know that I spend all my money on sweets,' he thought and hesitated, 'but come, I have only one life to live,' he said to himself, 'let me taste of the sweets; who knows, tomorrow I may be no more.' Standing in a corner, he stole a glance at the shop to see which was the cheapest thing he could buy. His eyes scanned the array of good things; rasgulas, gulabjamans and ludus. They were all so lushly, expensively, smothered in syrup, that he knew they certainly could not be cheap, certainly not for him, because the shopkeepers always deceived the sweepers and the poor people, charging them much bigger prices, as if to compensate themselves for the pollution they courted by dealing with the outcastes. He caught sight of jalebis. He knew they were cheap. He had bought them before. He knew the rate at which they were sold, a rupee a seer.

'Four annas' worth of jalebis,' Bakha said in a low voice as he courageously advanced from the corner where he had stood. His head was bent. He was vaguely ashamed and self-conscious at being seen buying sweets.

The confectioner smiled faintly at the crudeness of the sweeper's taste, for jalebis are rather coarse stuff and no one save a greedy low-caste man would ever buy four annas' worth of jalebis. But he was a shopkeeper. He affected a casual manner and picking up his scales abruptly, began to put the sweets in one pan against bits of stone and some black, round iron weights which he threw into the other. The alacrity with which he lifted the little string attached to the middle of the rod, balanced the scales for the shortest possible space of time and threw the sweets into a piece torn off an old *Daily Mail*, was as amazing as it was baffling to poor Bakha, who knew he had been cheated, but dared not complain. He caught the jalebis which the confectioner threw at him like a cricket ball, placed four nickel coins on the shoe-board for the confectioner's assistant who stood ready to splash some water on them, and he walked away embarrassed, yet happy.

His mouth was watering. He unfolded the paper in which the jalebis were wrapped and put a piece hastily into his mouth. The taste of the warm and sweet syrup was satisfying and delightful. He attacked the packet again. It was nice to fill one's mouth, he felt, because only then could you feel the full savour of the thing. It was wonderful to walk along like that, munching and looking at all the sights. The big signboards advertising the names of Indian merchants, lawyers and medical men, their degrees and professions, all in broad, huge blocks of letters, stared down at him from the upper stories of the shops. He wished he could read all the luridly painted boards. But he found consolation in recalling the arrangement he had made for beginning his lessons in English that afternoon. Then his gaze was drawn to a figure sitting in a window. He stared at her absorbed and un-self-conscious.

'Keep to the side of the road, you low-caste vermin!' he suddenly heard someone shouting at him. 'Why don't you call, you swine, and announce your approach! Do you know you have touched me and defiled me, you cockeyed son of a bow-legged scorpion! Now I will have to go and take a bath to purify myself. And it was a new dhoti and shirt I put on this morning!'

Bakha stood amazed, embarrassed. He was deaf and dumb. His senses were paralysed. Only fear gripped his soul, fear and humility and servility. He was used to being spoken to roughly. But he had seldom been taken so unawares. The curious smile of humility which always hovered on his lips in the presence of high-caste men now became more pronounced. He lifted his face to the man opposite him, though his eyes were bent down. Then he stole a hurried glance at the man. The fellow's eyes were flaming and red-hot.

'You swine, you dog, why didn't you shout and warn me of your approach!' he shouted, as he met Bakha's eyes. 'Don't you know, you brute, that you must not touch me!'

Bakha's mouth was open. But he couldn't utter a single word. He was about to apologize. He had already joined his hands instinctively. Now he bent his forehead over them, and he mumbled something. But the man didn't care what he said. Bakha was too confused in the tense atmosphere which surrounded him to repeat what he had said, or to speak coherently and audibly. The man was not satisfied with dumb humility.

'Dirty dog! Son of a bitch! The offspring of a pig!' he shouted, his temper spluttering on his tongue and obstructing his speech, and the sense behind it, in its mad rush outwards. 'I . . . I'll have to go-o-o . . . and get washed—d—d . . . I . . . I was going to business and now . . . now, on account of *you*, I'll be late.'

A man had stopped alongside to see what was up, a white-clad man, wearing the distinctive dress of a rich Hindu merchant. The aggrieved one put his case before him, trying to suppress his rage all the while with his closed, trembling lips which hissed like a snake's:

'This dirty dog bumped right into me! So unmindfully do these sons of bitches walk in the streets! He was walking along without the slightest effort at announcing his approach, the swine!'

Bakha stood still, with his hands joined, though he dared to lift his forehead, perspiring and knotted with its hopeless and futile expression of meekness.

A few other men gathered round to see what the row was about, and as there are seldom any policemen about in Indian streets, the constabulary being highly corrupt, as it is drawn from amongst rogues and scoundrels, on the principle of 'set a thief to catch a thief,' the pedestrians formed a circle round Bakha, keeping at a distance of several yards from him, but joining in to aid and encourage the aggrieved man in his denunciations. The poor lad, confused still more by the conspicuous place he occupied in the middle of the crowd, felt like collapsing. His first impulse was to run, just to shoot across the throng, away, away, far away from the torment. But then he realized that he was surrounded by a barrier, not a physical barrier, because one push from his hefty shoulders would have been enough to unbalance the skeleton-like bodies of the Hindu merchants, but a moral one. He knew that contact with him, if he pushed through, would defile a great many more of these men. And he could already hear in his ears the abuse that he would thus draw on himself.

'Don't know what the world is coming to! These swine are getting more and more uppish!' said a little old man. 'One of his brethren who cleans the lavatory of my house, announced the other day that he wanted two rupees a month instead of one rupee, and the food that he gets from us daily.'

'He walked like a Lat Sahib, like a Laften Gornor!' shouted the defiled one. 'Just think, folks, think of the enormity!'

'Yes, yes, I know,' chimed in a seedy old fellow, 'I don't know what the *kalijugs* of this age is coming to!'

'As if he owned the whole street!' exclaimed the touched man. 'The son of a dog!'

A street urchin, several of whom had pushed their way through people's legs to see the fun, took his cue from the vigorous complainant and shouted: 'Ohe, you son of a dog! Now tell us how you feel. You who used to beat us!'

'Now look, look,' urged the touched man, 'he has been beating innocent little children. He is a confirmed rogue!'

Bakha had stood mute so far. At this awkward concoction of the child's, his honest soul surged up in self-defence.

'When did I beat you?' he angrily asked the child.

'Now, now mark his insolence!' shouted the touched man. 'He adds insult to injury. He lies! look!'

'No, Lalla ji, it is not true that I beat this child, it is not true,' Bakha pleaded. 'I have erred now. I forgot to call. I beg your forgiveness. It won't happen again. I forgot. I beg your forgiveness. It won't happen again!'

But the crowd which pressed round him, staring, pulling grimaces, jeering and leering, and was without a shadow of pity for his remorse. It stood unmoved, without heeding his apologies, and taking a sort of sadistic delight in watching him cower under the abuses and curses of its spokesman. Those who were silent seemed to sense in the indignation of the more vociferous members of the crowd an expression of their own awakening lust for power.

To Bakha, every second seemed an endless age of woe and suffering. His whole demeanour was concentrated in humility, and in his heart there was a queer stirring. His legs trembled and shook under him. He felt they would fail him. He was really sorry and tried hard to convey his repentance to his tormentors. But the barrier of space that the crowd had placed between themselves and him seemed to prevent his feeling from getting across. And he stood still while they raged and fumed and sneered in fury; 'Careless, irresponsible swine!' 'They don't want to work.' 'They laze about!' 'They ought to be wiped off the surface of the earth!'

Luckily for Bakha, a tonga-wallah came up, goading a rickety old mare which struggled in its shafts to carry a jolting, bolting box-like structure and shouted a warning (for lack of a bell or a horn) for the crowd to disperse as he reined in his horse in time to prevent an accident. The crowd scattered to safety, blurting out vain abuse, exclamations of amusement and disgust, according to age and taste. The touched man was apparently not yet satisfied. He stood where he was though aware that he would be forced to move by the oncoming vehicle, as for the first time for many years he had had an occasion to display his strength. He felt his four-foot-ten frame assume the towering stature of a giant with the false sense of power that the exertion of his will, unopposed against the docile sweeper-boy, had called forth.

'Look out, eh, Lalla ji,' shouted the tonga-wallah with an impudence characteristic of his profession. The touched man gave him an indignant, impatient look and signed to him, with a flourish of his hand, to wait.

'Don't you thrust your eyeballs at me,' the tonga-wallah answered back, and was going to move on, when all of a sudden, he gripped his reins fast.

'You've touched me,' he had heard the Lalla say to Bakha. 'I will have to bath now and purify myself anyhow. Well, take this for your damned irresponsibility, you son of a swine!' And the tonga-wallah heard a sharp, clear slap through the air.

Bakha's turban fell off and the jalebis in the paper bag in his hand were scattered in the dust. He stood aghast. Then his whole countenance lit with fire and his hands were no more joined. Tears welled up in his eyes and rolled down his cheeks. The strength, the power of his giant body glistened with the desire for revenge in his eyes, while horror, rage, indignation swept over his frame. In a moment he had lost all his humility, and he would have lost his temper too, but the man who had struck him the blow had slipped beyond reach into the street.

'Leave him, never mind, let him go, come along, tie your turban,' consoled the tonga-wallah, who, being a Muhammadan and thus also an Untouchable from the orthodox Hindu point of view, shared the outcaste's resentment to a certain degree.

Bakha hurried aside and putting his basket and broom down, wrapped the folds of his turban anyhow. Then wiping the tears off his face with his hands he picked up his tools and started walking.

'You be sure to shout now, you illegally begotten!' said a shop-keeper from a side, 'if you have learnt your lesson!' Bakha hurried away. He felt that everyone was looking at him. He bore the shop-keeper's abuse silently and went on. A little later he slowed down, and quite automatically he began to shout, '*Posh*, keep away, *posh*, sweeper coming, *posh*, *posh*, sweeper coming, *posh*, *posh*, sweeper coming!'

But there was a smouldering rage in his soul. His feelings would rise like spurts of smoke from a half-smothered fire, in fitful, unbalanced jerks when the recollection of some abuse or rebuke he had suffered kindled a spark in the ashes of remorse inside him. And in the smoky atmosphere of his mind arose dim ghosts of forms peopling the scene he had been through. The picture of the touched man stood in the forefront, among several indistinct faces, his bloodshot eyes, his little body with the sunken cheeks, his dry, thin lips, his ridiculously agitated manner, his abuse; and there was the circle of the crowd, jeering, scoffing, abusing, while he himself stood with joined hands in the centre. 'Why was all this?' He asked himself in the soundless speech of cells receiving and transmitting emotions, which was his usual way of communicating with himself. 'Why was all this fuss? Why was I so humble? I could have struck him! And to think that I was so eager to come to the town this morning. Why didn't I shout to warn the people of my approach? That comes of not looking after one's work. I should have begun to sweep the thoroughfare. I should have seen the high-caste people in the street. That man! That he should have hit me! My poor jalebis! I should have eaten them. But why couldn't I say something? Couldn't I have joined my hands to him and then gone away? The slap on my face! The coward! How he ran away, like a dog with his tail between his legs. That child! The liar! Let me come across him one day. He knew I was being abused. Not one of them spoke for me. The cruel crowd! All of them abused, abused, abused. Why are we always abused? The santry inspector and the Sahib that day abused my father. They always abuse us. Because we are sweepers. Because we touch dung. They hate dung. I hate it too. That's why I came here. I was tired of working on the latrines every day. That's why they don't touch us, the high-castes. The tonga-wallah was kind. He made me weep telling me, in that way, to take my things and walk along. But he is a Muhammadan. They don't mind touching us, the Muhammadans and the sahibs. It is only the Hindus, and the outcastes who are not sweepers. For them I am a sweeper, sweeper—untouchable! Untouchable! Untouchable! That's the word! Untouchable! I am an Untouchable!'

Like a ray of light shooting through the darkness, the recognition of his position, the significance of his lot dawned upon him. It illuminated the inner chambers of his mind. Everything that had happened to him traced its course up to this light and got the answer. The contempt of those who came to the latrines daily and complained that there weren't any latrines clean, the sneers of the people in the outcastes' colony, the abuse of the crowd which had gathered round him this morning. It was all explicable now. A shock of which this was the name had passed through his perceptions, previously numb and torpid, and had sent a quiver into his being, stirred his nerves of sight, hearing, smell, touch and taste, all into a quickening. 'I am an Untouchable!' he said to himself, 'an Untouchable!' He repeated the words in his mind, for it was still a bit hazy and he felt afraid it might be immersed in the darkness again. Then, aware of his position, he began to shout aloud the warning word with which he used to announce his approach, 'Posh, posh, sweeper coming.' The undertone, 'Untouchable, Untouchable,' was in his heart; the warning shout, 'Posh, posh, sweeper coming!' was in his mouth. His pace quickened and it formed itself into a regular army step into which his ammunition boots always fell so easily. He noticed that the thumping of his heavy feet on the ground excited too much attention. So he slowed down a little.

He became conscious that people were looking at him. He looked about himself to see why he was arousing all that attention. He felt the folds of his turban coming loose over his forehead. He wanted to retreat to a corner and tie it up properly. But he couldn't stop right in the middle of the street. So he walked to a corner. Feeling that he might be observed, he assumed a look of abstraction, as if he was harassed by the thought of some important work he had in hand. And he stared round. He felt a fool knowing that he was acting. He unrolled his turban and began to wrap it hard round his head.

Anthropologists would like to believe, perhaps pridefully, that they, in E. M. Forster's words, "would have known enough about his troubles" to have written Bakha's story. In fact, a sensitive anthropological observer quite likely would have known enough—but it is unlikely that he or she, for reasons mentioned previously, would actually have attempted to write such an account.

Although we take pride in the fact that America is not a caste society and attempt to minimize the importance of **social class,** the differences between caste cultures and our own are by no means as great as they appear. Caste societies like India's are more flexible than is generally acknowledged, and social classes in the United States, especially if they are complicated by differences in color, are more rigid than we like to believe. For those on the bottom, like Bakha, the comparison is largely academic. Consider the picture of American society given in the following passage from James Baldwin:

> Now I am perfectly aware that there are other slums in which white men are fighting for their lives and mainly losing. I know that blood is also flowing through those streets and that the human damage there is incalculable. People are continually pointing out to me the wretchedness of white people in order

to console me for the wretchedness of blacks. But an itemized account of the American failure does not console me and it should not console anyone else. That hundreds of thousands of white people are living, in effect, no better than the "niggers" is not a fact to be regarded with complacency. The social and moral bankruptcy suggested by this fact is of the bitterest, most terrifying kind. [1962:62]

While it may be possible for a few to rise in a society through their own talent and initiative, the majority cannot. They may not be literally "untouchable" but they are, in practice, a kind of functional equivalent. It is an unpleasant subject, of course, like the sweeping of latrines, and our attitudes towards the "lower classes" are probably no more reasonable than the emotion-laden attitudes we have on the subject of elimination. With respect to the latter, three solutions for solving the problem of the Indian untouchable are suggested to the sweeper at the end of the book: embrace Jesus Christ, embrace Gandhi, or put in flush toilets! However tongue-in-cheek that remark may be, it does say something about the process of culture change.

For further works of a similar type, but dealing with Africans, see: Thomas Mofolo, **Chaka: An Historical Romance** (1931); Ferdinand Oyono's **Houseboy** (1966) and **The Old Man and the Medal** (1969); and Sahle Sellassie's **Shinega's Village: Scenes of Ethiopian Life** (1964). For a novel on Papua New Guinea see Vincent Eri's **The Crocodile** (1970). A collection of short stories and sketches on similar themes from Papua New Guinea can be found in **Black Writing from New Guinea,** edited by Ulli Beier (1973). Books by American Indian authors dealing with the same kinds of issues include James Paytiamo's **Flaming Arrow's People** (1932) and N. Scott Momoday's prizewinning **The Way to Rainy Mountain** (1969).

Other ethnographically oriented novels on India include **The Bachelor of Arts** (1954), **Swami and Friends: A Novel of Malgudi** (1954), and **The Man-Eaters of Malgudi** (1961), all by R. K. Narayan. There are also **Music for Mohini,** by Bhabani Bhattacharya (1968); **The Dark Dancer,** by R. Balachandra (1958); **Godan,** by Premchand (1963); **Nectar in a Sieve** (1956), by K. Markanday; **Chronicles of Kedaram,** by K. Nagarajan (1912), and many, many more. Anand himself has also written **The Village** (1939), **Across the Black Waters** (1940), **Coolie** (1936), and several others. An interesting ethnographic novel about witchcraft in India is Verrier Elwin's **A Cloud That's Dragonish** (1938).

For anthropological works dealing with the subject of caste see **Homo Hierarchicus,** by Louis Dumont (1970) and Nur Yalman's **Under the Bo Tree** (1971). Also **Caste and the Economic Frontier,** by F. G. Bailey (1957) and Morris G. Carstairs' **The Twice-Born: A Study of a Community of High-Caste Hindus** (1961). For a well-known account of caste in America see John Dollard's **Caste and Class in a Southern Town** (1957).

Some of the better ethnographic films on Indian life include **Day Shall Dawn** (1959), **North Indian Village** (1958), **Undala** (1968), **Calcutta** (1968), **Ganges, Sacred River** (1965), **India** (1960), and **North Indian Village** (1959).

13

The widow Fascide

ANN CORNELISEN*

Anthropologists in general have always been more interested in nonliterate peoples in remote corners of the world
than in their own cultures—or in cultures closely resembling
their own. This is doubtless a result of our fascination with
human differences and of our relative neglect of similarities.
Consequently, until fairly recently there have been few anthropological studies done in European countries or in the
United States.

Many people besides anthropologists have reason to
live for extended periods of time with others whose
customs are foreign to them and difficult for them to assimi-
late. Few, however, are as perceptive as Ann Cornelisen,
and even fewer can write with such clarity of what they
have experienced. Ms. Cornelisen traveled to Florence in
1954 with the original intention of pursuing an interest in
archaeology. She became interested in the Save the Children Fund, and during the next ten years she helped to establish nursery centers in the poverty-stricken regions of
southern Italy. She is an astute and sensitive observer and
eventually wrote the much-acclaimed **Torregreca: Life,
Death, Miracles** (1969), from which the following account
has been taken. Her long immersion in the culture and her ded-
ication to helping enable her to speak with unusual authority
on a culture that appears to have been badly neglected.

* From *Torregreca: Life, Death, Miracles* by Ann Cornelisen, by permission of Little,
Brown and Co. in association with the Atlantic Monthly Press. Copyright © 1969 by
Ann Cornelisen.

That afternoon I went to the old *case popolari*—the first of the post-war public housing—on the Appian Way, just where the houses of the town end, where each night the promenaders turn to start their course back to the Piazza. I always thought of it as the beginning of the dark.

My knock at the Widow Fascide's door was answered by the high eerie wails of formal mourning that swelled and shrilled ever faster to a crescendo of howls. I understood I was to wait. This was one of the conventions of Southern grief, which is not so much a personal torture as a public marathon.

(Every act, every gesture, every word is prescribed, and any deviation will rouse comment. The actual moment of death electrifies the mourners. They fling open the windows to let the dead man's spirit out and open the doors to invite people in; then settle down for the harrowing hours of the watch when the women chant, one singing the virtues of the dead man, the others wailing the chorus. They tear their hair, claw their faces, and weep until it seems they can mourn no more—but they do, through a long day and an even longer night. They will only stop when the body is in its coffin and borne away to the church on the shoulders of friends. So they wail on. They change off, and a new voice takes up the litany of virtues; the chant continues. But practical concerns are not forgotten for mummery. Arrangements are discreet. Hidden by the comings and goings of neighbors, clothes are sent out to be dyed, a coffin is ordered, a priest hired, bell ringers paid, and a Confraternity is found to walk in the procession. When it is all over, the death of the living begins. A widow may have no fire in her house for two months. She depends on neighbors for food. She may not play her radio for two years. She must always wear black, of course, but she must wear a black scarf over her head, even in her own house for six months, and outside for two years. She must never be seen. If she must shop, she does it before dawn or after dark. She may not go to the Piazza. She cannot go to a festa, a wedding, a christening or even a funeral. As Chichella Fascide told me once, "It's all set out like a bus schedule. The one who's underground is lucky. The one left behind dies slowly with everyone watching, checking, making sure you do it the right way—the Torregreca way." Slowly the restrictions dwindle away. In five years gold earrings may be substituted for black loops. A festa, even a wedding, is permitted. At the end of twelve years, or fifteen, a widow might put off her weeds if, by some chance, another close relative has not died, but she is old by then, set in her habits, cramped in her pocketbook and loath to give any ground for comment.)

Chichella Fascide was a fresh widow of four months. She was expected to spend her days wailing and could not open the door before she vocalized enough to satisfy her neighbors who appeared on their landings, craning their necks upward to inspect her visitor.

"Who are you?" "What do you want?" "What's she done?" they called at me like crows. Young women with high cheekbones and beak noses, they might have been Italian Indians. Their voices were shrill and at the same time flat, and sounded, as I found they always did even when asking the time, as though they were in the midst of a violent argument.

"I just want to talk to Fascide for a minute. I'm a friend of Don Luca Montefalcone's." In one voice they yowled, "Oyee, Chichella. Open up. There's a lady to see you. Oyee, Chichella . . ." but she already had. Black, peppercorn eyes were peering at me through a crack in the door. They showed no sign of tears. She opened the door further and inspected me as I inspected her. She was somewhere in her thirties, I guessed, and very solid, though she later insisted she had been terribly wasted by mourning. A delicate face accented by heavy eyebrows and a large but well-balanced mouth seemed mismated to a short, stocky body. Stubby fingers fumbled trying to knot her head scarf under her chin. She must not show her shiny black hair that was pulled into a bun at the back of her head.

"Well, you don't expect me to wear it *all* the time, do you?" She laughed, showing small, very white teeth. I remember being surprised at her broad, childlike fingernails and at her breasts, not that they were large, but they seemed very much in the way of her short arms. Her eyes twinkled at her own joke. "*Trase, trase . . .*" and a Niagara of words without meanings. Diphthongs tripped over diphthongs in what sounded like the spewings of an irate woman with a head cold. My first, full-dress encounter with the lingua franca of the peasants left me stunned. Dialects change from district to district and from town to town, and also, as I found out, in Torregreca from neighborhood to neighborhood. Chichella spoke pure "Tarnese," as she called it. She understood Italian, but even with intense concentration could not utter more than a sentence or two in what was supposed to be her native language. I grabbed at words: husband, *povertà*, *miseria*, and *piccinin*, her children. She never took her shrewd eyes off my face. The instant I opened my mouth she burst into tears and rocked her breasts back and forth, cradling them as though they were a baby. She moaned on the verge of wailing, but still she watched me, in no way hypnotized by her own expression of trauma. I could feel her determination. This was not just begging self-pity; she had a specific purpose and I wanted to know what it could be. I turned to go.

"Don't you want to see the apartment?" Grief could wait. I

thanked her, but explained I had only come to ask if she knew of anyone else who might want to rent an apartment, or better yet a small
house in town. Her eyes narrowed; this was not going as she had
planned. As I was saying that I understood her desire to stay in her
own home, I was grabbed and dragged into a small bare room lined
with wooden chairs. It had the air of a third class waiting room in a
railroad station and was surprisingly dark, although there was a
French door that led to a balcony where I could see a jumble of stovewood, derelict boxes and broken pots. Beyond, framed by two
more eggcrate buildings of the *case popolari*, was the Norman tower,
one-dimensional in the glare of afternoon light that could not penetrate the gloom of this dreary parlor. In the middle of the room was a
table with a crocheted doily so starched it provided a frill for the
plaster dog that nested in its center. Off in a corner on a stool was the
radio, put to bed like a parrot, with a black sateen cover, and over it
all loomed a dish cupboard which like the rest of the furniture had
been painted with ochre shellac and then grained by the dexterous
use of a comb. Creating this "pretend walnut" is an essential art in
the Torregrecas where almost no one can afford the real thing, but
to the uninitiated, the swirls and color bring on an attack of bilious
vertigo.

"See how neat it is?" It was. It had the impersonal order of any
room that is never used. I had finally understood what made the
room so dark; the walls were cocoa brown and furry from smoke.
"Come, now you must see the bedrooms." Obviously the doors had
been kept shut for the walls were less stained. Instead they were covered with a fluffy meringue of whitewash that had been lifted away
from the plaster by humidity. Near the ceiling there were speckles of
black mold. In one bedroom were a chest of drawers and a huge
"matrimonial bed" of tin "pretend walnut," covered with an immacu-
late, white cotton jacquard spread. In the other, which was much
smaller, there was a pathetic array of sleeping equipment: a trunk
with a lumpy sack of ticking arranged on the top, a deck chair
stretched to the maximum, and a chromium-framed, extendable love
seat. In both rooms; faded pictures of relatives, the men mustachioed
and uncomfortable looking in ties, the women very prim with religious medals strung around their necks, glimmered at me. Each was
lighted by a minute electric bulb poised at the end of a gooseneck of
thin metal piping. A plaque of Saint Anthony lighted from behind
beamed a saccharine blessing over the "matrimonial bed." Speechless, I went on to the bathroom which was narrow and basic: a half-
tub filled with water, a toilet without a seat, and a basin both of whose
faucets were lying, detached, in the depression made for soap. It was

all very clean. It went through my head that anyone who settled down there would be in full view of the traffic passing on the Appian Way. The kitchen was almost bare except for a sink and a miniature wood range which was the only form of heat and was also the source of the oily brownness covering the walls. A low cupboard with a two-ring gas burner set on top and some bowlegged chairs were the only furniture. There was another balcony with a morass of wild roses growing out of tin cans. Depression blanked out my mind.

"You see, it's clean. The mattress is new. You won't find anything better." She stopped. "I need the money. I'm a widow with four children . . ." and she began to moan.

A lightning resignation paralyzed my will for the first time. It was to become a chronic affliction of my life in Torregreca; after all, if I looked further, wouldn't I find the same kind of genteel squalor, probably dirtier, more dejected? "But you just want to rent a room. I need the whole thing."

She shook her head violently.

"You're willing to move out? How much do you want for it?"

So, standing there in the kitchen, we started the wrangle that is the crux of any deal. This was something she understood. Her eyes snapped at me as she explained how she had arrived at her price. I objected. She cried. I made a counter-offer; she protested. It was a play to her and she was Bernhardt. It took us probably thirty minutes to split the difference between her idea of the rent and mine. I promised a daily amount for the work she did for me. We agreed it would never take more than two hours, and I advanced part of the first month's rent to have the place completely whitewashed. Unless she were willing to have that done, I would not take it.

The neighbors had waited for news as long as they could and then wandered in to stand with blank faces as though they were waiting for a bus. Chichella was used to communal living, but I was not. I asked them to leave us to our discussion, and when they did not move, I led them by the hand to the door. A few minutes later others came in and we repeated the scene. Two crones, almost blind judging from the opaque look of their eyes, came in, walked up under my nose and asked, "Who are you?" Chichella had to scream a full explanation at them. Then I showed them out. The only person I was unable to depose was Chichella's sister, Tina, who had been alerted by the neighbors. She was younger than Chichella, tall and proudly erect with flashing blue eyes, tawny hair and perfectly modeled small features. She was the classic peasant beauty of romantic imagination, but she was also a shrew with a viper's tongue and a mulish will. My reaction was chemical, not logical; I disliked her on sight and I never had any reason to change my mind in the years that followed. That day she would not budge, though she was so busy fawning over me that she really caused little trouble. When I left it had been agreed everything would be ready for me in ten days. As casually as that I committed myself to Chichella's care, but it was probably inevitable because, as she told me months later, she had had a dream. She had seen the Madonna at the top of a long, long flight of stairs. She clambered up, but no matter how she tried she could never reach the top. Finally she stood still and heard the Madonna say, "When a stranger comes, do what he tells you and he will lead you to safety." Dreams are very important. Properly interpreted they can lead you to the right combination on the numbers wheel, tell you whom to marry, and what land to buy. I suspect they are more useful after the fact as a confirmation than as a guide, and I do not for one minute believe she dreamed of the Madonna. Had she known anything about the flight of birds, pagan augury would have done as well. She had made up her mind that I was the solution to her problems.

One afternoon ten days later I *did* move in with my trunks and supplies I had sent from my organization's stores: towels, washclothes, blankets and cotton yardage from which to make curtains. I was shocked to see that the chalky whitewash had brought out a feature of the apartment I had failed to notice; the doors and windows were a violent, sickening pea green. Chichella dithered around pulling out drawers to show me they were empty and lined with "clean" newspaper. She was careful to teach me how I could hang my clothes on great crosstie nails that stuck out from the walls where one least expected them. The trick was to do it without rubbing whitewash off on the shoulders of dresses and coats. Eventually, when we were muddling around in the dark, I flipped a light switch and was greeted with the distant twinkle of a ten-watt bulb. In the whole apartment there were three ten-watters and in the kitchen one seventy-five-watt bulb which, after I assured her I would pay the light bill, I was allowed to move from room to room. At that, it was not a very convenient arrangement and I soon put off unpacking until the morning and sent her home, which I realized meant a basement storeroom without light or water where she and three of her four children were camping like refugees. Left to myself there seemed little I could do. I made a cup of tea and then started circling around looking for a place to sit as a dog twists and turns and backs before he settles down. Finally I gave up and had my tea standing at the kitchen window. I think I had a wistful hope that a car or truck might go by, but nothing broke the stillness of the night except my neighbors' radios.

The light fixture in the bathroom was too high for me to change the bulb and I did not want to put on a tantalizing show for the neighbors anyway, so I settled for a sponge bath in the penumbra. It would have been possible in a familiar bathroom, but not there. I found a pot in a small pantry-closet off the kitchen. I was glad later that I had not been able to see the true condition of either the pot or the pantry. I heated some water, but it turned out there was no stopper for the basin. After bailing hot water into pitchers and buckets and mixing in cold I did get cleaned up. Remembering to leave the tub faucet open in case water came in the middle of the night, I went to bed. The new mattress which had been so stressed in our negotiations was in a sense new. It had been stuffed with fresh corn husks! They crackled and crunched and tickled me if I shifted my weight. From the bathroom came greedy sucking and burping noises. The ancestors glowing in their demonic lights seemed perched around the edges of the bed just waiting for me to close my eyes. I must have fallen asleep. The last thing I remember was the Voice of Moscow on my little transistor radio crooning the latest sins of the capitalist villains of my faraway country. I might as well have been on the moon.

I was not at all sure just where I was when a bus trumpeted under my window like an enraged elephant at two o'clock. It was the warning signal for passengers. At four, with the first streaks of light and the clip-clip of donkeys on their way to the fields I was up, planning the campaign which somehow must make this into a place to live.

For several days Chichella was very patient with me. She made me watch her washing dishes with detergent so that I would be convinced she had given up her method of wood ashes and sand. She made me smell the laundry for proof there was no bleach. In shopping she was less successful. There was no meat for sale, no *parmigiano* and no milk that was safe to drink. The butter was rancid from being too long in transit from the North. I refused to accept murky, raw olive oil, or pears of poured concrete. There was *pecorino* but it tasted of old cellars and bad drains. It seemed I would have to live on figs, spaghetti and eggs which cost the handsome price of ten cents each because they were "out of season." Absorbed with bending heavy wire for curtain rods and setting wooden plugs in the wall to hold the drapery irons, I still had mind enough to notice Chichella's ingenuity. She went around telling people that I planned to lay in a large stock of wine. Sample bottles began arriving and no matter how I insisted, there was no way for me to pay for them. When we were unable to attach the new toilet seat, she called a plumber who seemed determined to discuss the remodeling of the bath with me. Only when she started making signs behind his back did I understand; let him make the estimate and he would not only attach the seat, but the faucets as well. "He would never have come just to do our chores," was her lucid reasoning. If he did what suited him, we would do what suited us. After a lot of dickering and arguing with a carpenter who wanted to make me a "masterpiece of inlay" for a clothes cupboard, I ordered a monument of plywood that I planned to paint white and put in the bedroom. Until it came I lived from suitcases and Chichella had no chance to inventory my clothes, but when the final coat of paint was dry she was careful to be there "to help."

For a while she watched in silence. When she could stand it no longer, she said, "*Ma, Signo'*, are you going to open a store? And all those shoes! Nobody alive can wear more than a pair at a time. Why, I'd be rich if I had two pairs: one wet and one dry."

I did not try to explain. It is true I had fur-lined boots, mountain boots, heavy rubber-soled shoes, loafers, tennis shoes, high-heeled black, low-heeled black, brown, blue and I no longer remember what else, but she would never have understood that I used them all at various times and in various places. "Too bad," she muttered. "They're the right length, but they're too narrow." I turned to find her jamming her square feet into the only pair of Ferragamos I owned. Not long after, I realized that my slippers seemed, somehow, to be getting larger and larger. When I questioned her she pulled a very serious face. "But you wouldn't want me to track mud around the floor I've just mopped, would you?" I declared those slippers hers. She smiled innocently. We had started another variety of graft.

I had found an innerspring mattress at an exorbitant price in Torregreca. Rush-bottom chairs were being sent to me, but for a simple armchair and a reading lamp I had to go to Matera. When I had finished making the curtains and bedspreads, had scoured out all the cupboards, reorganized the kitchen and rigged up temporary bookshelves, I tackled the slow business of painting all the windows and doors. I had not thought to mention it to Chichella. It was not a question of having painters in; there are none in Torregreca. Painting is done by carpenters and they cannot conceive of working without boiled linseed oil that has a suspicious odor of fish and never, never allows the paint it has diluted to dry. It was just another chore for me to do before the curtains were hung and I could call the place more or less finished. At the same time I planned to repaint the border at the base of the walls that protects whitewash from the splashing tongue of the mop. In an effort to save money Chichella had done it herself—freehand—so that it looked like a profile of the Dolomites. With the first piece of furniture I moved I discovered she had also skipped those parts of the wall she expected to be covered. *Eh, be',* *pazienza!* I was resigned to the system. She had probably saved a dollar or two. A first coat was on the windows and I had started the doors when she stormed in, red in the face, her eyes snapping. My ear had improved, but it would have taken a native to understand her avalanche of Tarnese. One thing was clear: she wanted things left as they were. She eyed the curtains laid out on the bed and spewed again. There was no way to interrupt her, so I made a pot of coffee and suggested we sit down over it and discuss the situation.

"I've never had a cup of coffee in my life and I don't intend to start now!" was her answer. While she stood, and I sat drinking coffee I did not want with what I hoped was epic appreciation, I told her that the apartment would be as I wanted it for as long as I had it, but that I guaranteed I would leave money for replacing everything I had changed. She turned, stalked out and slammed the door. Knowing that the worst thing I could do was to show any doubt or lack of determination, I went back to painting. Late in the afternoon I hung white glass curtains and side curtains of the only material I had in quantity—a startling Kelly green cotton. I had finished in the sitting room and the bedroom when the front door opened.

"They say it's all right. It looks nice," Chichella panted.

"Who says?"

She led me to the window. Below in the courtyard were at least fifty neighbor women with their babies and their chickens milling around their feet. "*Complimenti, complimenti!*" one of them yelled. "*Stanno bene, stanno!*" screeched another.

"See what *my* signora can do?" Chichella shouted back. "She's clever, you'll see."

I felt like a disheveled Queen Elizabeth waving to the crowd. They waved back. Our problem was no more, the neighbors approved.

Chichella may have thought she could ride the crest of that wave, but she was soon enough in a deep trough of her own. She had found temporary work washing, by hand, all the hospital linen, whereupon those neighbors dubbed her "The Merry Widow"—she was not sticking to the rules.

Her days went something like this: at dawn she started splitting wood for the laundry boiler; from eight to two, after loading the wood up four flights of stairs to the loft, she shunted the mountains of bloody sheets and bindings from tub to tub, to boiler to rinse tub, and then to dry. At two she raced back to me, did my cleaning, collected my shopping list which she had to have someone read to her, and went off to the wife of a local official to wash the lunch dishes and sit with the baby for two hours. She did my shopping, and then tried to round up her own children and feed them.

During the two months she worked at the hospital, she was supposed to be paid $15 a month, though she never saw a penny of it until I complained to the director six months after she did the work. Her normal income was clear-cut and meager. I paid her $20 a month for the apartment and $12.50 for the chores she did. The woman whose dishes she washed seldom gave her more than 15 cents a day; half the time she paid her nothing. The family resources, then, were limited to $32.50 a month and an uncertain bit. A year later a government pension of $10 a month was added. According to her peers she should not even have had the $32.50, though she was expected to live somehow and pay her husband's debts—$1,000 of debts. Except for pasta, food in Torregreca was as expensive as in America. She had herself and three children to feed (the fourth lived with a sister-in-law) and clothe; school books to buy for the two boys who were in school and her rent on the apartment she rented to me was $5.

Now she was "The Merry Widow" and the few women who had called on her to sit gossiping in the evenings no longer came. Children threw stones at her and yelled *"puttana"*—whore. To go out in the streets, to work, meant she had already forgotten her husband, that she had a lover.

Sometimes when I came home in the evenings I stopped by her storeroom to say I was back. Always I found her sitting in her doorway looking with glazed eyes down the dimly lighted corridor. Against the dampness of the basement and the chill of summer evenings she wrapped a crocheted black wool scarf around her head and shoulders and around her three-year-old daughter Rosa, who refused to fall asleep anywhere but in her mother's arms. They molded together into one hunched, almost cringing figure of passive desolation. Chichella leaning her head against the door jamb might have been asleep, except that her eyes were very wide open and the deep lines around her mouth spoke of bitter, frightened thoughts. If I asked her about them she was evasive.

"I don't think. In my position it's better not to think. I just go over and over my life trying to find what I did wrong; what made God punish me."

When she could stand no more self-torture she went inside her storeroom and crawled onto the bed she shared with the three children. There, in sleep, they wrestled with each other all night for it was not a real bed but planks straddling two iron stands. During the day, so that the neighbors would not know the truth, she covered and padded it into softness. One end of the little room was reserved for the owner's goods: stovewood, burlap sacks of grain and a wine barrel. The rest was a clutter of pots and pans, many filled with water, and a bread chest on top of which was a gas burner. One of the unexplained miracles of Chichella was how she kept the children as clean and decent-looking as she did. Vincenzo was seven, a thin, tiger-eyed boy whose gaze was fixed on the toes of his scuffed shoes. For more than a year he refused to speak to me. Some childish vision of cause and effect had given him the idea that, having taken his home, I was also responsible for his father's death. Luigi was six and looked exactly like Chichella, but there was something especially appealing about his brown eyes and well-formed head with its thick mat of dark hair tinged white from his mother's ministrations of DDT. She was so sure he played in "dirty" places that even the dire warnings on the box which I read to her did not discourage nightly treatments against fleas and lice. Luigi was ingratiating to the point of being a juvenile boot-licker. The parish priest was sure he would enter the priesthood; his teacher knew he wanted to go to normal school; the *guardie* saw him a policeman. They all spoiled him, but Chichella might have saved her DDT because he and Vincenzo with single-minded concentration spent their free time at the market snitching figs or peppers or persimmons when the vendors' backs were turned. Their memories of childhood will, I think, be of unrelieved hunger punctuated by lickings for stealing or wearing out their shoes. Rosa was only three but already had the wide-eyed look of rage that was her mother's face for the world. As long as she had a hunk of bread to chew on life was bearable. Only when she was left without it did she become a problem, wandering around the neighborhood, squatting wherever the notion hit her and eventually, after spankings from her mother for not lowering her panties, leaving a trail of Kelly green panties that had been constructed out of scraps from my curtains.

Chichella kept the three children clean and fed as best she could, but more than that, from the quicksand of her own despair and loneliness she managed to give them security.

Death is an inevitable part of life, and since it awaits us all with total unconcern for status, social class, caste, or culture, it is the definitive equalizer. Although the deceased cannot participate, death is always acknowledged and ritualized as a rite of passage like birth and marriage. The observance of funeral customs, although these vary enormously,

187

seems to set man apart from other animals just as much as the ability to control fire or the possession of symbolic thought.

Funerals, of course, are for the living, and, as in this case, the dead might be seen as perhaps more fortunate than the living. Widowhood is always difficult, but there are few cultures where it is surrounded by quite so many rules, regulations, demands, and expectations—all designed, it would seem, to make life horribly unpleasant, if not impossible. This is the type of situation that is terribly difficult and even painful for the fieldworker. What is one to do? One may attempt to remain completely objective—simply standing by, experiencing oneself as some kind of inhuman spectator—or one can intervene to make another's life a bit more pleasant, thereby risking hostility, criticism, and jealousy from those in whose lives one is meddling.

This particular account raises another awkward point about fieldwork; the observer often has what seems a surplus of material comforts—in this case, shoes. Should one reduce one's possessions to the bare minimum—"go native," as it were, or simply ignore the disparity in wealth. The extent to which this is a problem varies from situation to situation, of course. At times the anthropologist literally has to hoard his possessions and eat in secret, as Turnbull says he was forced to do when working with the Ik (1972). At other times the fieldworker must make do with an inadequate diet or even go hungry for a time. As there is no real solution to these problems, each researcher is left to decide for himself. The decision doubtless affects the person's ability to achieve **rapport** and, consequently, the kinds of data that can be collected. It is not a trivial matter.

Ann Cornelisen has also written **Vendetta of Silence** (1971) and **Women of the Shadows** (1976). The latter book is a particularly evocative and moving portrait of the women of southern Italy, women like Chichella, tied to the sparse soil, the ungentle poverty, and hopelessness. An unusual account of urban Italian poverty is Morris L. West's **Children of the Shadows** (1957). A very sensitive account of urban Italian Americans is **Blood of my Blood,** by Richard Gambino (1974).

It is difficult to find other books to recommend that are truly the equivalent of **Torregreca.** Perhaps the closest examples in the literature of anthropology are the various village studies that have been written. A fine ethnography of a village in Sicily, **Milocca: A Sicilian Village** (1971), by Charlotte Gower Chapman, was completed in 1935, but its publication was unfortunately delayed for more than thirty years. On the subject of Europe in general, these studies include Frankenberg's **Village on the Border** (1957); J. A. Pitt-River's **The People of the Sierra** (1954); **Village in the Vaucluse,** by Laurence Wylie (1957); **Hal-Farrug: A Village in Malta,** by Jeremy F. Boissevain (1969); and **Vasilika: A Village in Modern Greece,** by Ernestine Friedl (1962).

Village studies made in other parts of the world include **Tepoztlan: A Mexican Village,** by Robert Redfield (1930); **Suye Mura,** by John F. Embree (1939); **A Chinese Village,** by Martin C. Yang (1945); **K'un Shen: A Taiwan Village,** by Norma Diamond (1969); and **Village Life in Northern India,** by Oscar Lewis (1965).

Some extremely interesting and ethnographically valuable personal accounts by nonanthropologists are Wilfred Thesiger's **The Marsh Arabs** (1964); Alan Villiers's **Sons of Sinbad** (1969); Jan Yoors's **The Gypsies** (1967); Gontran de Poncins's famous book on the Eskimo, **Kabloona** (1941); Farley Mowat's **People of the Deer** (1952); and Daisy Bates's account of her lifetime with Australian aboriginals, **The Passing of the Aborigines** (1967).

Some ethnographic films of interest include **The Visit** (1967), which deals with an immigrant's return to his village of origin in Italy, and **Bandits of Orgosolo** (1961), a film on Sardinia which is more ethnographic than the title suggests. Other films on village life in Europe include **The Village** (Ireland, 1969), **Anastenaria** (ecstatic religious ceremony in the village of Serres, Northern Greece, 1969), and **Land Without Bread** (Western Spain, 1932).

14

An excursion into the country

ELIZABETH WARNOCK FERNEA*

Rapport, which is so absolutely necessary for successful
anthropological fieldwork, is difficult to achieve, and even
after it has been gained there is still the possibility of destroy-
ing it with a single misstep. The following account, taken
from Elizabeth Warnock Fernea's **Guests of the Sheik: An Ethnography of an Iraqi Village** (1965), presents a striking illustration of this occupational hazard. Just such a disaster
nearly befell the author and her anthropologist husband, Robert Fernea, during their fieldwork in Iraq.

Like Margery Wolf, Elizabeth Fernea is an unusually
gifted writer, with the ability to very subtly inform us about
Arab culture while telling an interesting and entertaining
story. Arab attitudes towards women and the customs surrounding the veiling of Arab women have always been difficult for Europeans to understand. While it might seem incredible to us (living as we do in a culture in which both males
and females are allowed to go about almost as freely as
they choose) that an innocent drive in the country could
have potentially disastrous consequences, such restrictive
customs were common in the past and survive even now in
some parts of the world. Arab comprehension of our insis-

tence on **monogamy** and of our emphasis on the **nuclear family** is somewhat analogous to our understanding of **polygamy** and of the keeping of harems.

Guests of the Sheik: An Ethnography of an Iraqi Village is precisely what the subtitle suggests, but it is unusual because of the insight with which the characters are portrayed. We see them become involved, as individuals, with the Ferneas. We also gain a perspective—an understanding of Arab customs and of how Arabs feel about them—that we would not ordinarily get from a more academic account. We begin to appreciate how it is that attitudes of this kind are relinquished so reluctantly, even when societies are otherwise changing rapidly, a phenomenon called **cultural lag**. We also see how fortunate it is for anthropologists that people virtually everywhere can be exceptionally forgiving.

Aziza and I kept up our lessons twice a week that autumn, but it was usually I who went to see Aziza. Therefore I was surprised to find her at my door after lunch one afternoon. Laila, who had been visiting, sprang up in delight, pleased that the teacher, a person of some importance, should appear when she was present.

"Come for a ride with me," said Aziza. "It is such a fine day."

"A ride?" I echoed.

"Yes," replied Aziza. "My cousin is here from Diwaniya with his car and his driver. They are going partridge hunting along the canal. I will sit in the back seat to look at the view and I thought you might like to come. Do come, Beeja!" she urged, clapping her hands together. "The country will be beautiful today."

"I would love to," I answered. An excursion away from my house and garden would be a real event. But I turned to my visitor Laila.

"Laila must come too," said the kindly Aziza, and Laila beamed. "But," she added, "are you sure that your father would allow you to go driving with my cousin?"

"Of course, of course," said Laila.

When I remember that afternoon, I wonder what gave it such a luster. It had none of the characteristics of autumn afternoons to which I was accustomed—no brilliant leaves, no crisp winds or changing skies. Perhaps it was the light, the sunlight in Mesopotamia which warms without burning, which adds subtlety to what is usually an elemental landscape. For fall here is really spring. The year's principal crops are planted early in October. By the end of the month the brown fields that have baked under the summer sun are fuzzed with green. This thin dusting of green, the young barley and wheat and sesame plants, casts a gentle haze over the flat land. Even the uncultivated sandy sections develop shadows, and the sharp fronds and spiny trunks of the date palms look softer in outline. Gazelles race over the plains; the partridge nests in the new grasses. This is the best season of the year, for the heat has lifted and the icy muddy winter has not yet come.

Aziza's cousin, one rifle in hand and a second rifle on the seat beside him, rode in front with his driver. Both men wore tribal dress, almost identical with the garments worn by the men of the El Eshadda. For their tribe and the El Eshadda were members of the same tribal confederation. The cousin spoke occasionally to Aziza, but he was careful not to address Laila or myself. We sat silently, wrapped in our abayahs, enjoying a marvelous sense of release in the unexpected holiday.

We went as far as Seddara El Nahra, the point where the sluice gates of the El Nahra canal are located. Here a small rest house had been built in a large garden facing the canal; I knew this little house and garden well, for Jabbar, as irrigation engineer, had free use of the place and often brought his sister Khadija, Bob, and me here for picnics. Today, however, we passed on to a section of canal that I could not remember having seen before, and drove along for nearly half an hour until the cousin stopped the car near a plowed but unplanted field. Aziza indicated that we would get out and walk a little while the men went on ahead to hunt. In this way they would not intrude on our privacy while we strolled, and they would return for us when they had bagged a brace of partridge.

Strange as it seems to me now, I realized as we got out of the car and breathed deeply the country air how long it had been since I had had a chance to walk aimlessly for pleasure. It was not the sort of thing that ladies in El Nahra did; they were busy most of the day, and in their leisure hours they hardly felt the need of more exercise. Even if they had, they were expected to stay indoors with their families and not wander about in public view.

The three of us struck out over the furrows of the field, clutching our abayahs up slightly above the ankles so that we would not trip on the uneven earth. We walked away from the road toward the bank of an irrigation canal no longer in use. The bank formed a fairly high ridge where Aziza had suggested we might sit for a better view; from there we could easily see the car when it returned.

"How lovely it is," said Laila. It was the first time she had spoken since we had left my house.

"It is good for the mind, the countryside and its scene," said Aziza to me, in her stilted not-quite-colloquial English.

I looked about me and agreed.

Brown and green, the flat land stretched away to the horizon, a horizon which seemed only a flat base for the arch of the sky. Over and above the ridge toward which we walked the camel-thorn grew, its spiny branches picked out clearly against the wide emptiness of that cloudless sky. A few small undistinguished birds rose from the brush and whirred over our heads toward the water of the canal, and as we neared the bank we heard a deep, pulsating note.

"It is the calling of the partridge," said Aziza, and began telling me the Arabic names of the birds and plants. Laila was not listening; she walked along with her head down, apparently deep in thought; I had never seen her so quiet.

Suddenly over the ridge three children appeared, two barefoot boys with shocks of black hair and a girl in a ragged abayah, carrying a baby on her hip. They stopped dead at the sight of us, as surprised to see us as we were to see them in this apparently empty place. Aziza spoke to them, but they did not answer. After a moment of intense scrutiny, one of the boys bolted down and across the hollow of the unused canal. We were close enough to the bank to be able to see now two or three mud huts clustered on the far side of the canal. A scrap of green, raggedly outlined, marked the garden and I guessed that these were water squatters who had settled near the old canal in the hope of getting moisture from it. When the rains came, the land would just sustain a small crop without further irrigation.

While we watched, the boy disappeared into one of the huts and reappeared with a man. Laila looked frightened and turned to run but Aziza held her ground. The boy pointed, the man started toward us, then seemed to change his mind, for he retreated into the hut again and a woman emerged and came toward us, the boy running ahead and pointing.

"Stand still, Laila," said Aziza. "Where are you going?"

"Oh," cried out Laila, "someone will recognize me and tell my father I have been out wandering!"

"Then cover your face, you silly girl," replied Aziza in her severest, most schoolteacherish tone.

Laila stood still, but she covered her face with her abayah and turned away as the woman neared us.

"*Salaam alaykum!*" called Aziza cheerfully.

The woman did not reply. She had paused on the bank above to stare down at us, three ladies, wearing respectable abayahs, out walking in a strange field. Every inch of her thin, tattered figure seemed to question our presence. She peered over our heads to see if we had escorts, and even I turned around to search for a sign of the cousin's Buick. The road was empty.

Finally she returned our greeting.

"We are out walking because it was such a beautiful afternoon," offered Aziza.

"Where do you come from?" demanded the woman.

"Don't tell her, Aziza," pleaded Laila. "Please don't tell her."

But Aziza recounted in detail the story of our outing while the woman and the tousle-headed children listened; even the baby did not make a sound. After Aziza had finished, there was a long silence before the woman, her old-young face already set into harsh lines of hunger or pain or fear, switched her tattered abayah about her feet ever so slightly and said perfunctorily (she would have been violating all of her social codes had she done otherwise, even in this situation) "*Ahlan wusahlan*. Come and drink tea with us."

We declined with thanks and moved off, murmuring "God be with you" and "Peace be with you," farewells which were not returned. After crossing perhaps half the distance between the ridge and the road, we looked back. The woman and the children still stood in a line against the sky.

When we reached the road, the Buick still had not appeared, so I offered to take pictures of the girls. Laila refused, but Aziza posed by the little arched iron footbridge which crossed the canal; then she climbed the bridge to pose again, leaning on the railing and looking into the water romantically.

The Buick roared up just before sundown and we clambered gratefully in. It was good to be rescued on the lonely road as night approached and the only human habitation for miles those unfriendly families in the mud huts. It was very cosy in the car. The lights were on in El Nahra and it was actually dark when we reached my door. On impulse, I asked the girls to have supper with me, as Bob was eating in the mudhif.

Over cold chicken and salad, watered yogurt and tea, Aziza became quite eloquent. The subject was tribal purity, and Laila supported her effusively on every point. Neither girl, it appeared, would ever dream of marrying a man not of her own tribe.

"It is—it is—" fumbled Aziza, looking desperately for an explanation which might appeal to my strange Western mind, "it is like the British royal family," she finished triumphantly. "They do not sully their bloodlines. Why? Because they are proud of their lineage. That is the way we feel."

"But if a man from another tribe were very handsome and very rich would you marry him?" asked Laila.

"I might like to, if I saw him and fell in love with him," said Aziza.

"I would, if my father asked me to," burst out Laila.

"Any girl would do whatever her father asked," retorted Aziza, "but my father would never ask anything like that. In our tribe we are very tall and we want to keep the tallness."

"Of course," said Laila politely, and then to make amends she added, "your cousin is very tall."

"Yes," said Aziza.

At that moment Mohammed called through the shuttered window to ask if he could speak to me privately. I was surprised, for Mohammed never interrupted or intruded when I had guests, especially women. I excused myself, and Aziza asked me as I went out whether Mohammed could walk her home, as she did not like to return to the school alone in the dark.

Mohammed waited in the kitchen.

"Sitt," he burst out without even a prefatory greeting, "something very bad has happened."

"What?" I cried, my mind jumping to a vision of Bob lying dead in a ditch out in the middle of the plain.

"It is Laila," he said.

"Laila?" I echoed, in some perplexity.

"Yes, Laila. Isn't she in your room now with the schoolteacher?" I nodded.

"Didn't you take her with you this afternoon?"

"Yes," I said, still not understanding.

"You should not have done that," said Mohammed solemnly. "In fact, you should never have gone at all without asking your husband."

My first reaction was one of irritation. What right had Mohammed to tell me what I must and must not do?

"Thank you very much, Mohammed," I said as calmly as I could, "but I am sure my husband would not object. After all, I was with the schoolteacher, whom everyone respects."

Mohammed brushed my reply aside with a gesture of impatience. I could hardly believe that this was Mohammed, who never spoke like this to anyone, and had never presumed to discuss my conduct with me. But he continued firmly, "Sitt, you are a foreigner and although you wouldn't, I should think, want to ruin your good name, you don't have to live here. The schoolteacher's cousin is a very bad man; he drinks and gambles and stays with bad women in Diwaniya."

I opened my mouth to interrupt but Mohammed held up his hand warningly.

"Laila is in great danger," he said. "If anyone"—he paused and repeated "—anyone were to know that she went riding with a strange unmarried man without men from her family present, she could be killed. Her father would have to do it to save the honor of the other women of the family. Do you understand?"

Yes, now I did understand, with the sickening realization that one has as a child of being caught in an act of serious wrongdoing, conscious that there will be no discussions or excuses, no opportunity to explain. It is done and one is to blame and waits for punishment.

"What shall I do, Mohammed?"

"You must deny that Laila was with you. Say it was a cousin of the schoolteacher. I know Laila went and so do some of the children who saw you go, but I will deny it and so will the children because they like Laila."

"But Mohammed, she is here now, eating supper with me. Everyone will know that, and will see her leave."

Mohammed paused. "You could say that she came after the ride to eat supper with you," he decided. "Perhaps you had better explain to the schoolteacher."

I went in to Laila and Aziza, where they sat chatting happily, and told them what Mohammed had said. "We must swear it was a cousin of yours in the car, Aziza," I finished, "and all stick to that story."

"Yes," said Aziza.

Laila's holiday manner disappeared as I talked; she now rose abruptly, knocking her half-full glass of tea all over her abayah. I pushed my handkerchief at her, but she did not take it.

"Never mind, never mind," she said and wiped ineffectually at the wet abayah with her hand.

"I must leave," she said, shaking our hands perfunctorily and going out quickly.

Aziza and I were left looking at each other. "I should have known better," she said. "I know how conservative these people are; after all, I grew up as Laila did. That is why I made a point of asking whether her father would allow her to go. When she said yes, I was too careless to press it further.

"We must say nothing," she added. "The least they can do is to beat her. Let us hope they do nothing worse."

Mohammed coughed discreetly outside the window where he was waiting to escort Aziza home. He would walk, as he walked with me, a few steps ahead to lead the way; and he would wait until the school gate had clicked shut behind Aziza and only then return.

Aziza took my hand.

"I'm sorry our lovely afternoon finished this way," she said.

My face must have shown what I felt, for she added quickly, "Don't worry, please. If no one will admit that she went with us, it will be all right.

When Aziza had gone, I sat appalled at the possible consequences of my thoughtlessness. I tried to busy myself tidying up our two rooms, but I had a bad hour, alternately imagining Laila weeping and beaten, or Laila thrown into the canal and drowned (would they tie her hands and feet?). There should be something I could do to help, but, alas, there was nothing. What I had done could not be repaired by any words or action of mine.

Bob's appearance was hardly reassuring. He had just spent an extremely uncomfortable half hour in the mudhif being scolded by Nour for his husbandly neglect in letting me go out alone. Poor Bob had been at a disadvantage, but he had been away from El Nahra the entire afternoon and knew nothing of what had happened.

"I covered you, I think," Bob said, "by saying that I had told you beforehand that you could go, but I didn't know anything about the sheik's women, fortunately. When they asked me who was in the car with you, I said quite truthfully that I had no idea. But I have never seen Nour so upset. He spoke very abruptly. He has never acted this way in all the time we have been here."

Bob was as upset as I.

"I'm afraid you've made quite a blunder," he said. "You might have asked me before you went. You've made me look foolish and compromised your friend."

"I know, I know," I wailed, "but what can I do?"

He thought for a moment. "I think you probably should stay here, but I had better go back to the mudhif and act as if nothing were wrong. Maybe I can find out what is happening."

We both knew this was unlikely. Whatever Laila's punishment, it would be administered behind the high walls of her house. What actually took place would be known only long after.

Bob on his return had little to report. Nour had seemed calmer, but had repeated his earlier strictures on Bob's conduct. "Nour is being over conscientious because Sheik Hamid is in Baghdad," Bob said.

"If only the teacher's cousin hadn't been such a rake," he added, "I have the feeling it might not have been so bad. Nour may be afraid that the cousin will gossip about Laila and you in the Diwaniya coffee shops. Then the tribe will lose face. This business of the good name of their women being the honor of the tribe is no joke."

Neither of us slept much that night. I reproached myself again and again for being so thoughtless. After all, Aziza had asked Laila and she, Laila, had made her own decision about going. It was not all my fault. But I knew that I should have been perceptive enough to realize that it was an almost unheard of action for as sheltered a girl as Laila. I was older and, as a married woman, theoretically I was more responsible. On the other hand—and so I argued back and forth.

Mohammed, when he came in the morning, had not dropped his role of counselor-adviser. This must mean that the situation was still grave, but when I asked he said he did not know what had happened. He told me not to visit Laila's house but instead to visit the sheik's house. This seemed like a good way to appear unconcerned and a wise move in general, but I found it very difficult to walk up the path that morning, past Laila's house (what was going on inside?) and into Selma's courtyard. I sat down in the bedroom and prepared myself to face questioning. Selma and Samira sat with me, and Kulthum came in to drink tea. Several other women stopped momentarily, but an hour passed with no mention of yesterday.

Bob told me at lunchtime the men had stopped talking about it in the mudhif. I asked Mohammed at nightfall if he had heard any news.

"Laila is all right, I think," he said, "but she hasn't been out of her house all day, and neither have her sisters."

At this I felt a great sense of relief, although Mohammed warned me again never to mention the episode to anyone. It would, he said, be all right for me to visit Laila the next day.

Laila greeted me cheerfully. I had just about decided Mohammed had exaggerated the seriousness of the whole affair when Laila left the room, and her three older sisters came in and closed the door. They proceeded to give me the politest, most cutting lecture I have ever received.

I was thoroughly embarrassed as the girls pointed out the damage I had nearly done.

"We know that you don't understand our ways," said Fatima.

"We realize you didn't mean any harm," put in Nejla.

"We just wanted you to understand . . ." Sanaa left her sentence unfinished.

None of the three actually mentioned the facts of the case, and when I put in, rather crossly, that after all Laila had come of her own accord, they merely looked at their hands.

Finally Fatima said, "Yes Beeja, we know she should not have gone. We have scolded her already, but she is young and silly. You are older and a married woman and have been to school. If our father knew for certain, he would beat her very hard. We were all so frightened for Laila last night."

The three girls stared at me in a somber way, while I felt they were willing me to imagine the things that might have happened to Laila. I dropped my eyes before that steady, virtuous, oppressive gaze, saying I was very sorry for the trouble I had caused.

Fatima caught me by the hand. "We will never mention this again," she said.

Gradually our pattern of visiting re-established itself, the men in the mudhif no longer discussed the question, and I thought the incident forgotten completely. But two months later I was drinking tea with Selma. We were discussing I don't remember what, when she casually asked, "Who was in the car with you, Beeja, when Sitt Aziza took you for a ride?"

"Aziza's cousin from Diwaniya," I replied promptly.

"What was her name?" inquired Selma, pouring a little hot tea into the saucer and blowing it.

"I've forgotten."

"Many people say that it was Laila in the car," said Selma, offering a little of the cooled tea to her three-year-old daughter, who sipped it noisily.

"They are wrong," I lied.

One of the women said, "But my daughter told me she saw Laila get into the car."

"So did mine," put in another.

My uneasiness was growing, but Selma cut the two women short. "Didn't you hear Beeja?" she asked. "Are you calling our guest Beeja a liar?"

No more was said. But I began to realize that Bob and I would never be other than foreigners, even though our efforts to conform to the local customs might prove ingratiating. No one would seriously blame us for our lapses, but we had to recognize our responsibility when, on our account, other people were exposed to blame or shame or worse.

How little I really knew about the society in which I was living! During the year I had made friends, I had listened and talked and learned, I thought, a great deal, but the pattern of custom and tradition which governed the lives of my friends was far more subtle and complex than I had imagined. It was like the old image of the iceberg, the small, easily recognizable face on the surface of the water giving no idea of the size or shape or texture of what lies beneath.

In **Guests of the Sheik** we encounter yet another form of social organization, a large **nation-state,** which has as smaller political units within it tribal **confederacies** made up of tribes that seem to prefer but do not insist upon tribal **endogamy.** The tribes are broken down into smaller units that are already familiar to us—clans and lineages. Like all societies, the Iraqi group described here has a moral code that prescribes conduct, and this particular society possessed very highly developed concepts of hospitality and tribal honor. It is a characteristic feature of human social systems, which, unlike the social systems of insects, must be learned through socialization, that not only do we internalize the rules of our society but we come to believe they are **right.** This has much to do with our seeming inability to accept the customs of others.

The situation described in this selection underlines another important facet of fieldwork—the sex of the fieldworker. A male anthropologist, for example, often finds it difficult, and sometimes absolutely impossible, to work with female informants. Even if he can work with them he cannot readily obtain certain kinds of information. Female fieldworkers have problems as well, although they are of a different kind. Thus it is obviously desirable for both male and female investigators to work simultaneously. However, this has only rarely been the case, and the overwhelming majority of ethnographic accounts have come to us through the efforts of a single person. As the majority of anthropologists have always been male, it is unfortunately but realistically the case that the anthropological literature has a decidedly male bias.

The closing paragraph of Elizabeth Fernea's story is worthy of a second reading. The apt analogy with an iceberg points up on the one hand the complexity of cultures, and on the other the relative superficiality of our knowledge. However inadequate their accounts may be, anthropologists have been virtually alone in their attempt to overcome the superficiality.

The Ferneas have spent a great deal of time in the Middle East. In addition to **Guests of the Sheik** Elizabeth Fernea has written **A View of the Nile: The Story of an American Family in Egypt** (1970) and **A Street in Marrakech: A Personal Encounter with the Lives of Moroccan Women** (1975). Robert Fernea, with photographer Georg Gerster, has produced a delightful and informative book on Nubia, **Nubians in Egypt: Peaceful People** (1973). He has also written **Shayk and Effendi: Changing Patterns of Authority Among the El Shabana of Southern Iraq** (1970).

Anthropologist Carleton Coon wrote two early ethnographic novels dealing with a most unusual group of people in the same general area of the world. They are **Flesh of the**

Wild Ox: A Riffian Chronicle of High Valleys and Long Rifles (1932) and **The Riffian** (1933). True classics on the area include Charles M. Doughty's **Travels in Arabica Deserta** (1921) and **Seven Pillars of Wisdom,** by T. E. Lawrence (1935). A more recent and excellent book in this vein is **Arabian Sands,** by Wilfred Thesiger (1959). **Sons of Sinbad,** by Alan Villiers (1940), deals with seafaring Arabs, and another of Thesiger's books, **The Marsh Arabs** (1964), portrays a unique group of people inhabiting the marshes of Southern Iraq.

Still other books of more strictly anthropological interest about this general area of the world are Donald P. Cole's **Nomads of the Nomads** (1975); Vincent Crapanzano's **The Hamadsha** (1973); Alois Musil's **Manners and Customs of the Rwala Bedouins** (1928); **Arab Village,** by Richard T. Antoun (1972); Frederik Barth's **Nomads of South Persia** (1964); **Bedouin of the Negev,** by Emanuel Marx (1967); and Ibn Khaldun's three volume account, **The Muqaddimah,** translated in 1958.

A very early silent documentary film on this general region was **Grass** (1925), which depicts the struggle of an Iranian tribe to find grazing for its flocks and herds. **Land and Water in Iraq** deals with ecological factors in modern Iraq. Also see **A Day Among the Berbers** (1947) and **Kabylia** (also on the Berbers, 1947). **Sahara, La Caravane du Sel** (1969) deals with a Tuareg salt caravan, and **Touareg** (1940) is a more general treatment of the culture. **Islamic Mysticism: The Sufi Way** (1971) is a beautifully photographed film on one of the religions of the area.

15

Deprivation

RENA GAZAWAY*

Throughout the greater history of anthropological field-work, anthropologists have been far too busy—either in traveling in remote parts of the globe or attempting to "salvage" what was left of American Indian cultures before they disappeared entirely—to pay much attention to their own contemporary culture. Only in very recent years, as the seriousness of our own social problems was reaching a peak, have anthropologists done extensive ethnographic work in the United States. Since many anthropological research projects have been undertaken in response to felt "problems," the published results of these studies tend naturally to give a rather negative view of American culture. Thus the complaint is often voiced that social scientists "never say what is right about American culture." An anthropologist observing his own culture must almost inevitably appear to be a social critic. Indeed, as the following account demonstrates, it is often difficult not to be outraged as well as merely critical.

Rena Gazaway is a nurse who has also been trained in anthropology and education. She spent over a year in "Duddie's Branch," the Kentucky "hollow" which is the setting for the following passage from her book **The Longest Mile** (1969). The kind of poverty she depicts is often neglected due to the greater interest in urban poverty. The isolation of the "Duddie's Branchers," allows the author to observe them closely and to show clearly how a well-defined **subculture** such as theirs could come into existence and perpetuate itself. The reader learns, although he may not understand, how the more powerful parent culture contributes to the situation.

The Longest Mile is an unusual book, which very effectively combines statistics and tables with extremely moving descriptions of the plight of the hollows people. Rena Gazaway makes use of irony to cloak her natural feeling of outrage that such conditions can be tolerated in a supposedly "civilized" nation. Since she was raised in a very similar environment in Missouri, it is perhaps surprising that the author remains as objective as she does. The picture she gives us is a bleak one—one that seems to offer no promise of meaningful change.

> The three problems of the age—the degradation of man by poverty, the ruin of woman by starvation, and the dwarfing of childhood by physical and spiritual night.
>
> Victor Hugo
> **Les Misérables**

Press a handkerchief to your nose and plunge into the slick, muddy necropolis of the living dead—Duddie's Branch. The narrow artery that dissects the ripe community is a fetid, honeycombed, mile-long creek bed of slime stippled by debris-draped rocks. A miasma of malodorous mortals and garbage slams into your stomach the deeper you penetrate and even the packs of limp-tailed ravening dogs slink about with compressed nostrils. On wintry mornings, pungent waves of wood smoke scald your throat and when the sun burns off the pearl from the dense atmosphere, a microcosm of poverty is exposed between gloomy canyon walls. Tarpaper shanties, tilting drunkenly on rock stilts, huddle along the scabrous banks of the creek and trash is strewn about with riotous imagination: under the dwellings, on the porches, in the yards, on the banks, in the stream. Shells of abandoned automobiles, silhouetted against the opaque horizon like squat sepulchers, are left to corrode and crumble in the Valley of the Poor.

The substandard houses rival the trash for space. Two thirds (65.5 per cent) of the fifty-five dingy shacks cling to the very edge of the Branch; 70 per cent are separated from one another by fewer than two yards and 16 per cent are removed from their neighbors by an additional yard or two. A coal storage shed and a chicken coop also serve as dwellings, but these structures are not included in the total number of residences. All of the shelters are constructed of random combinations of old, weathered boards (some have a clapboard lean-to attached to the back or side), but none is insulated. Only 12 per cent have the benefit of exterior finish, while the rest are partially protected with flapping sheets of tar-treated canvas. When dry twigs are not available to start a fire on cold mornings, the inhabitants rip off chunks of the tarpaper for fuel and spasmodic wisps of blue-gray smoke soon begin to writhe from clay pipes that protrude from the huts like Penrose drains. Little by little, the exterior reverts to rough lumber and even houses that are painted fall prey to the uncompromising weather that claws away enamel and denudes wood.

No surfaced paths lead to or around any of the hutches. A few flat stones have been dropped in the black pool the hollowers euphemistically call a yard, but these are glazed over with a slippery film of wet clay. Charybdis and Scylla await you. "Better take t' th' mud," Jabe counseled. "Footin' hain't fur sure on 'em thar rocks." But I tried. After two or three hard falls, a laceration or two, and soiled clothing, I sensed the wisdom of his recommendation. "Hit's better t' git mud on just 'em shoes than t' spread hit all over," he reasoned.

In the dwellings that have windows, the general tendency is to install the type that do not open because they are cheaper and easier to cobble in. Except for letting in light, they say, there is no need for windows—the flies will just have to come in through the door. Ventilation is no problem; construction defects are so extensive that air, snow, rain, dust, and small creatures circulate freely through every part of the house.

The adequacy of the shelter is proportionate to the degree of discomfort. If a leak from the roof trickles into the room, measures are taken to keep the bed dry. If the leak is not above the bed, it is left to drip and find a hole in the floor boards to escape through. "Hain't no use hurryin' hit by sweepin'; hain't got nothin' to sweep with nohow." What about a mop? " 'Em things costes money 'n' I hain't never had a hankerin' fur fancy things. Hain't no need wastin' stren'th t' do somethin' nature's plannin' on doin' anyways. Th' warter'll creep yander through 'em cracks.

"You's gotta keep movin' if'n you's wanta keep outta th' way'a 'em drippin's. I knows whar they is 'n' if'n hit's measly rain I sits in 'at thar place, but if'n hit's a hard rain I runs outta places t' sit. Sometimes I cain't git th' younguns off t' larnin' 'cause they's duds gits froze on 'em while they's sleepin'. But if'n we stirs early we kin git th' ice thawed out 'n' they kin wiggle in 'em. 'Course if'n hit's bad cold, they's plum froze agin w'en they gits t' school."

The houses all lean backward or forward and you soon become accustomed to walking uphill or downhill in them. Since well-being is not immediately threatened, floor joists are not repaired.

"Somethin's bound t' give 'way 'neath thar one 'a these days," Al perceptively noted.

"Shouldn't you take a look and fix it now?"

"Nope. Cain't be sure w'at's gonna need fixin' first. Hain't plannin' nothin' till I's sure."

Al's equilibrium has to operate on a full-time schedule too. He notes his shack is "leanin' right smart." But as long as it is still standing, he figures he won't bother it.

The first and only step to Meander's door is three feet in height. If you are wearing a tight skirt, you can ascend it best by being launched from a pogo stick.

"Why in the world did you build your step so high?" I demanded.

"'At way I only needs one t' git t' m' door. 'Sides, I 'uzn't plannin' on nobody comin' in but me 'n' I's got long laigs."

My head collides with the ceiling in Willis' house. I have the choice of a possible spine curvature from standing in a stooped position throughout the visit or being rendered anemic by the legions of aggressive bedbugs which engage a vicious assault the moment I sit down until I leave. A considerable number of suicide squadrons embed themselves in the seams of my clothing and carry the battle to my camp.

"We's all built low t' th' ground, 'n' figgered thar warn't no point in buildin' a tall roof," Willis apologized. "Hit heats easier low down 'n' you's cain't live near th' roof nohow."

The broken-down stoves cannot compete with the wind that whistles through the shacks and the inhabitants stay cold all winter. You don't expect to thaw out until summer, I am told, so you just heat the spot that is coldest. At first, this was impossible for me because I was literally cold all over. I took to wearing thermal underwear and socks, lined boots, and wool suits in order to be reasonably warm. I even slept fully clothed and kept shifting position during the night to distribute the reflective heat of my body to different areas. My early reluctance to sleep in boots was shattered the first morning I tried hobbling about on two functionless appendages at ten degrees below zero.

Fuel represents such a large financial investment that the coal pile is a status symbol in the Branch. The few families that can afford to purchase a ton at a time would not think of storing it; it is left in the open for their neighbors to envy. If the coal reserve is modest, it is concealed. Letcher kept his two or three bushels in an old car body whose interior accessories were all missing.

"What happened to the insides?" I asked.

"We burnt w'at we could 'n' junked th' rest," he answered.

One of the doors had also vanished. Letcher explained that since none of the doors could be tightly shut, it made no difference if one was altogether removed, and why bother opening it each time coal was needed?

Most of the families have no fuel supply at all, but collect the small pieces of coal that fall from trucks as they round curves on the highway. They go out daily and search the highways for enough pieces to fill half a gunny sack, which is about all they can carry on their backs. In severe weather they must go foraging two or three times a day.

I was walking toward my jeep, having just watched a late, late movie on television with one of the families, when I caught sight of Willis walking down the Branch.

"Are you heading out?" I shouted to him.

"Reckon, Jerry's croupin' so we's gotta have a fire. I's borryin' some snake oil, too, if'n I gits up inta th' next Branch."

"At two o'clock in the morning?"

"They's prob'ly not sleepin' no how. Mostly huddlin' in this cold."

I drove him to his sister-in-law's shack in the next Branch. He opened the door without knocking.

"It might be better to knock," I advised.

"Nope. They's hain't got no gun. Anyways, they's slow t' stir w'en hit's cold."

It was as frigid inside the house as it was outside and I stood shivering while Willis conformed to prescribed protocol before making his request. On the return drive, I expressed concern that he would be unable to find coal in the dark.

"Reckon I won't look fur litterin's now; hit's too cold. I'll jist borry a piece hyur 'n' thar on my way in. Won't need much till sunup w'en I kin scour th' highway. Don't never need much nohow, 'cause we's only got one room and they's seven 'a us fur huddlin'."

Willis' story is typical of the hollow. The shapes and sizes of the dwellings vary, but the majority are overcrowded. In 67.7 per cent of the families, three or more persons sleep in one room and in 20 per cent anywhere from five to ten or more people share the same quarters. The houses cannot be classified in terms of rooms because one chamber usually serves multiple purposes—sleeping, eating, living, cooking, bathing; the homes must be classified in terms of space. The living area considered minimal for human requirements is 102 square feet per person, but statisticians seldom poll the Duddie's Branchers. Jude and his wife always have twelve children at home, and when their married daughter, her husband, and child stay with them—which is most of the time—the minimum space requirement is 1,794 square feet for seventeen persons. There are only 343 square feet of space in Jude's house, or an 81 per cent deficit of the minimum need.

Privacy, a retreat from noise and confusion, and a place for the children to play are not available. Youngsters are sent out even in raw weather to allow mothers and fathers a brief respite from the din and overcrowding. The unwholesome sleeping arrangements cannot be modified so easily, and parents and children of different sex sleep in the same room frequently in the same bed. Many times I have bedded down in the middle of a urine-soggy mattress with three children on either side of me and two or three at my feet. We all slept in the fetal position, not through choice but through necessity. If by "stirrin' time" we were one degree removed from paralysis, we had the rest of the day in which to coax our numbed limbs to respond to mental commands.

The living deficiencies are not confined to comfort and space. Water is a scarce and, for the most part, impure resource in the Branch. All but one of the twenty-three sources supplying the area have been tested for bacteriologic quality. Three contained potable water, three were questionably potable, and sixteen were contaminated. Five of the former are sufficient in quantity and serve eighteen per cent of the population. The remaining 82 per cent make do with polluted and/or insufficient water. The least brackish must be used for human consumption and parceled out frugally; miners and students attending one-room rural schools must furnish their own daily water requirements, which they carry in a jar. Many of the families use the contents of the creek several times over, even when it looks and smells like sewage: first, for washing hands, then for washing dishes; next, fruit jars are washed in it, after which it is used to wash the laundry; finally, it waters the livestock or a bite-sized garden plot.

During the time I lived in the Branch the creek was very low for a few weeks and what little water remained was as thick and dark as chocolate milk. Despite its appearance, the residents continued to avail themselves of it by siphoning off the top with a Coca-Cola bottle. I asked one boy how long it took to fill a tub in this manner. "If'n I gits hit filled afore you's drive up th' Branch, hit don't take more'n two hours," he solemnly replied. "But if'n you's stirs up th' mud, hit takes a heap longer."

The expense of drilling and the uncertainty of finding water are significant factors in discouraging the Branchers from sinking wells. Beyond that, they have adjusted to their desertlike existence and the need for an abundance of water rates low on their priority list; anything in excess of drinking and cooking requirements is not considered essential. No one can divine whether their sanitation would be improved if water were plentiful, but as the situation stands now, they bathe remarkably infrequently. "'Udn't be much reasonin' t' usin' a bucket 'a warter jist fur warshin' up with. We'uns hain't much fur takin' off our duds nohow," declared Dana. "Scourin' younguns is a waste 'a time too. They's dirty filthy agin afore you's gits 'em clean th' first time. I jist scours up th' ones 'at's goin' schoolin'.'"

Although four of the dwellings have kitchen sinks, only two have running water (the quantity of which varies with the weather). Three of the sinks drain directly under the houses, and one drains into the Branch. I mentioned the virtues of a drainage system to Claude, who does not endorse extravagant expenditure of energy. "If'n th' warter gits t' crowdin' me 'r m' shack, reckon I'd stir 'n' send hit headin' out."

"But what if it ran across Tiny's yard?"

"'At 'ud be his problem. If'n I's rid 'a hit, hain't my worry."

None of the fifty-five households has an inside toilet and only one has a privy that can be described as "good," and one other as "fair." Twenty-one of the families use toilets that are unfit for waste disposal and thirty-two families have no privy. The rocky nature of the soil partially accounts for the absence of suitable pit toilets; the other reason is that most of the hollowers fail to see the advantage of building a facility to satisfy their simplest needs. "Hain't no use buildin' fur somethin' nature's s'posed t' take care of. 'Sides, thar hain't no sense in pilin' shit in one place; hit'll stink if'n you's do."

On the basis of this simple philosophy, the somewhat seasonally related use of the toilets is easily understood. They are occasionally utilized in the summer, but outhouse traffic is light in cold weather or rain—particularly to those conveniences without roofs. Human excreta is consumed by the dogs which, in the words of a Brancher, "gotta eat somethin'." But the dogs do not dispose of it quickly enough; it is very much in evidence in the houses, on the porches, and in the yards.

To ascertain the value dimension of an inside toilet, I asked Shelly what he thought one would cost.

He scratched his head. "Heap 'a skin, I reckon."

"If someone gave you one, what would you do with it?"

Shelly was baffled. "Hain't 'xactly sure. Figger I'd not be a-needin' hit, so I'd prob'ly swap hit fur somethin'."

"Who would want it in the Branch?"

"Reckon nobody," he admitted.

"Then with whom would you swap?"

"Jist anyone."

"Anyone, Shelly?"

He deliberated. "Nope. Jist th' feller w'at's got somethin' I wants."

"Like what?"

"Hain't knowin' till I sees w'at th' feller's swappin'," he concluded.

Swapping personal, household, and food items is a general pattern of behavior for most of the men, many of the children, and some of the women. Commodity foods are the most prevalent items of barter, but the frequency with which other articles show up for interchange gives rise to suspicion. Gid Shifter suddenly began displaying a Winchester rifle in the Branch and said he paid ten dollars for it. During the next few days the weapon was swapped back and forth among almost all the families in the neighborhood, with a swap value of eight to ten dollars, until it ultimately became the property of Judey Shifter. Another time, a new television set (acquired for twenty-five dollars) went the rounds for several weeks before it found a permanent home. Although the men never specifically say that most of the barter articles are stolen, the admission is implicit in their general talk and in the low rate of exchange placed on them. Stolen goods are prized as a medium of interchange because they are cheap and can be traded back and forth for small sums of money that can be used to purchase clothing and essentials otherwise unobtainable.

Television sets are popular trade merchandise; it is not unusual to go up the Branch in the morning and see a television set in one home and find the same set in another house on the way down in the evening. The precise number of utilitarian appliances is extremely difficult to determine. Most of the families have radios and television sets, but the majority do not operate—in fact, the cabinet is generally all that remains of the original product. The same situation is true for the cars that stand idle in the hollow. Not only are they not in running condition, they have not enjoyed that distinction for some time. Washing machines constitute another perplexing statistic; almost every porch supports one, but only a few are operative. On one of my visits I asked Marshall why Alice did the laundry by hand when they had a washing machine. Hearing that it had not worked properly for quite some time, I was then curious why it was kept on the porch.

"Reckon hit jist's well set thar's somewhar else. Leastaways, hit's ketchin' a heap 'a things thar hain't room fur otherwise."

Alice washed a few pieces of clothing, emptied the tub into the yard, and sank down on the porch. I referred to the mound of dirty laundry relaxing against the washing machine.

"We's plannin' on warshin' 'em if'n we needs 'em n' if'n we has th' washer a-runnin' 'n' if'n we has soap 'n' if'n we has warter."

"And if you don't get all those things?"

"Cain't rightly tell w'at'll be, then," she calmly responded.

The amount of water available for laundry purposes is the most portentous determinant of how much and how frequently it is done. When the Branch is high there is no problem, but when it is running low this activity is sharply restricted and it is not unusual for the family wash to be done only once every five or six weeks. There is no staggering accumulation of laundry because none of the families has much to accumulate—no tablecloths or napkins, rarely sheets and pillowcases, only a few towels and washcloths, scarcely any underwear, not one sleeping garment, and not more than one change of apparel per person. The most obvious effects of the infrequent washdays are seen in the grimy clothing the people wear and in the two or three towels that serve all family members until they are rigid with use. Notwithstanding the small laundry, this chore is still oppressive. Every wife in the Branch does the washing in the yard all year round because there is not enough space to do it inside or a stove capable of heating a tub of water. The women build a fire close to the creek where the water is most accessible and keep filling and heating their tubs as they need them. The entire wash is done by hand and spread over bushes or on fences to dry.

Most of the work in the hollow descends upon the females who, in addition to the laundry, do the housekeeping, yard duties, and gardening. They are also responsible for collecting coal, getting food supplies, cooking and serving the meals, carrying water from the well or creek, building and tending the fire, and caring for the children. The older daughters are of little assistance, spending most of their time in play activities. Because of the primitive manner in which the tasks are performed, the most routine housekeeping chore is difficult. Few households have more than one pan or a skillet in which to cook food or a bowl or a place in which to prepare it. In the summer the women peel potatoes and string beans on the porches, but in cold weather they must do everything inside. Eating utensils are likewise sparse; when I ate meals with a family I was the only one who sometimes ate from a plate or pie tin and had either a fork or spoon. Everyone else dipped into the pot of beans or gravy with his hands or used the bare breastbone of a chicken as a scoop. I talked to Elsie about applying for a job in Shade as a waitress, and explained the duties. The idea of furnishing each customer with a set of silverware was intimidating. "I sure hain't knowin' w'at outside fellers eats with; I hain't never used nothin' 'ceptin' fingers fur eatin'. Bestes I's findin' a feller fur marryin' 'n' hankerin' fur holler livin'." A few chipped cups without handles are owned by some of the families, but never did I see a saucer. Tin cans are often substituted for cups. The dearth of cooking and eating implements is not of much concern since few homes have kitchen cabinets or other storage places in which to keep them when they are not in use. Dishwashing, therefore, is not a time-consuming task, but it is done in such a perfunctory fashion that even the little time spent in this effort is wasted. In lieu of a sink, dishes are washed in a pan of cold or tepid water. No soap is used to make the job easier, nor are the utensils ever scalded or rinsed to make them more sanitary. As a result, they usually carry stubbornly encrusted remnants of one meal over to the next. The skillet in which corn bread is mixed and cooked is never washed or even wiped out and one generation could well be digesting grains of an adherent layer that fed a previous generation.

The rewards for being a hollow wife must be more spiritual than material. Even the tension-releasing exercise of gossiping conveniently is denied her; there is not one telephone in the neighborhood and all communication is entirely by word of mouth.

Electric lines were run through Duddie's Branch in 1952 and some of the families do pay for this service. Others benefit by having "borried from th' light line. Figgered 's long 's hit's passin', might jist 's well take some 'a hit." The ingenuity of the functional illiterate to tap a power feed line for electric current without the protection of insulated gloves or tools, knowledge of electric power, and understanding of distribution patterns is mystifying. A number of the families, however, neither pay for electricity nor borrow it—they still depend on coal-oil lamps for illumination. "We beds down early so that hain't no need fur dark-seein'. Hain't got nothin' much t' see in hyur nohow."

The truth is grossly understated. With few exceptions, the housekeeping is shocking and the filth defies description. The air is foul with the stifling odor of dried urine, stale cooking, unwashed bodies, dirty clothing. The incomprehensible chatter of children at play drifts through boards and breathing is further endangered as the dust they stir up seeps through the crevices. A wide variety of bugs and rodents, which claim squatter's rights to every corner and loose board, leisurely emerge from their territories and trek to the generous hunting ground—the floor. Food particles are so bounteous that all species grow and multiply in harmony, and even the bedbugs are defiantly secure. Their hosts bear the badges of battle but have neither the means nor the knowledge to exterminate the night-marauding armies. Because they are unequipped to counterattack, the Branchers regard all insects as immortal foes—especially the flying kind that "kin make a hole in you's faster'n a woodpecker kin bore out a livin' tree. Thar hain't no leaves t' fall off w'en we's dyin', but we's dyin' jist as daid."

The floors of the shacks are made of roughly sawed boards between which fissures have been created by the natural aging of the wood. Some of the surfaces are concealed with well-worn linoleums that have molded themselves to the contours of the "humpin' timbers." Cracks also develop in the walls and ceiling and the cold air comes whipping through those that are not invested with cardboard, newspaper, or pages from magazines. Decorating paper is seldom employed; when it is, several different patterns and colors are often seen in one room. Other coverings are used as well. Since none of the houses has closets, anything that is not being worn or that can be hung is suspended from nails. Family portraits also often adorn the walls; pictures of deceased relatives are most often displayed, and those of dead children apparently have more emotional significance than photographs of adults consigned to coffins.

Coal- or wood-burning stoves are used for both cooking and heating purposes. Two families have electric ranges and upon delivery were told that special electrical wiring was required. It took several months for them to save enough money to have the appliances properly installed. A number of the homes have electric refrigerators, but there are many which do not even have iceboxes.

Crude, hand-made tables and benches are found in many homes. They are made of scrap lumber and are neither painted nor stained. Some families own a backless chair or two, but lard cans substitute as a seating facility with astonishing regularity. Dwellings contain filthy, decrepit couches and a few have old, banged-up dressers tucked away in a corner. The most common piece of furniture is a bed, and no other appointments are seen in any of the homes beyond the insufficient, well-worn pieces mentioned.

Personal possessions are as skimpy and shabby as the furnishings. In answer to her teacher's question as to why she was absent from school for two days, Kizzie replied that her dress was being washed and it took one day for the washing, a second for drying. Her shoes were so broken down and shapeless, it was little short of miraculous that she could keep them on her feet. Most clothing is purchased from secondhand stores and, even though it is less expensive than new merchandise, the prices often exceed the value of the item. Faded dresses with missing buttons and belts cost from ten cents to a dollar and none of the clothing is cleaned or washed before it is put up for sale. Children's used shoes are in such poor condition that they are generally rejected, but new shoes that cost two dollars cannot withstand the daily punishment of mud and water for any length of time either. Most children, and some adults, walk about barefooted or in raggedy, soiled tennis shoes several times too large or a size or so too small. Only one man in Duddie's Branch has a wool suit and overcoat, both old but serviceable.

Such grooming articles as nailfiles, hairbrushes, deodorants, and razor blades are seldom acquired. "Rags, dirt, whiskers—we lives like this. You know how much shavin' costes?" Most of the Branchers will spend a lifetime without ever having brushed their teeth and the snags they might retain at the time of their demise will give the grim reaper little cause to wonder where the yellow went. The consequences, however, will be slight: they rarely have an opportunity to bite into anything more solid than blue gravy. It made such a regular appearance at meals that I became one of the most expert finger gravy eaters in the Branch. I learned to eat the thick type in short order and after a brief training period I mastered the technique of eating the thin, watery variety without losing a drop in transit. In the beginning, the blue gravy on three of my fingers provided an interesting contrast with my dirt-blackened hands; after eating several meals of very thin gravy, the trio of digits began to regain a normal appearance, after which the contrast was dramatic indeed. Much to my chagrin, I was unable to match the Branchers' skill in bread-sopping; I could never accurately estimate how much gravy the bread would support or where it was most apt to buckle when overburdened.

When pinto beans make the menu, nothing else does. Sometimes a microscopic piece of pork is available to add flavor to the unwashed pintos. Potatoes, green beans, tomatoes, and sweet corn furnish a refreshing change in the summer. Most commodity foods are staples, and the canned meat is far from a favorite among the recipients. Nonetheless, their very survival depends on the surplus foods and they have no alternative but to overcome their aversion to them. As Herb delphically submitted, "If'n a poke's got nothin' in hit, hit cain't stand up." Those who are ashamed of being on welfare hide the commodities in the hills and return for what remains of them after it is dark. If another resident discovers the cache he is not above helping himself to the most desirable goods and converting them into cash. One day I saw Winn, a ten-year-old, in a clump of trees guarding the family supply of surplus food. I asked him why he was not in school and he told me that he had accompanied his mother for their allotment but that she had to walk six miles farther on to care for an ailing parent. He was waiting for her to help him carry the groceries home.

"What if someone were to come along and take some of your commodities, Winn?" I asked.

"Reckon I'd not be doin' nothin' if'n th' feller 'uz bigger'n me; I'd jist be seein' him takin' 'em. But Paw 'ud hide me fur losin' our grub."

The miners are addicted to a high-glucose diet. Mr. Hiram is of the opinion that sweets are digested easier than anything else in the poorly ventilated shafts. I was in the store a few times and took note of what the men bought for lunch—a pie, an apple turnover, a jelly roll, and nothing more. One man who always took a Pepsi-Cola to work had to stop drinking them when he was transferred to a low coal vein; the combined height of his head and the tilted bottle amounted to more than the sixteen inches from the bottom of the tunnel to the top.

Filth, overcrowding, discomfort, hunger, thirst, rags—these are the ingredients of deprivation; the Duddie's Brancher is its product and a one-way journey to the human slag heap is his destination.

Reva was only six years old when I first saw her, but even at that age she had reached the point of no return. Enormous, deep-set eyes seemed to occupy her entire face and she had not started to school yet because of her small stature; chronic malnutrition had delayed her growth to half of what is considered normal. She lives in a 10 × 10-foot shack with her parents and eleven brothers and sisters.

Reva was always the first to sight me on my way up the Branch and she would run barefooted through the snow or frozen mud to clasp my hand. Jude, her father, told me that he worked in the mines for thirty years (employment records indicate eight or fewer years for short periods) before his poor lungs forced him to quit. He is emaciated and haggard and appears to be fifteen years older than his actual age of forty-three. The army rejected him in 1940 and he considers this unfair. "They's ejected me fur nothin'. Hit warn't 'cause 'a m' shootin', neither—I's right good gunnin'."

"They must have said why they wouldn't accept you."

"They jist mouthed 'at I warn't physical."

The only time he had been away from Earle County was shortly after the army turned him down; he and some other men went to Baltimore to find work but no one would hire them. On his way back to the Branch he stopped in Indiana and tried unsuccessfully to get a job on the railroad. He attended school for three years and thinks that he finished the third grade. Layuna, his wife, has no education.

For a long time this family lived on commodities amounting to thirty-nine dollars a month. The supplies never lasted more than two weeks and Layuna would have to secure an emergency order. Much of the food was thrown out because they either did not know how to prepare it or they did not like it.

The only water available to them is a bucket a day they get from neighbors—when all is well. When the donors are temperamental, they go without water. "If'n they's a mite friendly, we gits drinkin'."

The children are covered with big sores and are often sent home from school because of them. Layuna could not treat the youngsters properly because she never had enough medicine. Although the salve is free, it is only distributed in two-ounce tubes and the amount was not enough to cover the sores of even one child. In addition, each round trip to pick up the ointment cost a dollar and a half. Every time I went into town I would stop for the medicine and once I asked the workers why Layuna was not given an adequate supply.

"If she were, she'd sell it instead of using it on the kids."

I knew that this would not be the case, but kept silent.

I was able to talk a physician friend out of a one-pound jar of the medication and told Layuna that he had sent it to her. All the scabs had to be removed before the ointment was applied, so I had Jude cut the children's hair close to their scalps. It took me one day to remove the crusts from four heads and the next day I tackled four more. The neighbors were not cooperative at this time, so I made compresses from Branch water to soak off the incrustations. Much to my surprise, their scalps remained intact and the scabs finally loosened. When the medication was used up, Layuna asked me to "'preciate 'at feller fur hit."

If these people are not low family on the Branch totem pole, they are but a millimeter away. Their regular welfare applications have not been approved in ten years. "'Em fellers jist hain't took no likin' fur us'ns." One physician reports that Jude is physically sound, while another says that he is unable to work. Jude volunteered to enter a tuberculosis sanatorium so that he could qualify as "disabled," but chest X rays disclosed no evidence of tuberculosis and a test of his "spittin'" was negative.

He returned to the mine long enough to earn "rockin' chair" money, at which time he would quit. When the money gave out, he would work again for a while and this was his schedule for some time. But for many years now the mine operators will not hire him because of his erratic work pattern.

He "borrows" electricity from the REA line and the children scavenge coal along the highway. The fuel is so precious to them that they use it only when Layuna cooks and the children must stay in bed most of the time in order to keep warm.

Most of their children have been delivered at home by the local midwife. The babies come often and are thin and frail and prone to long periods of diarrhea. Layuna does not take them to the clinic because she cannot pay "fur haulin'." When Keith was a year old he weighed only sixteen pounds and could not stand even when holding onto something. He was extremely anemic and malnourished from the daily doses of Castoria his mother gave him to get rid of worms. The Health Department provided Layuna with Duofoam birth control cream, but she refused to use it because she did not think that anyone should "stick somethin' in you's body. I hain't usin' hit; I hain't aimin' hit up me."

Layuna keeps hoping that someday they will live better and she often wonders if anything would improve the children's health. "One 'a 'em nursin' wormans sayed vitins [vitamins] lackin'. If'n I's knowin' 'em, reckon Jude 'ud dig 'em up in 'em fur hills. Hain't costes nothin' then."

One day I asked her what she would most like to have if she were granted one wish. In a home where there was so little, I was curious to hear what she would want.

"Hain't big."

"I don't think I can guess, so you had better tell me."

"Hit 'ud be a picher 'a you."

I tried to bury my emotion. "Oh, Layuna, what good would that do you?"

"If'n you's headin' out fur long, I's still got you's hyur, in a way."

Her wish was granted.

I have sent several people to the hollow and always request that they check on Layuna for me. She never fails to point to my picture on the wall and tell them that I have a house in the head of the hollow, "'ceptin' her hain't hyur 'nuf fur suitin' us'ns." My place is the only one referred to as a "house"; all the others are called "shacks."

"Right nice fixin's in hit, 'ceptin' no picher maker [television]. But I's glad. 'At way we's gits her fur watchin'. Mouths she's from th' 'versity, but she hain't never claimin' high-like. Her's our'n. Hain't naty one afore her took no likin' fur holler folkses. We's prayin' fur her's stayin', 'ceptin' she's claimin' job workin' somewhars. We's hain't th' missin' kind 'a folkses, 'ceptin' we's missin' a heap fur her."

And I miss them and I ache for them. I can hold out my hand for Reva to clasp, but I cannot hold her back from the inevitable journey she has already begun.

The journey that Reva has begun, of course, will lead her inevitably into the same cycle of poverty in which the other Duddie's Branchers are trapped. This cycle is sometimes referred to as the **"culture of poverty."** Some would argue that people can break out of such a culture if they wish, but this claim has little basis in fact for the vast majority. It is a notion that assumes that such subcultures exist only because of lack of motivation on the part of the poor, and it ignores entirely the economic and social factors that bring about and perpetuate such conditions. One could learn much about poverty by studying the affluent, the sources of their wealth, and the means they employ to keep and increase it. But the wealthy are not seen as a "problem" and, in any case, they are not as amenable to investigation.

The Duddie's Branchers are only one example of what are essentially "surplus populations," those for whom society has little use and who for that reason have been left behind. They are mostly unskilled, poorly educated individuals for whom there is no demand in a society that operates at a high level of technological complexity and efficiency. More and more people are squeezed into this category each year. There is no relief in sight for these people, and even now we know far too little about them.

There is certainly no lack of books on poverty in the United States. They have been especially abundant in recent years because of the much ballyhooed but now failed "war on poverty." For good descriptions of white poverty see **Hard Living on Clay Street,** by Joseph T. Howell (1973); **How the White Poor Live,** by M. and P. Pilisuk (1971); **Night Comes to the Cumberlands,** by Harry M. Caudill (1962); and **Whitetown USA,** by Peter Binzen (1970). For an interesting account of the effects of poverty and discrimination on the personality of blacks see Allison Davis and John Dollard, **Children of Bondage** (1940). Also see Ulf Hannez's **Soul Side: Inquiries into Ghetto Culture and Community** (1969), and **Manchild in the Promised Land,** by Claude Brown (1965). For an account of the American Indian's experience of urban poverty see the collection edited by J. O. Waddell and Michael Watson, **The American Indian in Urban Society** (1971).

There are at least two informative films on this particular version of poverty: **Appalachia: Rich Land, Poor People** (1969) and **Mountain People** (1974).

16

A day with Soledad

OSCAR LEWIS*

The cultures we have been reading about—from the small and technologically unsophisticated to the large and technologically complex—may be placed on a rough continuum. Some anthropologists have compared cultures in precisely this way, in terms of a **folk-urban continuum** (Redfield, 1953). In this view it is argued that **folk societies** have a number of characteristics that distinguish them collectively as an **ideal type** and that set them apart from urban societies, which are seen as essentially opposite to the ideal. Folk societies are said to be small, isolated, nonliterate, kinbased, conventional, not highly mobile, and personal (with face-to-face interaction between all or most of the members). They are also said to be homogeneous, in that the members are all of the same ethnic group, the same religion, and so on. The economic system is a simple one, there is little **division of labor,** and there are no great discrepancies in wealth among the members. Urban societies are clearly different.

This widely held view is, unfortunately, in many ways a romanticized one, that tends to picture small-scale societies as being much more harmonious than they actually are. One of the most telling criticisms of the concept is that its proponents attempt to characterize urban societies by the simple assertion that they are the opposite of the folk soci-

* From La Vida, by Oscar Lewis. Copyright © 1965, 1966 by Oscar Lewis. Reprinted by permission of Random House, Inc.

ety, rather than on the basis of independent research on real urban societies. Nonetheless, it is clear that a concept like the "culture of poverty" would make little sense in many of the cultures we have considered.

The person who first developed the concept of a culture of poverty, Oscar Lewis, was also an innovator in the presentation of ethnographic materials. Beginning with **Life in a Mexican Village** (1951), he began to work in great detail with families and individuals. This led to **Five Families: Mexican Case Studies in the Culture of Poverty** (1959), **The Children of Sanchez** (1961), **Pedro Martinez** (1964), and then to **La Vida: A Puerto Rican Family in the Culture of Poverty —San Juan and New York** (1965), from which the following selection has been taken.

Most of these works employ extended life histories that are linked together by virtue of the fact that the individuals recounting them are related to each other. This provides us with more than one view of the same situation and also brings out aspects of the dynamics of interpersonal and family relationships not usually presented. The books are unusually powerful because Lewis typically allows the people to speak for themselves. Much of the text is transcribed directly from recorded interviews, the author adding only some judicious editing and some descriptive passages of his own. A great deal of basic ethnographic information is included in the following passage, which at the same time gives considerable insight into what it is like to be one of the urban poor.

Rosa hurried along Eagle Avenue toward Soledad's house. It was almost nine o'clock and Soledad and her daughters had to be at the Public Health unit by nine-thirty. Rosa had agreed to go along as interpreter. Soledad lived in a four-story tenement in a Puerto Rican neighborhood in the Bronx. Her narrow, ground-floor railroad apartment consisted of a small living room in the front, a kitchen and bathroom in the rear, and two windowless bedrooms between. The living-room window, close to the street, was covered by a screen of heavy chicken wire. In the summertime when the window was kept open and the Venetian blind pulled up, passers-by could easily look into the apartment and Soledad could carry on conversations with her friends outside.

This April morning* the blinds were closed. Rosa entered the tenement hallway, went directly to the kitchen door in the back, and knocked. Soledad's sister-in-law, Flora, a short, thin, pleasant-faced woman of about thirty, opened the door. "Good morning, Rosa," she said with a smile. "I'm coming along too, to see if they'll take the stitches out of Gabi's head." Gabriel, Felícita's seven-year-old son, had come from Puerto Rico a few days earlier to stay with his uncle Simplicio and Flora. The day he left Puerto Rico, Gabriel had fallen and cut his head, and the cut had required nine stitches.

Rosa sat down at the kitchen table. Although the kitchen was clean and cheerful-looking, she saw several cockroaches crawling on the walls and over the sink. On one side of the crowded room were a china cabinet, a large four-burner gas stove, and a table and three chairs. On the outer wall a combination sink and washtub was partially blocked by the refrigerator, making the washtub inaccessible. Soledad often washed clothes in the bathtub. The kitchen walls had just been painted a bright green. They were decorated with religious calendars, plastic flowers, a fancy match holder, a plaster plaque of brightly colored fruit, and a new set of aluminum pans. Fresh red-and-white curtains hung at the window. The linoleum, although worn, was scrubbed clean. On a shelf above the kitchen door stood an improvised altar for Saint Expedito, who brings luck to gamblers. On the altar, before a small straw cross, Soledad kept as an offering a glass of rum, cigarettes, coins, dice, playing cards, and bread and butter.

"Hello, Rosa, I'm almost ready," Soledad called from the far bedroom. "Just wait till I get shoes on these little bitches."

In a few minutes Soledad appeared with her three daughters and her nephew Gabriel. Soledad was an attractive, full-bodied mulatto woman, about five feet four inches in height. She had a broad face with high cheekbones, deep-set dark eyes and a short, slightly flat nose. Her hair, normally brown and kinky, had been straightened and tinted a coppery hue. Today she had it done up in two buns behind her ears.

"Well, let's go or we'll be late and then heaven knows when we'll get out," she said. "Those people fill out forms like the devil."

The three women walked together while the children, dressed in inexpensive though clean clothes and new shoes, skipped on ahead. Catín, Soledad's adopted daughter, was eight and a half years old. She was olive-skinned, with straight brown hair and large brown eyes. Her

*1964.

thin body and plain face had a pinched, sickly look and she walked with a limp because one leg was shorter than the other. Six-year-old Sarita, the prettiest of the sisters, was a slender, small-boned child, with blue eyes, white skin and abundant light-brown hair. Toya, who was only four years old but looked older and larger than Sarita, was an attractive, dark-skinned, robust child with a round face, bright black eyes and tightly curled black hair. Gabriel, also dark-skinned, with closely cropped black kinky hair and several front teeth missing, was dressed in a new gray wool suit, red plaid vest, white shirt and black shoes—the outfit he had worn on the plane.

"Oh, my God, I wonder what they'll tell me at the Health Bureau," Soledad said as they walked along. "If Catín is sick, I'm going to write my mother such a letter! She was the one in charge and she abandoned the child to go off with that *teenager*. She loves her husband more than her grandchild. But she'd better look out. If you harm a child you pay dearly for it. I wonder what came over my mother to take up with that *teenager*."

"He works, doesn't he?" Flora answered. "He gives her what she needs. That's what counts. Nothing else matters. Well, who am I to talk? When I first saw Simplicio he was a tiny boy, and now he's my husband."

"But, Flora, how can you compare your marriage to my mother's?" Soledad protested. "The difference between you and Simplicio isn't so great."

"Well, everyone to his own taste," Flora replied. "Isn't that right?"

"Yes, everyone to his taste, but wait until that kid grows up," Soledad said cynically. "He's bound to meet some young girl and then a kick in the ass is all Nanda can expect. He'll get rid of her. As for me, I've always said I like old men. When I break up with a man, I don't want him to be able to call me 'old hag.' Let him look at himself and see who's younger."

They arrived at the Public Health unit and were told by the receptionist to take the elevator to the second floor.

"Oh no, I won't go up in that!" Soledad protested. "Suppose it gets stuck between floors? I'm always dreaming that I'm in an elevator that keeps going up and down, up and down. Or else up and up without stopping."

"Oh, come on, Soledad!" Flora said, and they all crowded into the elevator.

They were given turn number 7 and sat down to wait. "Ay, I don't like to come to the doctor," Soledad said. "I wonder why I get so scared?"

To pass the time, Soledad began to tease Gabi. "What's the matter with you? You're trembling."

"I was born trembling," the boy answered.

"Ah, you're scared," Soledad said, taking his hand in hers. "That must mean you ran away from something in Puerto Rico. You've got a woman down there, haven't you? Whose wife did you steal, eh?"

"I didn't, Aunt Soledad, really I didn't do anything."

"Yes, you must have seduced some girl. We'll have to send you back to Puerto Rico."

"I won't go back," the boy said, looking worried. "I was hungry there, and everybody beat me, Cruz, Fela, and all of them. I won't go back."

"All right, you can stay here and be my pimp," Soledad said. "you love me, *papito*, don't you?" And she kissed him.

The boy wiped away the kiss. "I won't. I won't be your pimp."

"Oh, yes, you're going to be my man," Soledad insisted, pressing his little hand on her stomach.

"Don't be so fresh with him" Flora said. "He might begin to get fresh himself."

"Oh, when will we get out of here?" Soledad said impatiently. "I can't bear waiting." She fell silent for a few moments. Then she said, "You know, I made a vow to go on my knees from my house to Saint Peter's church if Catín comes out of this well. I wouldn't stop at the greatest sacrifice for my daughter. If He died nailed to the cross for His children, there's nothing wrong in my going to Saint Peter's on my knees. If I had money I'd have Catín treated by good doctors. I'd give my life for that child."

"Did I tell you what Nanda said when I wrote her that Catín was sick?" Flora asked."

"Yes. How could Nanda say that Catín got sick because I beat her! What wickedness! I never beat that child. If a person got sick from beatings, I'd be dead by now. Nanda gave me enough of those."

Finally Soledad's turn came. A tall Negro woman in a navy-blue uniform handed her paper jackets, saying, "Here, put these on the children." Then she began to fill out a form for Soledad, beginning with her name and address.

"And how many children have you?"

"Four."

"Names?"

Soledad gave the children's names, explaining that her son, Quique, was in Puerto Rico with his father.

"How come this little girl's last name is Alvarado?"

"Because she isn't my own daughter. I adopted her," Soledad answered.

"Well, I'd better put them all down as Ríos," the woman said. "What's your husband's name?"

"My husband is dead."

"What did he die of?"

"In an accident." Soledad answered the woman's questions rather sullenly. "What busybodies these people are!" she said in an aside to Rosa. "You'd think I was being jailed for murder."

The attendant asked if Soledad was getting welfare aid. Soledad replied that she was not. "Don't you know you qualify for it?"

"Forget it," Soledad said shortly. "As long as I can work to support my children, I don't want *welfare*. Not the way they treat you."

"Have the children been in contact with anyone who had tuberculosis?" the woman asked.

"Well, yes, with a cousin of mine in Puerto Rico a long time ago. But it was the school doctor who told me to bring the children here." The attendant went out and a doctor came in to give the children the tuberculin test. He then sent them to an adjoining room for chest X-rays, telling them to come back for the results a week later, on Friday.

Before they left the Health Bureau, Soledad spoke to the attendant who had filled out their forms. "Could you take care of my nephew? All he needs is to have these stitches cut."

"No, not here," the woman answered. "You'll have to take him to a hospital for that."

"But we can pay," Soledad said.

"No, we can't do it here," the woman repeated impatiently, waving them out.

"What sons of the great whore they are, all of them! They should have a bomb dropped on them," Soledad exclaimed. "Look," she said when they were outside, "I'm going to cut Gabi's stitches myself. I just know they won't do it at the hospital either. They don't want to take care of him."

Sarita, skipping ahead, stopped in front of a chewing-gum vending machine. "*Mami*, give me a penny," she begged.

"A knife in your back is what you'll get," snapped her mother. "Let's go over to Third Avenue. I have to pawn my ring because I'm flat broke. That stupid husband of mine hasn't sent me a thing. I guess he expects me to live on air."

At the pawnshop Soledad stood admiring her ring while the proprietor waited on other customers.

When it was Soledad's turn, she held out her ring.

"How much do you want for it?" the pawnbroker asked.

"Seven."

"Four."

"All right. Give it to me and let's get it over with." She took the bills and the ticket and put them in her purse. "Let's go to the stationery store and buy some stamps," she said.

Inside the store some small religious pictures caught Soledad's eye. "Say, how much do these cost?"

"Thirty-five cents each."

"I'm going to buy one for Fernanda," she said. "You know, she's writing to me again. It's a miracle. The wings of her heart must have started fluttering." She chose a picture and wrote on the back of it, "Nanda, I am sending you this Saint Anthony so that he will get you lots of sweethearts. Save him as a keepsake from your daughter Soledad."

Leaving the store, she said to Rosa, "Saint Anthony gets sweethearts for you if you stand him on his head. But he's a bad saint. They say the men you get through him always beat you. I'm so unlucky with men, damn it! There hasn't been one good one except for Tavio, and he died. Good things never last."

They passed a Chinese woman and her two children. "Sainted Virgin, that woman looks like the devil's own mother!" Soledad said. "I wouldn't bear a baby to a Chinaman even if they tied me up. They say Chinese men are good husbands and all that, but they're so ugly!"

"I have to go home and cook Simplicio's dinner," Flora said abruptly. She took Gabriel by the hand and turned to leave.

"Yes, go along and take good care of your husband," Soledad called mockingly after her. Then she said to Rosa, "Ay, let's go to the park awhile so the children can get some sun. They're always shut up in the house."

When they reached the park Soledad broke into a run and raced the children to the swings. She picked each one up, set them on the swings and began pushing them. Then, smiling, she stopped Toya's swinging in order to hug the child. "This is *mami's* littlest girl. *Mami's* little Toya. Come, give me a real lover's kiss on the mouth like in the movies." Toya kissed her mother full on the mouth.

"Ummm, good!" Soledad said, licking her lips.

She went to Sarita, who was in the next swing. "Get down, get down!" Holding the child in her arms, she pulled down her panties and kissed her buttocks. Then she touched the little girl's vagina. "And who does this little kitchen belong to?"

"Don't be so fresh, *mami*," the little girl said, squirming free.

Soledad ran to Catín and hugged and kissed her. "Ay, this daughter is almost a young lady already."

"*Mami*, swing me on your lap," Catín said.

Soledad sat down on a swing and took Catín on her lap. As they swung, Soledad looked childishly happy; she laughed aloud like a little girl. After a time Catín slipped from her lap and ran with her sisters to the slides. Soledad began to swing high. When she tired of it she abruptly jumped from the swing and announced, "We're going now."

Outside the house they met Rosalía, an old, stout Negro woman who was a friend and neighbor. She was dressed in black as usual.

"Hello, my darling! How are you?" Soledad called, running up to hug and kiss the woman.

"Keep off, sugar, you aren't my husband," Rosalía said good-naturedly.

"You know you're my darling," Soledad answered as she hurried into the house. She unlocked the kitchen door and went straight to the bathroom. When Rosa and the girls came into the kitchen, they heard her urinating. "I can't hold my urine very long," she said when she came out. "They must have hurt my bladder when they operated on me."

Soledad went to her bedroom and threw herself face down on the big double bed. Because she seemed tired, Rosa tried to keep the girls in the kitchen, but after a few minutes they went to stand quietly beside the bed, looking at their mother with anxious faces. The room was very small and the bedroom set almost completely filled it. Between the bed and the matching dresser there was a space of only sixteen inches, and here the girls lined up. The foot of the bed was so close to the chest of drawers that the two bottom drawers could not be opened more than three inches. There was no closet; clothes were hung from hooks on the wall. Over the bookcase headboard, a shelf held several suitcases and cartons. Underneath the shelf behind a short plastic curtain, a bar had been suspended to hold more clothing.

On top of the chest Soledad had arranged a number of religious objects to form an altar. In the center were statuettes of Jesus, the Sacred Heart, Saint Felícita, the Virgin of Carmen, and the dark-faced Saint Martin of Porres. Around these figures were two candles in candleholders, a vase of artificial flowers, a small crucifix, a paperweight with the figure of Jesus, a gold ceramic incense burner, a bottle of French perfume and three gracefully draped rosaries. On the wall above the chest were eight religious pictures: the Virgin,

Saint Martha, Saint Michael Archangel, the African Saint Barbara, the Heart of Jesus, the Child with the Torch, the Three Virtues—Faith, Hope and Charity—and a large Brazilian picture showing the Virgin as the Queen of the Sea who cast down stars that turned to roses.

Two prayer books lay open on the altar, one opened to "Prayers to the Guardian Angels," the other, a spiritist gospel, opened to "Instructions of the Spirits: In Gratitude for Children and Family Bonds." A glass of water to "catch evil spirits" stood next to the books. Each week Soledad poured the old water down the toilet and refilled the glass.

After watching her mother for several minutes, Catín said timidly, "What's the matter, *mami?*" Toya, who often demanded caresses, said, "*Mami,* please give me a kiss."

Soledad opened her eyes and said crossly, "Oh, go away and leave me alone! I'm all right." Seeing Rosa, she sat up and added, "I'll have to go to the old man. No matter how I stretch them, four dollars won't be enough for the whole week. Oh, I'm all screwed up!"

Suddenly she gathered the children into her arms. "But look at the treasures I have. Aren't my little girls pretty? There's just one thing missing, and that's my son, my only male child. I gave him my tits until he was five years old. Oh, Rosa, you don't know how much a mother loves her children! Look, want to see how beautiful Quique was when he was a baby?"

She got out a photograph album from a suitcase under the bed. Leafing through the album, she showed Rosa pictures of Quique at different ages. Then she came to some pictures of Octavio, her dead husband. In one photograph which had the words "My Heart Is Yours" inscribed on it, he was shown leaning against a counter. In another he and Soledad were together, she in a maternity dress and he proudly touching her stomach. On other pages Octavio's death was recorded. One showed his coffin covered with flowers; there were other photos of the grave. Soledad began to cry, silently at first. She shut the album, flung herself on the bed and sobbed, not caring who heard her. The children, who had wandered off to play, came running in.

"*Mami,* what's the matter? Why are you crying?"

Soledad drew Toya into her arms. "Come here, my little Toya. Where's your *papá?*"

"They killed him. They shot him dead."

"Yes, they did, they shot him dead." Soledad let the child go and turned to Rosa. "I loved that man and I still do," she said. "He was so affectionate, so nice to me. What a thing to happen! He's buried in the cemetery at La Esmeralda. We used to go there to talk and we'd play hide and seek and cowboys and Indians. He'd pretend to shoot me and I'd drop on the ground and then he'd pick me up."

Soledad fell silent for a moment, then stood up and freshened her makeup before the mirror. "Come out with me to call El Polaco," she said to Rosa. "I'll see if he asks me to go over. I just have to get hold of some money." The two women went to a telephone in a nearby store. Soledad dialed a number and then said engagingly. "Hello, lover, how are you? . . . Well, I was wondering about you, too. . . . You don't say! But that's no problem because I'll make it go down in no time at all. I'll be right over, O.K.? See you, darling."

Soledad hung up, and she and Rosa hurried back to the apartment. "Do me a favor, Rosa, and stay with the children? I'll wash up and leave and come right back with some money." The children asked where she was going and she told them she had to buy something in El Barrio. She reminded Catín to tidy up the house and she warned all the girls that they must behave well. When she was gone, the children went back to playing with her old pocketbooks and shoes.

Rosa began to make the beds, and the three girls helped her. Catín tidied the jumble of cosmetics on Soledad's dresser—the small-sized jars and tubes of creams and pomades, the make-up lotion, hair spray, wave set, deodorant, nail polish, powder and perfumes, almost all of the Avon brand. There were also two large eau de cologne bottles and a small bottle of Lanvin perfume. A cracker tin held hair curlers and bobby pins, and a cardboard box was filled with several lipsticks, pins, jewelry, buttons, combs and odds and ends. There were several paperback books, love stories in Spanish and two in English that a neighbor had given to Soledad.

When the bedrooms were neat, Rosa and the girls washed the breakfast dishes and made lunch. Rosa fried some pork chops and bananas, setting aside enough for Soledad. After lunch Rosa lay down on the bed to rest and the girls crowded around her, hugging her and demanding to be kissed.

Rosa was teaching them the English alphabet when Soledad returned at two o'clock. She had been gone an hour and a half.

She came into the bedroom, gave the children some cookies she had bought and sent them to the kitchen, saying, "Don't come in here until I say so." She lit the two candles and knelt with bowed head in front of the altar for several minutes. She did this whenever she was unfaithful to her husband. As there were no prayers in either of her prayer books for a situation like this, she just remained silent until she felt better. When she left the bedroom to go to the kitchen to eat her lunch, her face was serious but she seemed calm.

"*Mami*, where have you been?" Catín asked.

"Don't ask questions. What a little busybody you are!"

"But what were you doing, *mami?*" Sarita said.

"Nothing. It's none of your business. Run away and play."

When the children had gone to the living room to watch television, Soledad said to Rosa, "Look, I got my fifteen dollars. It only takes a little while, because he comes right away."

Someone knocked on the kitchen door and Soledad opened it to Rosalía. "Hello, my love. You can't live without me, eh? What's new?"

"Oh, go to hell," Rosalía answered.

"Don't say that. I want you to take good care of your you-know-what, because it belongs to me."

"And since when have you become a lesbian, you shameless hussy?" Rosalía said, laughing. "Aren't you ashamed of yourself? How's your husband?"

"With a stiff prick, I suppose, since I'm not there to give him anything."

"Have some respect, dirty mouth!"

"Ay, Rosalía, that's the way we talk in La Esmeralda. You talk even worse, because you're from Loíza Aldea, where people aren't civilized yet."

"Now look," Rosalía said, "I came here forty years ago. I've never been back to Puerto Rico and I never will go back. Not even when I die. I want to be buried here where it's cold so the worms won't eat me."

"I want to die in my own country. Me buried here? Oh no!"

"Do you know how much it costs to ship a body to Puerto Rico? About fifteen hundred dollars."

"Don't be a damn fool," Soledad said. "Do you think I'd let myself die here? What an idea! The minute I feel even a little bit sick, I'll fly right back to Puerto Rico."

"I don't even remember what Puerto Rico's like. To tell you the truth, I don't even like to eat green bananas."

"Why, you shameless creature! You don't deserve to live. To think that a countrywoman from Loíza Aldea shouldn't like green bananas! There's nothing better than a dish of fresh-cut green bananas boiled with codfish. Oh, well, let's skip it. Want some coffee? Some soup? A banana?"

"No, no."

"Well then, eat shit if that's what you want. Toya, come over here. Don't you want to make *caca?* Rosalía feels like eating some shit."

"All kidding aside, I don't like to eat in anybody else's house," Rosalía said. "Not since I visited some people and found a gob of phlegm in the kitchen sink. I haven't eaten outside my own house since then."

"*Ave María!* Don't be so finicky. Water cleans anything."

"Oh no, I can't stand dirty habits, like people brushing their teeth over the kitchen sink. Listen, that girl of yours, the dark one, is getting fresh. She won't pay any attention to me any more."

"Tell Benedicto," Soledad said indifferently. "He's the one that spoils her. If I spank Toya, Benedicto practically eats me alive. He'd let her throw the doors out of the windows if she wanted to. But if Sarita, the white one, does anything at all, he spanks her right away. Do you think it's because of Toya's color that he likes her better? She's dark like him."

"That's what it is. You see, a white person sooner or later is going to call a Negro '*nigger.*' You mark my words. A white person will always throw your color up to you. Well, I have to go now. I'm waiting for my son and he's due to show up any minute."

"Oh, drop it, Rosalía," Soledad said. "Do you think that boy is still a baby? He must be twenty-eight years old. He's off some place screwing a girl. Or do you put out for him yourself?"

"Damn it, Soledad, have a little more respect for my son!" Rosalía said in real annoyance. "I love that boy like he was God, girl."

"All right, you love him like God, *chica,* but for God's sake, let loose of him," Soledad answered.

A few minutes after Rosalía had gone there was another knock on the door, and Soledad opened it this time to Elfredo, a white-skinned, baby-faced, dark-haired young man. He was a numbers runner and Soledad bought a number from him almost every day. Today she asked for three numbers, paying fifteen cents each.

After she had finished her business with Elfredo, Soledad suggested that they go into the living room. She sent the children back to the kitchen and sat down with Elfredo on a bulky black sofa in front of the window. Rosa took a large blue chair in the opposite corner. This chair stood in front of the livingroom door, which Soledad kept permanently locked. An orange chair in another corner was occupied by a life-sized doll dressed in black and yellow tulle. A false fireplace covered almost the entire left-hand wall; on the mantel was a profusion of photographs, ceramic figurines of a lion and a panther, a little boat in a stemmed glass, a set of toy animals and, in the center, an African voodoo doll which Benedicto had brought from Brazil. The plaster doll had two faces, a black one on one side and a brown one on the other. Soledad turned the faces around each week. She had more faith in this doll, she said, than in her two black saints. A coffee table that stood in front of the fireplace held a crocheted doily, a set of glass ashtrays shaped like butterflies, and various inexpensive ceramic objects. End tables holding similar objects stood beside each of the big chairs. On one of the end tables there was also a record player; a stack of records was piled on the shelf beneath. A television set occupied a corner between the coffee table and the sofa. The walls also were decorated with objects, a cheap tapestry of "The Last Supper," artificial flowers, ceramic plaques, small pictures, some tiny straw hats, and two necklaces of multicolored plastic fruit with bracelets to match. On the window sill, partly hidden by the cretonne drapes, stood a green plant, some artificial flowers in a brightly painted vase, and a ceramic figure of a naked woman sitting on a beer barrel. A washable gray rug covered the small space in the center of the floor.

The television set was still turned on and they all watched a scene in which a young girl was contemplating suicide because her father had been killed for selling stolen goods and she was left alone and penniless.

"Dope! Idiot!" Soledad said, switching off the set impatiently. "How can she think of killing herself? She shouldn't be such a coward. You have to face whatever life brings. Hell, some people shit on themselves over every little thing that happens to them. I say put a good face to bad times. No trouble lasts a hundred years."

Elfredo looked at Soledad admiringly and said, "You know, Soledad, I wouldn't mind getting married to you."

"How can you say such a thing to me? And with all those sweethearts. Really, how can you? I have four children."

"That's nothing. If you love the hen, you love her chicks."

"You know very well that I have a husband."

"Yes, and I know something else, too. I know you aren't happy with him." He moved closer to Soledad on the sofa. "Come on, give me a kiss."

Soledad leaned back to avoid him but he kissed her on her closed lips anyway.

"I have to go now," he said. "It's getting late and I have to turn in these numbers. But I'll be back tomorrow and I'll be much hotter then."

"It's time for me to leave too," Rosa said. "Will you walk me to the bus, Elfredo?"

They went through the two darkened bedrooms. There was a strong stench of urine from the children's bed. "Those girls are real pissers," Soledad said. "I'll have to change their sheet tomorrow."

In the kitchen, the children were coloring pictures on the floor. Soledad said good-bye to Rosa and Elfredo and double-locked the door behind them.

There has been considerable controversy over the so-called culture of poverty in recent years. Oscar Lewis has been acclaimed by some, but rather soundly criticized by others. The fact is that in spite of many recent studies of urban poverty, we still know far too little about the ways in which such a culture affects those who are a part of it. For perhaps the most cogent critiques of the concept of the culture of poverty see Charles Valentine's **Culture and Poverty: Critique and Counterproposals** (1968) and the volume edited by Eleanor B. Leacock, **The Culture of Poverty: A Critique** (1971).

For some films of special relevance see **Prejudice Film** (1973), **Right to be Different** (1972), **Storm of Strangers** (1970), and **Hunger in America** (1968). Films that deal with particular ethnic groups include **Harvest of Shame** (Mexican-Americans, 1960), **Forgotten Americans** (American Indians, 1968), **Spend it All** (Cajuns, 1970), **Sam** (Japanese-Americans, 1973), and **Nothing But a Man** (Blacks, 1963).

The ethnocentrism of the poor and uneducated, expressed here by Soledad and Rosalia, is relatively easy to understand. Not easy to understand is the ethnocentrism of the more educated and presumably better informed, as in the examples with which we opened this book. Even the brief glimpses of life assembled here should make it plain that all people share a fundamental humanity, no matter how much it may be obscured by cultural overlay. The very fact that anthropologists have been able to make contact, live, communicate, empathize with, and be accepted by peoples everywhere, no matter how different they may appear, is in itself proof of this, although it is most probably not yet fully appreciated. All people must be born of woman, and the overwhelming majority share the experience of being raised in some type of family. All must be **enculturated,** most inevitably mature, marry, procreate, and die. No evidence supports the view that anyone exists who does not feel both physical pain and mental anguish, even though thresholds may vary somewhat. Although some people may accept death more stoically or fatalistically than others, there are none (with perhaps rare exceptions in almost all cultures) who are truly indifferent to death. In spite of what we may wish to believe, there is no satisfactory or convincing evidence that different mental processes or lesser "intelligence" are characteristic of any particular group or groups. Nowhere do people lack a moral code and some basically "religious" sentiment. All people possess some means of social control and some sense of "legality" and of group welfare. All have well-developed systems of kinship and recognize mutual rights and obligations. All provide for the well-being of their citizens—although some, it appears, provide more than others.

Still, there is variation—incredible and perplexing variation—in both individuals and groups. Whereas the social systems of animals are **species specific,** those of humans are not. Whereas the behavior of animals can be said to be programmed primarily by nature, the behavior of humans is largely programmed by culture. To understand this, and to use that understanding for the benefit of all, is what anthropology is all about.

Glossary

Acculturation The process of cultural transmission that occurs when two different cultures are in continuous firsthand contact.

Affinal Relations that come about through marriage rather than through blood.

Age Mates Individuals of roughly similar ages who are bound to each other through the sharing of common experiences such as having been initiated at the same time. Also referred to as *age grades* or *age sets*.

Agnates Persons descended in the male line from a common ancestor. Also termed *patrilineal kin*. Agnates can be contrasted with *cognates*.

Ancestor Worship A religious system that venerates the deceased members of the family or group.

Anthropology Broadly, the scientific study of man. Anthropology is ordinarily broken down into archeology, physical anthropology, linguistics, and social or cultural anthropology.

Avunculo-Virilocal A rule of residence whereby the married couple live with the husband's *matrilineal* kin.

Bilocal A rule of residence whereby the couple live by turns with the husband's and the wife's kin.

Caste A hierarchical type of social organization in which groups are assigned a ranked and presumably fixed status depending on their origins. Hereditary occupations for caste members are common, and there are often dietary restrictions and beliefs about pollution.

Clan A *unilineal* descent group, either patrilineal or matrilineal, within which the precise connections with the ancestral founder, real or putative, are unknown. A clan can be said to be *localized* when the majority of the adults of one sex live together in one place. A clan is *dispersed* when both sexes are scattered over a wide area. Clans are most commonly but not invariably *exogamous*.

Cognates Persons descended from a common ancestor or ancestress. Descent may be traced through males exclusively, females exclusively, or males and females indifferently. Thus cognates include the agnates, *uterine kin*, and all other *kin*.

Compound A type of living arrangement in which the members (usually a *nuclear, extended,* or *polygamous* family) live together in a number of huts or buildings enclosed by a common wall or fence.

Confederacy A league of two or more groups, such as tribes, usually formed for purposes of offense or defense.

Consanguineal Relationships established by ties of blood.

Corporate Group A recognized body of individuals who for some purpose or purposes act together as a single entity. Often the *clan* or *lineage* are corporate groups and their members are considered to be *jural equals*.

Cultural Lag Refers to the fact that some elements or aspects of a culture do not change at the same rate as others with which they may or may not be *functionally related*.

Cultural Relativism The position that there is no single scale of values for all cultures, hence that particular customs, beliefs, and practices must be judged in relation to the cultural context in which they occur.

Culture There are many definitions, but no single accepted definition. The most important elements of the concept are shared behavior and ideas that are cumulative, systemic, symbolic, and transmitted from generation to generation extragenetically.

Culture Change Aside from the obvious meaning, this refers to a recognized subfield of study within the profession of anthropology.

Culture Contact Occurs when members of one culture discover members of another for the first time. Such contact ordinarily then becomes permanent although there may be an interval of years before that transpires.

Culture Hero A mythical person, sometimes a god, who is believed responsible for the group's present position and for the things they possess.

Culture of Poverty A distinctive design for living which results from economic deprivation and which, although it allows the poor to survive, also ties them to their poverty.

Culture Shock The psychological shock felt when one enters an unfamiliar culture.

Descent A relation mediated by a parent between a person and an ancestor. Thus a grandparent is a person's nearest ancestor.

Divination A magical technique for reaching a judgment about something unknown. Divination is extremely widespread, and a great variety of techniques have been reported.

Division of Labor The breaking down of a process or of an employment into parts, each of which is performed by a separate person. Also is used to refer to the specialization of roles that occurs in different societies so that, for example, women plant gardens while men do the hunting, certain individuals become curers while others do not, and so on.

Duolocal A residence practice whereby a married couple do not set up a common household, but continue to live in their respective *natal* homes.

Emic   A term originated by the linguist Kenneth Pike, which refers to the subjective meanings shared by speakers of the same language. It has now come to be descriptive of the meaning of almost any form of behavior as that meaning is perceived and understood by the participants in the culture, rather than by observers or outsiders.

Enculturation   The process whereby man achieves competence in his culture.

Endogamy   The process of marrying within some specified social group.

Ethnocentrism   A view of things in which your own culture is seen as the center of everything and others are evaluated with reference to it.

Ethnographic Novel   This is distinguished from an ordinary ethnographic work because in addition to describing another way of life, it also has developed characters and a plot.

Ethnographic Present   The period of time an ethnographic work describes, regardless of when it was actually written.

Ethnography   A written description of a particular culture.

Ethnohistory   The reconstruction of a past way of life from verbal, written, and other materials.

Ethnomedicine   The cross-cultural study of medical beliefs and practices.

Etic   A term used originally by the linguist Kenneth Pike for the formal analysis and categorization employed by linguists when attempting comparisons. It has also come to have the meaning of something as it is perceived and understood by an outside observer, rather than by the participants themselves.

Extended Family   A family consisting of two or more close relatives along either the male or female line, their spouses and children. For example, a man, his wife, his children, his sons and sons' wives.

Exogamy   The process of marrying out of some specified social group.

Fieldwork   The anthropological method of research that involves prolonged residence in the community being studied.

Folk Society   Defined as an ideal type, this is a society contrasted to our own urban type. It is said to be small, isolated, personal, based on kinship, homogeneous, usually nonliterate, static, and with informal modes of social control and face-to-face interaction between all or most of the members. There are other criteria as well, depending on the particular authority consulted.

Folk-Urban Continuum   An idealized construct with folk society at one end of a continuum and urban society at the extreme opposite end.

Functional Equivalent   A custom or practice that appears to have the same purpose or reason for being as another.

Functionally Related   Related in such a way that a change in one part or dimension will bring about a change in another.

Horticulturalists   People whose primary mode of subsistence comes from tilling the soil with simple implements that can mostly be worked by human power.

Hunting and Gathering Society A society in which the principal mode of subsistence comes from hunting and from the gathering of plant and other foods.

Ideal Type A hypothetical construct that represents a highly abstracted version of something that either exists or is supposed to exist. Folk society, for example, is an ideal type which for heuristic purposes "stands for" a large number of societies said to approximate it.

Incest Taboo A prohibition against sexual relations and/or marriage with certain categories of kinsmen.

Informants Persons used as sources of information by social scientists and others. Usually an anthropologist cannot personally interview everyone in a culture and comes to utilize a number of "key" informants who are willing and able to impart specialized or detailed information about their culture.

Instinctive A term ordinarily used to refer to what appears to be automatic and unlearned behavior.

Jural Equality The condition existing when the members of a group such as a clan or lineage are regarded as legally or conceptually equal. Thus, for example, satisfactory revenge can be taken on a group by killing any member of the group and not necessarily the original culprit.

Kinship The social recognition and expression of genealogical relationships that are both *consanguineal* and *affinal*. Kinship ties can be based on supposed as well as on actual relationships.

Kinsmen Those people who are related to an individual through affinal, consanguineal or adoptive ties.

Life History A biographical account of a person's life written by another when the subject is an illiterate.

Lineage A *unilineal* descent group, patrilineal or matrilineal, within which the specific connections with the founding ancestor are known and the members can say exactly how they are related to each other.

Matrilineal Tracing descent through the female line.

Matri-Uxorilocal A rule of residence whereby the couple live with the wife's matrilineal kin.

Monogamy The marriage of one man to one woman.

Natal Pertaining to birth. Your natal home is your place of birth; the term can also refer to the place you have come to regard as your home.

Nation-State A large group of persons who share a common language and geographical area, and who recognize some central authority with ultimate legal, military, and administrative power.

Neolocal A rule of residence in which a married couple move away from their kin and set up housekeeping in a new place.

Nomadic A group that practices regular changes of locale that are correlated with variations in the food supply.

Nuclear Family A married couple with their children. Also called the elementary family.

Pastoralists A group practicing a form of economy in which the bulk of the food supply comes from domesticated animals.

Patrilineal Tracing descent through the male line.

Patrilocal Residence A rule of residence whereby a married couple live in the community of the husband's patrilineal kin. The terms patrilocal and matrilocal have been replaced in recent years with *virilocal* and *uxorilocal* respectively. These terms are used in compounds such as *patri-virilocal, avunculo-virilocal*, and *matri-uxorilocal*. Residence can also be said to be *bilocal, neolocal,* and *duolocal*.

Patri-Virilocal A rule of residence whereby the couple lives among the husband's patrilineal kin.

Personal Equation The degree to which research is influenced by personality factors of the investigator.

Phratry Two or more linked clans which are joined by some common belief that they are (usually distantly) related in some way.

Polyandry The marriage of one woman to two or more men.

Polygamous Family A type of composite family in which two or more nuclear families are linked through a common spouse.

Polygamy Any form of plural marriage.

Polygyny The marriage of one man to two or more women.

Primitive This term has been used in the past to describe a "native," non-literate small, or "backward" population. It is no longer very commonly used by anthropologists because of the negative and erroneous implications that such people have somehow not evolved culturally.

Primitive Band The most fundamental social group beyond the individual family. The type of social organization found where hunting and gathering form the basis for subsistence.

Primogeniture A system of inheritance in which the oldest heir (usually a son) is favored.

Rapport The relationship established between two or more people based upon common thought, interest, or sentiment. In anthropology, the relationship established between the fieldworker and the people he is working with.

Rites de Passage This term was given by Van Gennep to the ceremonies that occur at key periods in the life cycle such as birth, puberty, marriage, and death. Such rites are seen as helping to ease the emotional trauma of moving from one status to another.

Ritual of Rebellion A rite in which essentially powerless individuals in a society are enabled to symbolically rebel against authority or some other source of their helplessness.

Role A particular behavior pattern associated with a *status*.

Scarification The cutting of the skin for ritual purposes. It can also refer to cutting the skin for beautification, self-torture, or other reasons.

Segmentary Lineage System A form of social organization in which there is no central authority and in which the lineages combine at different levels for common purposes.

Shaman A medicine man. A person with supernatural power who is able to effect cures.

Social Class The position an individual or group holds in a society at some level of the economy. Class is defined in terms of power, income, wealth, prestige, or some loose combination of such things.

Social System The system constituted by the interactions of individuals whose relationships to each other are defined by a code of culturally prescribed expectations and behaviors.

Socialization The process whereby individuals learn to adapt themselves to their society.

Sorcery Magical techniques for causing injury, illness, death, and other misfortunes.

Species Specific Applies to particular behavior patterns that are associated with a single species and that are followed by the members of that species predictably and consistently.

Status A position in a social system. Statuses can be either ascribed or achieved. For example, the ascribed status "old man" is given to a person merely because of his age, whereas the status of "doctor" must be achieved by completing medical school, etc. The term status is also used in connection with the notion of prestige or rank as, for example, when we speak of a "status seeker."

Subculture A subdivision of a national culture defined by regional, class, ethnic, or other such factors that make it recognizably different in important respects from the wider culture in which it is found.

Subincision A ritual operation on a male initiate in which an incision is made on the lower side of the penis.

Subsistence Farming Tilling the soil by means of relatively simple technology, in such a manner as to produce only the essentials of life.

Totemic Ancestors A totem is an object that has a special mystical significance for a particular group. Often the totem is an animal or plant which may not be consumed by the members of the group with which it is identified. A member of the kangaroo totem, for example, believes that the kangaroo was an ancestor and that he must observe certain kinds of ritual behaviors towards it.

Tribe There is no commonly held definition of a tribe, but the term is generally held to apply to a social group with a common and acknowledged territory, cultural homogeneity, and a common language. The families and communities that make up the tribe are linked through a variety of economic, religious, social, and kinship ties.

Unilineal In one line, of males exclusively or of females exclusively.

Universals of Culture This refers to those behaviors, beliefs, practices, and so on, that might be found in all cultures. The *incest taboo*, for example, is found in some form in all known human groups.

Uterine Kin Persons descended in the female line from a common ancestress. The term matrilineal kin has the same meaning.

Witchcraft Harming or otherwise exercising control over another person through personal (supernatural) powers believed to be part of the witch's person. Witchcraft is often distinguished from sorcery in that a person can be unaware of being a witch and thus can unintentionally harm others, whereas sorcery is always intentional.

REFERENCES

Achebe, C.
1959 Things Fall Apart. New York: Astor-Honor, Inc.
1961 No Longer at Ease. Greenwich, Connecticut: Fawcett Publications.

Alegria, C.
1941 Broad and Alien the World. New York: Farrar & Rinehart.

Anand, M. R.
1933 Untouchable. Bombay: Kutub-Popular.
1936 Coolie. London: Lawrence and Wishart.
1939 The Village. London: J. Cape.
1940 Across the Black Waters. London: J. Cape.

Andrist, R. K.
1964 The Long Death: The Last Days of the Plains Indian. New York: Macmillan Publishing Co.

Antoun, R. T.
1972 Arab Village. Bloomington: Indiana University Press.

Bailey, F. G.
1957 Caste and the Economic Frontier. Manchester: Manchester University Press.

Balachandra, R.
1958 The Dark Dancer. New York: Simon & Schuster.

Baldwin, J.
1962 Nobody Knows my Name. Boston: Beacon Press.

Balikci, A.
1970 The Netsilik, Garden City, New York: Natural History Press.

Bandelier, A. F.
1890 The Delight Makers. New York: Dodd, Mead & Co.

Barth, F.
1964 Nomads of South Persia. Oslo: Universitetsforlaget.

Bates, D.
1967 The Passing of the Aborigines. 2nd ed. New York: Praeger Publications.

Beal, M. D.
1963 I Will Fight No More Forever. Seattle: University of Washington Press.

Beier, U. (ed.)
1973 Black Writing from New Guinea. St. Lucia, Queensland: University of Queensland Press.

Benedict, R.
1934 Patterns of Culture. New York: Mentor Books.

Berndt, R. and C.
1952 The First Australians. Sydney: U. Smith

Beti, M.
1958 Mission to Kala. London: Heinemann.

Bhattacharya, B.
1968 Music for Mohini. Bombay: Jaico Publishing Co.

Binzen, P.
1970 Whitetown USA. New York: Random House, Inc.

Biocca, E.
1970 Yanoáma: The Narrative of a White Girl Kidnapped by Amazonian Indians. New York: E. P. Dutton & Co.

Birket-Smith, K.
1959 The Eskimo. London: Methuen.

Boas, F.
1964 The Central Eskimo. Lincoln: University of Nebraska Press.

Bohannan, L.
1958 "The Political System of the Tiv." In J. Middleton and D. Tait (eds.), Tribes Without Rulers. London: Routledge & Kegan Paul.

Bohannan, P.
1954 Tiv Farm and Settlement. London: Her Majesty's Stationery Office.
1957 Judgment and Justice Among the Tiv. London: Oxford University Press.

Boissevain, J. F.
1969 Hal-Farrug: A Village in Malta. New York: Holt, Rinehart & Winston.

Bowen, E. S.
1954 Return to Laughter. New York: Anchor Books.

Bowers, A. W.
1950 Mandan Social and Ceremonial Organization. Chicago: University of Chicago Press.

Briggs, J. L.
1970 Never in Anger. Cambridge: Harvard University Press.

Bronowski, J.
1962 "Science, the Destroyer or Creator." In E. and M. Josephson (eds.), Man Alone. New York: Dell Publishing Co.

Brown, C.
1965 Manchild in the Promised Land. New York: Macmillan Publishing Co.

Brown, D.
1971 Bury My Heart at Wounded Knee. New York: Holt, Rinehart & Winston.

Brown, P. & G. Buchbinder (eds.)
1976 The Ideology of Man and Woman in the New Guinea Highlands. American Anthropological Association Monograph.

Buck, P.
1931 The Good Earth. New York: John Day.

Burridge, K.
1973 Encountering Aborigines. New York: Pergamon Press.

Burrows, G.
1898 The Land of the Pigmies. New York: Thomas Y. Crowell Co.

Callado, A.
1970 Quarup. New York: Alfred A. Knopf.

Carstairs, M. G.
1961 The Twice Born: A Study of a Community of High-Caste Hindus. Bloomington: Indiana University Press.

Castaneda, C.
1968 The Teachings of Don Juan: A Yaqui Way of Knowledge. Los Angeles: University of California Press.
1971 A Separate Reality: Further Conversations with Don Juan. New York: Simon & Schuster.
1972 Journey to Ixtlan. New York: Simon & Schuster.
1974 Tales of Power. New York: Simon & Schuster.

Catlin, G.
1844 North American Indians. London.

Caudill, H. M.
1963 (1st ed.) Night Comes to the Cumberlands. Boston: Little, Brown & Co.

Chagnon, N.
1968 Yanomamo: The Fierce People. New York: Holt, Rinehart & Winston.
1974 Studying the Yanomamo. New York: Holt, Rinehart & Winston.

Chapman, C. G.
1971 Milocca: A Sicilian Village. Cambridge, Mass.: Schenkman Publishing Co.

Cole, D. P.
1975 Nomads of the Nomads. Chicago: Aldine Publishing Co.

Coon, C.
1932 Flesh of the Wild Ox: A Riffian Chronicle of High Valleys and Long Rifles. New York: William Morrow & Co.
1933 The Riffian. Boston: Little, Brown & Co.
1956 A Reader in General Anthropology. New York: Henry Holt & Co.

Cornelisen, A.
1969 Torregreca: Life, Death, Miracles. Boston: Atlantic Monthly Press.
1971 Vendetta of Silence. Boston: An Atlantic Monthly Press Book.
1976 Women of the Shadows. Boston: An Atlantic Monthly Press Book.

Crapanzano, V.
1973 The Hamadsha: A Study in Moroccan Ethnopsychiatry. Berkeley: University of California Press.

Curtis, E. S.
1907–1930 The North American Indian. Cambridge: The University Press.

Dark, E.
1941 The Timeless Land. New York: Macmillan Publishing Co.

Davis, A. and J. Dollard
1940 Children of Bondage. Washington, D.C.: Prepared for the American Youth Commission, American Council on Education.

de Poncins, G.
1941 Kabloona. New York: Reynal & Hitchcock, Inc.

Diamond, N.
1969 K'un Shen: A Taiwan Village. New York: Holt, Rinehart & Winston.

Dollard, J.
1957 Caste and Class in a Southern Town. New York: Anchor Books.

Doughty, C. M.
1921 Travels in Arabica Deserta. New York: Boni and Liveright.

Driberg, J. H.
1930 People of the Small Arrow. New York: Payson & Clarke Ltd.

du Chaillu, P. B.
1900 The World of the Great Forest. New York: Charles Scribner's Sons.

Dumont, L.
1970 Homo Hierarchicus. Chicago: University of Chicago Press.

Ekvall, R. B.
1952 Tibetan Sky Lines. New York: Farrar, Straus & Young.
1954 Tents Against the Sky. London: Victor Gollancz.
1968 Fields on the Hoof. New York: Holt, Rinehart & Winston.

Elkin, A. P.
1938 Australian Aborigines. Sydney: Angus and Robertson.

Elwin, V.
1938 A Cloud That's Dragonish. London: John Murray.

Embree, J. F.
1939 Suye Mura. Chicago: University of Chicago Press.

Eri, V.
1970 The Crocodile. Milton, Queensland: Jacaranda Press.

Evans-Pritchard, E. E.
1940 The Nuer. London: Oxford University Press
1951 Kinship and Marriage Among the Nuer. London: Oxford University Press.
1958 Witchcraft, Oracles and Magic Among the Azande. London: Oxford University Press.

Fernea, E. W.
1965 Guests of the Sheik: An Ethnography of an Iraqi Village. New York: Doubleday & Co.
1970 A View of the Nile: The Story of an American Family in Egypt. New York: Doubleday & Co.
1975 A Street in Marrakech. New York: Doubleday & Co.

Fernea, R. A.
1970 Shayk and Effendi: Changing Patterns of Authority Among the El Shabana of Southern Iraq. Cambridge: Harvard University Press.

Fernea, R. A. and G. Gerster
1973 Nubians in Egypt. Austin: University of Texas Press.

Flornoy, B.
1953 Jivaro: Among the Head-Shrinkers of the Amazon. London: Elek.

Forster, E. M.
1933 Preface to *Untouchable* by Mulk Raj Anand. Bombay: Kutub-Popular.

Frankenberg, R.
1957 Village on the Border. London: Cohen.

Frazer, J. G.
1890 The Golden Bough.

Freuchen, P.
1931 Eskimo. Translated by A. Paul Maerker-Branden and Elsa Branden. New York: H. Liveright.
1961 Book of the Eskimo. New York: Fawcett Crest.

Friedl, E.
1962 Vasilika: A Village in Modern Greece. New York: Holt, Rinehart & Winston.

Gambino, R.
1974 Blood of my Blood, The Dilemma of the Italian-Americans. New York: Doubleday & Co.

Gay, J.
1973 Red Dust on the Green Leaves. Thompson, Conn.: Interculture Associates.

Gazaway, R.
1969 The Longest Mile. New York: Doubleday & Co.

Geertz, C.
1965 "The Impact of the Concept of Culture on the Concept of Man." Pp. 93–118 in John R. Platt (ed.), New Views of the Nature of Man. Chicago: University of Chicago Press.
1973 The Interpretation of Culture. New York: Basic Books, Inc.

Gould, R. A.
1969 Yiwara: Foragers of the Australian Desert. New York: Charles Scribner's Sons.

Hannerz, U.
1969 Soul Side: Inquiries into Ghetto Culture and Community. New York: Columbia University Press.

Harner, M. J.
1972 The Jivaro. New York: Doubleday & Co.

Harris, M.
1971 Town and Country in Brazil. New York: W. W. Norton & Co.
1975 Cows, Pigs, Wars and Witches. New York: Vintage.

Hart, C. and A. Pilling
1960 The Tiwi of North Australia. New York: Holt.

Heider, K.
1970 The Dugum Dani. Chicago: Aldine Publishing Co.

Henfrey, C.
1964 Through Indian Eyes: A Journey Among the Indian Tribes of Guiana. New York: Holt, Rinehart & Winston.

Henry, J.
1941 Jungle People. New York: Vintage Books.

Herskovits, M. and F.
1934 Rebel Destiny: Among the Bush Negroes of Dutch Guiana. New York: McGraw-Hill Book Co.

Hogbin, I.
1970 Island of Menstruating Men. San Francisco: Chandler.

Honigmann, J.
1976 "The Personal Approach in Cultural Anthropological Research." Current Anthropology 16, 2.

Houston, J.
1971 The White Dawn. New York: Harcourt, Brace, Jovanovich, Inc.

Howell, J. T.
1973 Hard Living on Clay Street: Portraits of Blue Collar Families. New York: Anchor Press.

Hughes, C. C.
1974 Eskimo Boyhood. Lexington: University of Kentucky Press.

Huxley, F.
1966 Affable Savages. New York: Capricorn Books.

Jenness, D.
1959 The People of the Twilight. New York: Macmillan Publishing Co.

Jones, R. and S.
1976 The Himalayan Woman: A Study of Limbo Women in Marriage and Divorce. Palo Alto: Mayfield.

Kelley, J. H.
n.d. Four Yaqui Women. Manuscript.

Khaldun, I.
1958 The Mugaddimah. 3 vols. Translated from Arabic by Franz Rosenthal. London: Routledge and Kegan Paul.

Kiki, A. M.
1968 Kiki: Ten Thousand Years in a Lifetime. New York: Praeger Publications.

Kittredge, G. L.
1929 Witchcraft in Old New England. Cambridge: Harvard University Press.

Klass, S. S.
1964 Everyone in this House Makes Babies. New York: Doubleday & Co.

Kluckhohn, C.
1944 Navajo Witchcraft. Boston: Beacon Press.

Kluckhohn, C. and D. Leighton
1946 The Navaho. New York: American Museum of Natural History.

Kramer, J.
1970 Honor to the Bride Like the Pigeon that Guards its Grain Under the Clove Tree. New York: Farrar, Straus & Giroux.

Kroeber, T.
1961 Ishi in Two Worlds. Berkeley: University of California Press.

Kuper, H.
1965 Bite of Hunger. New York: Harcourt, Brace & World, Inc.
1970 A Witch in My Heart. London: Oxford University Press.

LaFarge, O.
1929 Laughing Boy. Boston: Houghton Mifflin Co.

LaGuma, A.
1967 A Walk in the Night and Other Short Stories. London: Heinemann.

Lamb, F. B.
1975 Wizard of the Upper Amazon: The Story of Manuel Cordova-Rios. Boston: Houghton Mifflin Co.

Lame Deer and R. Erdoes
1972 Lame Deer: Seeker of Visions. New York: Simon & Schuster.

Langness, L. L.
1965 The Life History in Anthropological Science. New York: Holt, Rinehart & Winston.
1967 "Sexual Antagonism in the New Guinea Highlands: A Bena Bena Example." Oceania 3:161–177.

Laughlin, E. D.
1943 The Yaqui Gold. San Antonio, Texas: The Naylor Co.

Lawrence, P. and M. Meggitt (eds.)
1965 Gods, Ghosts & Men in Melanesia. London: Oxford University Press.

Lawrence, T. E.
1937 Seven Pillars of Wisdom: A Triumph. New York: Doubleday, Doran & Co., Inc.

Laye, C.
1954 The African Child. London: Collins Fontana.

Leacock, E. (ed.)
1971 The Culture of Poverty: A Critique. New York: Simon & Schuster.

Lee, R. B.
1965 Subsistence Ecology of the Kung Bushmen. Ph.D. dissertation, University of California, Berkeley. Ann Arbor: University Microfilms.

Levi-Strauss, C.
1961 A World on the Wane. New York: Criterion Books.
1969 The Raw and the Cooked. New York: Harper & Row Publishers, Inc.
1973 From Honey to Ashes. New York: Harper.

Lewis, O.
1951 Life in a Mexican Village. Urbana: University of Illinois Press.
1959 Five Families: Mexican Case Studies in the Culture of Poverty. New York: Basic Books.

1961 The Children of Sanchez. New York: Random House, Inc.
1964 Pedro Martinez. New York: Random House, Inc.
1965 Village Life in Northern India. New York: Vintage.
1965 La Vida: A Puerto Rican Family in the Culture of Poverty—San Juan and New York. New York: Random House, Inc.

Linderman, F. B.
1962 Plenty Coups: Chief of the Crows. London: Faber.

Lockwood, D.
1962 I, the Aboriginal. London: Cassell & Co.

Lowie, R. H.
1912 Social Life of the Crow Indians. In Vol. 9, Part 2, Anthropological Papers. New York: American Museum of Natural History.
1922 Religion of the Crow Indians. In Vol. 25, Part 2, Anthropological Papers. New York: American Museum of Natural History.
1956 The Crow Indians. New York: Holt, Rinehart & Winston.
1963 Indians of the Plains. New York: The Natural History Press.

McHugh, T.
1972 The Time of the Buffalo. New York: Alfred A. Knopf.

McLuhan, T. C.
1971 Touch the Earth: A Self-Portrait of Indian Existence. New York: Outerbridge & Lazard.

Markandaya, K.
1956 Nectar in a Sieve. New York: Signet.

Martins, H.
1965 Nongalazi of the Bemba. Ilfracombe, Devon: Arthur H. Stockwell, Ltd.

Marx, E.
1967 Bedouin of the Negev. Manchester: Manchester University Press.

Matthiessen, P.
1962 Under the Mountain Wall. New York: Viking Press.
1965 At Play in the Fields of the Lord. New York: Random House, Inc.

Maybury-Lewis, D.
1965 The Savage and the Innocent. New York: The World Publishing Co.

Mead, M.
1930 Growing up in New Guinea. New York: William Morrow & Co.

Meggers, B.
1971 Amazonia. Chicago: Aldine Publishing Co.

Meggitt, M.
1962 Desert People. Chicago: The University of Chicago Press.
1964 "Male-Female Relationships in the Highlands of Australian New Guinea." American Anthropologist 66, 4, Part 2:204–224.

Metayer, M.
1966 I, Nuligak. Canada: Martin Associates, Ltd.

Mofolo, T.
1931 Chaka: An Historical Romance. London: Oxford University Press.

Moises, R., J. H. Kelley and W. C. Holden
1971 The Tall Candle: A Personal Chronical of a Yaqui Indian. Lincoln: University of Nebraska Press.

Momaday, N. S.
1969 The Way to Rainy Mountain. Albuquerque: University of New Mexico Press.

Morgan, L. H.
1877 Ancient Society. Chicago: Charles H. Kerr Co.

Morris, D.
1967 The Naked Ape. New York: McGraw-Hill Book Co.

Mowat, F.
1952 People of the Deer. Boston: Little, Brown & Co.

Murdock, G. P.
1934 Our Primitive Contemporaries. New York: Macmillan Publishing Co.

Musil, A.
1928 Manners and Customs of the Rwala Bedouins. New York: Czech Academy of Sciences and Arts and Charles R. Crane.

Nabokov, P.
1967 Two Leggings: The Making of a Crow Warrior. New York: Thomas Y. Crowell Co.

Nagarajan, K.
1912 Chronicles of Kedaram. Bombay, New York: Asia Publishing House.

Narayan, R. K.
1954 The Bachelor of Arts. East Lansing: The Michigan State College Press.
1954 Swami and Friends: A Novel of Malgudi. East Lansing: The Michigan State College Press.
1961 The Man-Eaters of Malgudi. New York: Viking Press.

Neihardt, J. G.
1951 When the Tree Flowered: An Authentic Tale of the Sioux World. New York: Macmillan Publishing Co.
1961 Black Elk Speaks. Lincoln: University of Nebraska Press.

Nelson, R. K.
1969 Hunters of the Northern Ice. Chicago: University of Chicago Press.

Norbu, T. F. and C. M. Turnbull
1968 Tibet. New York: Clarion.

Opler, M.
1965 An Apache Life Way. New York: Cooper Square Publishers.

Oswalt, W. H.
1972 Other Peoples, Other Customs. New York: Holt, Rinehart & Winston.

Oyono, F.
1966 Houseboy. London: Heinemann.

Paytiamo, J.
1932 Flaming Arrow's People. New York: Duffield & Green.

Pilisuk, M., and P. (eds.)
1971 Poor Americans: How the White Poor Live. Chicago: Distributed by Aldine Publishing Co.

Pitt-Rivers, J. A.
1954 The People of the Sierra. Chicago: University of Chicago Press

Premchand
1963 Godan. Bombay: Jaico Publishing House.

Pruitt, I.
1945 A Daughter of Han. Stanford: Stanford University Press.

Putnam, P.
1948 "The Pygmies of the Ituri Forest." Pp. 322–342 in C. Coon (ed.), A Reader in General Anthropology. New York: Henry Holt.

Radin, P.
1927 The Story of the American Indian. New York: Liveright Publishing Co.

Rasmussen, K.
1908 The People of the Polar North, A Record. London: K. Paul, Trench, Trubner & Co., Ltd.

Rattray, R. S.
1935 The Leopard Priestess. New York: D. Appleton-Century Co.

Read, K. E.
1952 "Nama Cult of the Central Highlands: New Guinea." Oceania 23, 1:1–25.
1955 "Morality and the Concept of the Person Among the Gahuku-Gama." Oceania 25, 4:233–282.
1959 "Leadership and Consensus in a New Guinea Society." American Anthropologist 61, 3:425–436.
1965 The High Valley. New York: Charles Scribner's Sons.

Redfield, R.
1930 Tepoztlan: A Mexican Village. Chicago: University of Chicago Press.
1953 The Primitive World and Its Transformations. Ithaca, New York: Cornell University Press.

Reichel-Dolmatof, G.
1971 Amazonian Cosmos. Chicago: University of Chicago Press.

Richter, C.
1953 The Light in the Forest. New York: Alfred A. Knopf.
1966 A Country of Strangers. New York: Alfred A. Knopf.

Ritzenthaler, P.
1966 The Fon of Bafut. New York: Thomas Y. Crowell Co.

Rorabacher, L. E. (ed.)
1968 Aliens in their Land. Australia: Cheshire.

Ruesch, H.
1950 Top of the World. New York: Harper & Row Publishers, Inc.

St. Augustine
The City of God.

Sandoz, M.

1942 Crazy Horse, the Strange Man of the Oglalas. Lincoln: University of Nebraska Press, 1961.

1953 Cheyenne Autumn. New York: McGraw-Hill Book Co.

Schapera, I.

1930 The Khoisan Peoples of South Africa: Bushmen and Hottentots. London: G. Routledge & Sons, Ltd.

Schebesta, P.

1933 Among Congo Pygmies. London: Hutchinson & Co., Ltd.

1936 Revisiting my Pygmy Hosts. London: Hutchinson & Co., Ltd.

Schmaier, M. D.

1960 "Conrad Richter's The Light in the Forest: An Ethnohistorical Approach to Fiction." Ethnohistory 7, 4:327–398.

Sellassi, S.

1964 Shinega's Village: Scenes of Ethiopian Life. Los Angeles: University of California Press.

Sewell, T.

1963 Yaqui Gold. Denver: Sage Books.

Simpson, C.

1954 Adam with Arrows. Sydney: Halstead Press.

Siskind, J.

1973 To Hunt in the Morning. New York: Oxford University Press.

Souter, G.

1963 New Guinea: The Last Unknown. Sydney: Angus & Robertson.

Spencer, B. and F. J. Gillen

1898 The Native Tribes of Central Australia. London: Macmillan & Co., Ltd.

1927 The Arunta: A Study of a Stone Age People. London: Macmillan & Co., Ltd.

Spicer, E. H.

1940 Pascua, A Yaqui Village in Arizona. Urbana: University of Illinois Press.

1954 Potam, A Yaqui Village in Sonora. Menasha, Wisconsin.

Stefansson, V.

1913 My Life with the Eskimo. New York: Macmillan Publishing Co.

1922 Hunters of the Great North. New York: Harcourt, Brace & Co.

Thesiger, W.

1959 Arabian Sands. London: Penguin.

1964 The Marsh Arabs. London: Penguin.

Thomas, E. M.

1959 The Harmless People. New York: Vintage Books

Turnbull, C. M.

1961 The Forest People. New York: Clarion.

1962 The Lonely African. New York: Clarion.

1965 Wayward Servants. New York: The Natural History Press.

1972 The Mountain People. New York: Simon & Schuster.
1976 Man in Africa. New York: Anchor Press/Doubleday.

Underhill, R.
1940 Hawk Over Whirlpools. New York: J. J. Augustin.

Valentine, C.
1968 Culture and Poverty: Critique and Counterproposals. Chicago: University of Chicago Press.

van der Post, L.
1958 The Lost World of the Kalahari. London: Hogarth Press.
1961 Heart of the Hunter. London: Hogarth Press.

von Fürer-Haimendorf, C.
1964 The Sherpas of Nepal. Berkeley: University of California.
1975 Himalayan Traders. New York: St. Martin's Press.

Villiers, A.
1969 Sons of Sinbad. New York: Charles Scribner's Sons.

Waddell, J. O. and M. Watson (eds.)
1971 The American Indian in Urban Society. Boston: Little, Brown & Co.

Wagley, C.
1964 Amazon Town. New York: Alfred A. Knopf.

Warner, L.
1958 A Black Civilization. New York: Harper.

Wells, A. E.
1971 Men of the Honey Bee. Adelaide: Rigby.

West, M. L.
1957 Children of the Shadows. New York: William Morrow & Co.

Williams, M.
1964 The Stone Age Island. New York: Doubleday & Co.

Wissler, C.
1917 The American Indian. New York: Oxford University Press, 1938.

Wolf, M.
1968 The House of Lim. New York: Appleton-Century-Crofts.

Wylie, L.
1957 Village in the Vaucluse. Cambridge: Harvard University Press.

Yalman, N.
1971 Under the Bo Tree. Los Angeles: University of California Press.

Yang, M. C.
1945 A Chinese Village. New York: Columbia University Press.

Yoors, Jan
1967 The Gypsies. New York: Simon & Schuster.

Yueh-Hwa, L.
1947 The Golden Wing. London: Kegan Paul, Trench, Trubner & Co.